WRITING THE
CHARACTER-
SCREENPLAY

DATE DUE

FE 12 '09			
NO 2 4 '10			
DE 5 '11			
JA 3 '12			
AP 17 '12			

DEMCO 38-296

WRITING THE CHARACTER-CENTERED SCREENPLAY

ANDREW HORTON

University of California Press
Berkeley   Los Angeles   London

University of California Press
Berkeley and Los Angeles, California

University of California Press, Ltd.
London, England

Copyright ©1994 by The Regents of the University of California

Library of Congress Cataloging-in-Publication Data
Horton, Andrew
    Writing the character-centered screenplay/Andrew Horton.
      p. cm.
    Includes bibliographical references and index.
    ISBN 0-520-08457-8 (alk. paper)
    1. Motion picture authorship. 2. Motion picture plays-
Technique. 3. Characters and characteristics in motion
pictures. I. Title.
PNI996.H67 1994
808.2'3—dc20
                                 93-37307
                                     CIP

Printed in the United States of America

    4 5 6 7 8 9

The paper used in this publication meets the minimum requirements
of American National Standard for Information Sciences—Permanence
of Paper for Printed Library Materials, ANSI Z39,48-1984 ♾

for Sam

THELMA

I guess I went a little crazy, huh?

LOUISE

No . . . You've always been crazy. This is just the first chance you've had to really express yourself.

Callie Khouri, *Thelma & Louise*

• • •

I've managed to live my life among multiple contradictions, without ever trying to rationalize or resolve them; they're part of me and part of the fundamental ambiguity of all things.

Luis Buñuel, *My Last Sigh*

• • •

In most good stories it is the character's personality that creates the action of the story. If you start with a real personality, a real character, then something is bound to happen.

Flannery O'Connor, "Writing Short Stories"

CONTENTS

ACKNOWLEDGMENTS

Many, beginning with my students, have helped shape my thinking about screenwriting.

But I would specifically like to acknowledge my patient wife, Odette, for the hours, days, and weeks she helped make it possible for me to write when I'm sure she had other things she would rather be doing.

At the University of California Press, editor Edward Dimendberg has been a strongly supportive partisan guiding this project through from concept to final rewrite. My manuscript readers also had important and often hard criticism that ultimately has, I think, paid off well. Special appreciation also to Rebecca Frazier, the managing editor, and Paula Cizmar, my copy editor, at the Press.

I wish to salute the following friends and colleagues who have read parts or all of the manuscript in various forms and have helped point toward wiser avenues of development: Paul Lucey at the University of Southern California; John Belton at Rutgers University; author Eileen Lottman in New York; Stuart McDougal, a kindred screenwriting soul at the University of Michigan; William Coveny, Vice President for Current Programming at Fox Broadcasting; Selise Eisman, Program Director at the Directors Guild of America; former students Kathleen Orilion, Jennifer Kim, Liz DeLuna, Francisco Castro, Bob Surgi; my colleague John Biguenet at Loyola; Dr. Amit Kshetarpal; screenwriters Rick Blackwood, Tom Rickman, Steve Tesich, Dick Blackburn, Ibolya Fekete; director-writers Srdjan Karanovic, Gyorgy Szomjas, Rajko Grlic, Slobodan Sijan, and George Roy Hill.

Finally, there would be no book if it were not for the pleasure of the give and take I have enjoyed with all my screenwriting students over the years at Loyola University of New Orleans, the University of Michigan, the University of New Orleans, Louisiana State University, Brooklyn College (CUNY), the Academy of Dramatic Arts of Belgrade, as well as those I've taught from Russia, Greece, and several other countries. All of you helped write this book with your energy, insight, hard work, and originality.

I also dedicate this to screenwriters everywhere who realize that Homer, Sappho, Murasaki, Shakespeare, Moliere, Tolstoy, Dickens, Austen, Chekhov, Marquez, Alice Walker, Milan Kundera, Italo Calvino, and Kate Chopin were some of the greatest script weavers even though many lived before the age of flickering images.

As always, of course, a special thanks to Preston Sturges's scripts, films, and carnivalesque and healing laughter. And especially to Luis Buñuel who so uncompromisingly and playfully answered "that call to the irrational" on film and in life.

INTRODUCTION

> What we need today is no less than a revolution. We need to do violence to the cliche, create havoc with the tried, the tired, and tested.
>
> Larry Gelbart

Producers who murder screenwriters. Screenwriters who spend their lives "pitching" rather than writing. Studios that endlessly recycle films that unimaginatively copy previous movies.

Such is the stuff of Michael Tolkin's devilishly accurate satire of The Industry, *The Player*, which delighted and horrified audiences in 1992. Tolkin's script provided director Robert Altman with a new opportunity to do what he had done years ago for a whole generation in his earlier films: he took on American cliches and destroyed them by placing them before us in such exaggerated or perhaps not exaggerated detail that we could laugh out loud and see beyond the cliches.

The destruction of cliches in character, story, and structure is at the center of this study. More specifically we are interested here in creating stronger, more vivid, and challenging characters in screenplays that go beyond what Larry Gelbart calls the "tried, tired, and tested."

I am speaking of films such as *Casablanca, It Happened One Night, The Quiet Man, High Noon, The Treasure of the Sierra Madre, Mildred Pierce, On the Waterfront, The Return of the Secaucus Seven, Thelma & Louise, Down by Law, The Silence of the Lambs, sex, lies and videotape, Boyz N the Hood, Unforgiven* or, from abroad, *The Crying Game, Wild Strawberries, The Bicycle Thief, Closely Watched Trains, Tokyo Story, Rules of the Game, Breathless, 400 Blows, The Loneliness of the Long Distance Runner, Cinema Paradiso, Europa Europa, The Gods Must Be Crazy, The Time of the Gypsies, Little Vera,* or *My Life as a Dog.* Then, too, there are those rare television series such as "Northern Exposure," "M*A*S*H," "Hill Street Blues," and "Rosanne," together with such quality miniseries as *Lonesome Dove.* All of these films and television projects please audiences, win awards, and linger in our memories long after most other films have been forgotten.

These films and programs cross many genres and numerous national borders. But they share a sense that, as Flannery O'Connor says, "it is the character's personality that creates the action of the story" and not the other way around. If much of Hollywood's fare has become plot centered *at the expense of character*, I wish in this study to suggest strategies and concepts that will help any writer develop more fully realized characters. This does not mean that we should fail to pay attention to story and structure and other elements. Far from it. In fact, our focus on character should help you see narrative from perspectives that go beyond many of the cliches that are often served us on the screen. But we should be able to listen to "other" voices, too. For example, surrealist director Luis Buñuel described his concept of screenwriting in this remark about his famous debut film, *Un Chien andalu* (*Andalusian Dog*, 1929), which he wrote with his friend Salvador Dali:

> Our only rule was very simple: No idea or image that might lend itself to a rational explanation of any kind would be accepted. We had to open all doors to the irrational and keep only those images that surprised us, without trying to explain why. (Buñuel 1983, 104)

Admirable advice for writers. But, of course, threatening advice to studio heads and producers. At least they *think* such advice is dangerous. That's why cliches and stereotypes are so comforting, after all!

Writer-director George Roy Hill whose career has included some of the best-loved Hollywood films of the past twenty-five years—*Butch Cassidy and the Sundance Kid*, *The Sting*, *The World According to Garp*, and *Slaughterhouse Five*—said that he had only seen one film in 1991 that interested him: *Cinema Paradiso* (Hill 1991). It struck me as ironic but not surprising that none of the recent Hollywood fare made it onto his list. For although we can admire the razzle-dazzle special effects of a *Batman* or *Ghostbusters* or *Terminator 2*, or the set design in a *Dick Tracy* or *Edward Scissorhands*, it is more than a bit troubling that these films don't really stick *with* us for very long *as strong stories about real human beings we care about who are experiencing difficult (comic or dramatic) and moral straits.* And yet, by and large, the pop genre films that Hollywood has churned out in recent years are the products of the "Hollywood formula," which is preached in numerous "how to" books lining bookstore shelves everywhere.[1]

Cinema Paradiso (written and directed by Giuseppi Tornatore, 1989), in contrast, is an Oscar-winning story about a boy whose father has not

---

1. I have reviewed many of the "how to" script books in my review essay, "The 'How to Write the Best Ever Screenplay' Book Biz." *Cineaste* 19, nos. 2–3 (Winter 1992–1993): 12–14.

returned from the war; the boy grows up in the movie theater (thus the title) of a small Italian town, befriended by an aging projectionist. It's an extremely simple tale. Yet you cannot forget it once you've seen it. Why? Various answers come to mind, but at the center of them all is the BOY himself. We remember him, his face, his actions, his moods, his character. And we remember him so because we *know*—whether we can articulate it or not—that his character touches what Flannery O'Connor (46) identified as "those underground springs that give life." *Cinema Paradiso* is only partially about cinemas and paradises. It is much more importantly, on a *core experience* level, about a young boy who must grow up without a father. It is this core experience that is an important key to his character and thus to the film itself. Without it, we would have a light story full of nostalgia for old movies.

It is this sense of struggle at the heart of character and narrative that Bruno Bettelheim had in mind in speaking of the very real need children have for fairy tales in his study *The Uses of Enchantment: The Meaning and Importance of Fairy Tales* (1989). We could easily substitute "the typical contemporary Hollywood film" for what Bettelheim attacks: modern children's literature, which, he points out, robs children of "the deep inner conflicts originating in our primitive drives" (10). We can substitute "character-centered script" for "fairy tale" when Bettelheim writes that "the fairy tale, by contrast, takes these existential anxieties and dilemmas very seriously and addresses itself directly to them" (10). Such inner anxieties and dilemmas are clearly not the stuff of action/adventure/plot-driven films.

But they are the territory of the character-oriented project. One critic recently observed that Hollywood executives appeared to be learning that "big bucks don't necessarily mean big bucks, that production costs have gotten out of hand and that smaller, more human movies are a better bet in tough times" (Hinson 1990).

> Character is the vital material with which an author must work.
> Lajos Egri, *The Art of Dramatic Writing*

If you want to write a screenplay, then write a screenplay! In fact, if you want to make a film, simply make one. You don't NEED a screenplay; you just need film, a camera, and money to develop and print the film.

Jean-Luc Godard used to say some of his best films had no script at all: just notes scribbled on paper napkins at whatever café he stopped at for coffee on the way to shoot. The truth is, however, that most filmmakers don't work this way: for artistic and commercial reasons both, they prefer to have a written script of what the movie will be before the cameras roll. Certainly producers feel this way. And thus the need for writers.

Nobody *needs* to read a book about how to write in order to write. Yet once you've plunged into writing the feature screenplay for the first time, you are more than likely bound to discover parts of the process that are hard, that you feel insecure about, that others feel you need work on. That's when seasoned advice and guidance can help. This book is offered in such a spirit for the new and the experienced screenwriter alike. Use as you see fit: some may wish to follow the step-by-step schedules offered in part 3 whereas others may find it more profitable to dip and browse. You choose. If several thoughts or suggestions prove useful, I will be pleased. If a handful of pages help you with your scripts, it's time to open a good bottle of wine.

Writing what has become the three-act, plot-driven Hollywood script in its most crass form leads to what I call the microwave script. That is, the attempt to make a meal instantly by simply throwing elements together according to a set recipe, setting the timer, and zapping it all for a brief time. Some dishes may taste OK concocted this way. But given the choice, I'll take a stove-cooked, half-improvised, half-planned meal any day.

I live and write in New Orleans, not Los Angeles. That means that cooking, eating, and jazz matter. Sure, people may reheat coffee in the microwave, but no self-respecting New Orleanian would make a gumbo or a jambalaya or a crawfish bisque in THAT machine! For many of the best Creole dishes, what you need to start with is the ROUX, which is the flour and butter (or oil) sauce that is simmered slowly until it turns just the right shade of rich brown (hazelnut) before anything else is added.

The roux is the spine, the core characteristic, of your characters and script. As one New Orleans cookbook says, "It's surprising to realize that gumbo is a dish that has a sauce—the roux. Properly prepared, *the roux is completely absorbed, but its taste and texture are an essential part of the gumbo*" (Collin and Collin 1989, 111; italics my own).

There you have it.

· · ·

Let us outline our character-centered project more specifically as we set forth to do battle with cliches and stereotypes.

CHARACTER NOTE #1
THE CHARACTER-CENTERED SCRIPT PORTRAYS CHARACTER NOT AS A
STATIC STATE OF BEING BUT AS A DYNAMIC PROCESS OF BECOMING WHICH

WE WILL CALL THE *CARNIVALESQUE*: IN BRIEF, THE CARNIVALESQUE DESCRIBES AN ONGOING, EVER-CHANGING STATE IN WHICH CHARACTER IS RECOGNIZED AS BEING MADE UP OF MANY "VOICES" WITHIN US, EACH WITH ITS OWN HISTORY, NEEDS, FLAVOR, LIMITATIONS, JOYS, AND RHYTHMS.

We will discuss the carnivalesque in more detail in part 1. The study of character almost necessarily brings to mind theories of psychology and even psychoanalysis as developed by Freud, the post-Freudians, and others. Although these theories have their uses, they are not, however, the center of our study. Rather we will draw particularly on the contributions made by the Russian theoretician Mikhail Bakhtin whose discussions of language, literature, identity, culture, and carnival versus noncarnival-oriented societies bear directly on our discussion of screenwriting.

Again it is helpful to refer to the carnivalesque environment of New Orleans in which I live, for, unlike Los Angeles, New York, and the rest of the United States, the whole culture of the "Crescent City" is organized according to what happens before Mardi Gras or after Mardi Gras, the carnival day that occurs each year on "Fat Tuesday," the day before Ash Wednesday.

Chris, the laid-back 1960s-styled articulate D.J. in television's "Northern Exposure," has a firm grasp on everyone's need for the carnivalesque. In the "Spring Break" episode (1991) he remarks:

> Spring is about to spring—Persephone's coming back. And here in Cicely, the ice is groaning—about to break with that exquisite, deafening roar. It's a time for madness. A time for our fangs to come down and our eyes to glaze over—so the beast in us can sing with unmitigated joy. (beat) Yes, ecstasy, I welcome thee.

Chris then emits a wolf howl. A sense of the carnivalesque is, in fact, what is most attractive about "Northern Exposure." One of the four main writers on the show, Diane Frolov, identifies the ideology of their concept as "a nonjudgmental universe" (1992, 266) where different personalities, races, ages, types can coexist, learn, and support each other as a *community*.

Furthermore, in tune with the carnivalesque:

CHARACTER NOTE #2
THE CHARACTER-CENTERED SCRIPT TAKES CHANCES.

In reviewing the "disaster" of the Hollywood movie business in early 1992, Jeffrey Goodell in *Premiere* concluded that "to win you have to gamble" (1992, 32). And John Taylor in *New York* magazine noted in the fall of 1991 that with so many big studios in trouble, studios would "love to give a Woody Allen movie their special spin" (23), referring to the low-budget, character-driven films that Woody has always made.

What was one of the most debated points of *Thelma & Louise*? Simple: "Why did they have to drive off into the Grand Canyon?"

Because it was their character given the circumstances:

> LOUISE
>
> We're not giving up, Thelma.
>
> THELMA
>
> Then let's not get caught.
>
> LOUISE
>
> What are you talkin' about?
>
> THELMA
>
> (indicating the Grand Canyon)
> Go.
>
> LOUISE
>
> Go?
>
> Thelma is smiling at her.
>
> THELMA
>
> Go.
>
> They look at each other, look back at the wall of police cars, and then look back at each other. They smile.[2]

Thelma and Louise took chances. And so did Callie Khouri in this, her first screenplay, for she consciously set out to write something that was off the chart from what had been seen before. Said Khouri simply: "*I had nothing to lose*" (1991; emphasis my own). "Nothing to lose" became, of course, "everything to gain" as she walked off with the Oscar for Best Original Screenplay in 1992.

Khouri took the plunge that many critics, including Wolf Schneider, the editor of *American Film*, have said more writers today *should* take:

---

2. Callie Khouri, *Thelma & Louise*, Final Shooting Script, 5 June 1990. All quotes from this version of the script.

"Playing it safe often means replaying the same thing . . . Maybe, if all of us who told stories took more risks, if we looked inward into our psyches instead of outward to the structure set by others' success, we would find more to say."

Too few Hollywood films in the late 1980s and early 1990s have taken chances. Even at the beginning of the 1980s, critic and novelist David Thomson observed that "movies are nearly at an end" (1981, 23). His reasoning? "The climactic crisis of American film is that the movies were unworthy of a culture dependent on imagination," he explains. And he concludes by speaking of films that are much closer to those we are discussing: "I suspect that they (American films) have never been worthy, but that they have come close enough, often enough, to tempt anyone interested in a communication that might touch everyone." The character-centered script is definitely interested in that kind of emotional power that connects with a widely varied audience, if not literally "everyone."

CHARACTER NOTE #3:

IN THE CHARACTER-CENTERED SCRIPT, WE AND THE CHARACTERS ARE
CONFRONTED WITH DIFFICULT AND OFTEN CONTRADICTORY MORAL
CHOICES.

Late in *sex, lies and videotape*, the "stranger," Graham, who has been videotaping Ann, the repressed wife of his once-best friend, speaks (as he tapes himself!):

GRAHAM
All right, you want to talk about lies, let's talk about lies, Ann. Let's talk about lying to yourself. You haven't been able to sleep with your husband because you're no longer in love with him, and maybe you never were. You haven't been honest with yourself in longer than you can remember.

To which Ann, who has been overly reserved the whole time till now, replies:

ANN
(heated)
Yeah, you're right. But I never claimed to *know* everything like you, and have all these little *theories*. I'm still learning, I know that. But I don't feel like I've wasted time. If I had to go through my marriage to get to where I am right now, fine.

Ann moves in closer, burrowing, her eyes on fire.

ANN

But *you*. You have wasted nine *years*. I mean, that has to be some
sort of weird record or something, nine years. How does *that* feel?

Graham says nothing. Ann picks up the camera and points it at him.

GRAHAM

Don't do that. (Soderbergh 1990, 159)

Ironically, for a film with such a provocative title, Steven Soderbergh's
popular "off-Hollywood" film, made in his native Baton Rouge, has two
main characters—Graham and Ann—who are both frigid and concerned
with the seeming lack of morality of those (Ann's sister and husband)
who are having an affair with each other. Consequently the whole film
becomes a witty, insightful meditation on the 1980s American "yuppie"
and self-gratification morality.

Likewise *Boyz N the Hood* (written and directed by John Singleton,
1991) places its young, black, male, South Central Los Angeles teenager
in the midst of a life-and-death moral dilemma. That this character-
centered drama of our times speaks strongly to its audiences was tragi-
cally clear in the subsequent outbreaks and even deaths during the opening months of its release in 1991. As producer Steve Nicolaides (1991)
stated, however, the violence was not caused by an irresponsible use of
violence in John Singleton's film. As he noted, any Schwarzenegger film
has much more "violence" in it. What affected viewers was rather the direct honesty and truth of the violence presented in all its contemporary
moral complexity. Clearly the film comes down on the side of breaking
the chain of violence for young black males as represented in the father's
strong, if somewhat "preachy," closing speech. How painfully accurate
Singleton's sense of character and place became clear in the spring of
1992 as we all kept many of his prophetic images in mind as Los Angeles
burned.

Aristotle helps on this point. He wrote that "virtually all the distinc-
tions in human character are derived from the primary distinction between goodness and badness which divides the human race" (1947, 6).

CHARACTER NOTE #4
THE CHARACTER-CENTERED SCRIPT OFTEN BREAKS SOME OR MANY OF
THE SO-CALLED "RULES" OF HOLLYWOOD SCRIPTWRITING.

It is in the spirit of the carnivalesque to adhere to no set rules. Good
screenwriters, like jazz musicians, are aware of the codes, modes, traditions of genres, trends, but go beyond them. Thus it has been a "rule" of

Hollywood for years that "westerns don't sell" and another often-stated dictum that "historical dramas are a no-no," and yet *Dances With Wolves* (Michael Blake 1990) and *Unforgiven* (David Webb Peoples 1992) proved everybody wrong. The Civil War has been taboo (on the premise of "who cares anymore?"), but *Gone With The Wind* (Sidney Howard et al. 1939) is still the film that along with *Casablanca* (Julius and Philip Epstein and Howard Kotch 1942) and a few others many feel represent "Hollywood" at its best.

Back to carnival in New Orleans once more. Yes, you can buy a guide to parade routes for the organized carnival clubs (called "krewes"). *But the more exciting carnival-within-a-carnival has to do with New Orleans African-American clubs organized as "Indian tribes" which have no parade route at all but which wander as they wish throughout the day!* There are no schedules, rules, routes, obligations on Mardi Gras day for these tribes that cultural historian George Lipsitz (1990) has studied carefully. Noting that these tribes consist of working-class blacks who collectively "author an important narrative about their own past, present, and future" (296), he underlines the multivoiced *character* of such events as drawing on "music, costumes, speech, and dance."

In other words, the Mardi Gras Indians create their own rules as they fashion their collective tribal identity.

CHARACTER NOTE #5

THE CHARACTER-CENTERED SCRIPT IS AWARE THAT THE CHARACTERS' LIVES ARE STRONGLY AFFECTED BY CORE CHARACTERISTICS AND EXPERIENCES THAT THE AUDIENCE AS WELL AS THE CHARACTERS THEMSELVES MAY OR MAY NOT COME TO IDENTIFY AND UNDERSTAND.

The Crying Game (1992), written and directed by Neil Jordan, surprised many in The Industry: this small character-centered British "foreign" film proved it had "legs" with a mass audience and won an Oscar for Best Original Screenplay in 1993. Beyond the many controversial topics that the film embraces—from politics and religion to race and homosexuality—there is the strong pull of the characters as developed and presented to us. By film's end, the various "surprises" in Neil Jordan's script seem, upon reflection, *inevitable given Fergus's character*. We may ask: Why is such a person in the IRA in the first place? Why doesn't he follow orders as he should? Why does he decide to fulfill a dying "enemy's" wish to visit his girlfriend? And why, once an identity secret is revealed, does he decide to stay?

Many lesser scripts would have explained all: perhaps Fergus was beaten as a child or he lived through his own tragic love affair or we see in a series of flashbacks that he has always been kind to animals but was forced into becoming an IRA hit man against his will. Whatever. But it is a measure of Neil Jordan's success that he has created a Fergus vivid and convincing enough, that we sense the core experiences and characteristics without fully knowing or understanding them. We have no such simple flashbacks or easily identified Freudian complexes drawn for us. But the narrative of the film traces a character who comes finally to appear in our minds as someone with a strong core from which his behavior and actions are drawn.

One further example. At the end of a recent term teaching an Introduction to Film class, I asked students to vote for their top three favorite films seen that semester. The field of contenders included *The Godfather, Rear Window, King Kong, Citizen Kane, All the President's Men, Desperately Seeking Susan,* an early Fellini film, an early Renoir movie, and a recent Hollywood-Yugoslav production, Emir Kusturica's *Time of the Gypsies* (Columbia Pictures, 1989). There was no contest. *Time of the Gypsies* won hands down.

How could this be? What did this seemingly unknown film made for $2 million with an unknown Yugoslav cast speaking in Romany have that *The Godfather* and even *Citizen Kane* didn't? Students answered: a deeply affecting sense of mystery about the human condition that nevertheless rang true to them. The film haunted them: they could not forget it. This tale of contemporary Yugoslav gypsies who sell their own children into slavery in Italy grabbed them and took them through comedy and pathos to places they'd never been before. The film took chances and those risks paid off (seen from today's perspective, of course, the film also seems prophetic in suggesting the kind of struggle that has led to the violent and bloody collapse of Yugoslavia).

Think how this is true in *The Silence of the Lambs* (Ted Tally 1991) as well. Although we come to realize that a core experience for Clarice, the main character, has to do with her need to reconcile the death of her father, a law enforcement officer, there are many questions left unresolved, untouched. What of her *mother*, generally considered the most important influence on a child's development, especially that of a young woman? That significant fact is never touched upon, and although Clarice's exterior goal is reached—to become an FBI agent—we sense that she still has miles to go before her odyssey is completed.

This point is made even more clearly in relation to the character of Hannibal Lecter. Not only is he on the loose by the end of the film ("having a friend for dinner"), but *we never come close to understanding his core character or experiences: we sense the gap between his intense understanding of human nature and thus his ability on the one hand to help others heal themselves and, on the other hand, his own personal need to kill and violate.*

This realm between what we know and don't know of a character brings us to a final note:

CHARACTER NOTE #6
THE CHARACTER-CENTERED SCRIPT SUGGESTS THAT BEYOND CORE CHAR-
ACTERISTICS AND EXPERIENCES, THERE IS MYSTERY AND A REALM OF THE
UNRESOLVED—THAT AREA THAT WE CANNOT FULLY OR TOTALLY KNOW,
UNDERSTAND, EMBRACE.

William Goldman coined a phrase often repeated in Hollywood in *Adventures in the Screen Trade*: "NOBODY KNOWS ANYTHING." He was referring to the entire American movie industry. Our character note #6 suggests a variation on Goldman's Law: *None of us ever completely knows anybody, including ourselves.* "Truly the beauty of life is its uncertainty," says the ancient Japanese poet Yoshida Kenko. Approach character as a question rather than a statement. This book is about understanding and learning to write scripts that might have the same lasting and deeply satisfying appeal that *The Silence of the Lambs, Cinema Paradiso, Thelma & Louise, Time of the Gypsies*, and, on television, "Northern Exposure" have had for millions. But I want this to be more than a "how to" book. I am also interested in the WHY in a broad context that goes beyond the boundaries of traditional Hollywood cinema.

• • •

The character-centered script is not a registered trademark or a recognized division with a label in all Blockbuster video shops. Furthermore, it's important to remember that classical Hollywood films traditionally built their appeal around strong characters and appealing stars. Thus no simple line can be drawn between Hollywood versus European or non-Hollywood independents. And certainly all the points made in this book could be applied to building characters within plot-oriented action/adventure films as well. But I have used the term "character-centered" because it best describes the kind of films I like to see—and so do many others—both from Hollywood and from elsewhere. Plus, this is the type of film I enjoy writing.

Note also that an emphasis on character in this book does not exclude the need for a carefully worked-out narrative structure or for any of the other elements that make up the rich gumbo of filmmaking. There can be no fully drawn character without a narrative point of view, a story structure, a sense of place and pace. Even (and maybe more accurately, "especially") in a film such as Louis Malle's *My Dinner With Andre* (1982), in which two actors, Andre Gregory and Wallace Shawn, talk with each other for 110 minutes over dinner, a finely etched narrative—both verbal and visual—is at play. As part 2 of this work makes clear, structure does count, and it counts significantly for the total shape and effect of a script. Within this context, however, I wish to focus on the need to develop stronger and more imaginative characters.

> Movies have largely lost interest in character. It is not without significance that two of the most publicized characters in the cinema of the last few years have been a shark and a mechanical ape.
>
> Larry McMurtry, "Character, The Tube, and the Death of the Movies," in *Film Flam*

Let's be even more specific. The basic premise of this book is simple: there is a large gap between the typical plot-driven films, especially those produced by Hollywood, and those movies that actually win Academy Awards and other prizes around the world. Yes, I'm talking about a clear double standard. Hollywood is an industry, and most of the films produced there are aimed at the Box Office and not the Academy Awards or the Cannes Film Festival or even the San Francisco International Festival. Yet the pictures we remember and which the Academy most often turns to when it takes a closer look at the end of each year tend to be narratives about strongly etched characters. And because these stories concern *people we care deeply about*, they have *emotional and moral resonance*: we replay them again and again in the cinemas of our mind.

This cannot be said of many films in the theaters today, a fact that has begun to be reflected in declining box office and video rental returns. After all, I enjoyed taking my five-year-old son to *Teenage Mutant Ninja Turtles II: The Secret of the Ooze* (Todd W. Langen 1991) when it was released. But would anyone dare distinguish between the character traits of Leonardo, Michelangelo, and the rest? Remember, in contrast, that Disney managed to make each of the dwarfs in *Snow White* (1937)— Doc, Happy, Sleepy, Sneezy, Grumpy, Bashful, and most especially Dopey—stand out in our memories because of a few sharply etched character strokes. (Note that writers of animation are still not represented by the Writers Guild of America. Story-script credit for *Snow White* lists Ted Sears, Otto Englander, Earl Hurd, Dorothy Ann Black, Richard Creedon, Dick Richard, Merrill de Maris, and Webb Smith as adapters of the Brothers Grimm story.)

In this context, consider the MOUNTAIN the aspiring screenwriter must climb today to create a film with such resonance and with characters who remain with us long after the credits have faded on the screen.

OBSTACLES TO WRITING THE CHARACTER-CENTERED SCRIPT

General

1. THE INFLUENCE OF TELEVISION

Television, at least in the United States, works against character-centered scripts because it prefers SITUATION-centered shows and nonthreatening characters who do not rock the boat for either viewers or sponsors. Thus, there is a certain national homogenized sameness and narrowness of range in character depiction. Exceptions such as "Northern Exposure" test the boundaries of television writing, but in general, the middle of the road, middle-brow approach to narrative and character robs writers of the chance to create a true *polyphony*: a chorus of many voices free to speak as they wish.

There is one very bright exception to the above, as Larry McMurtry has pointed out and proved with the filming of *Lonesome Dove*, the script for which was based on his own novel: the television miniseries. The miniseries has allowed good writers an excellent chance to develop character to a greater extent than most films, simply because in a miniseries, writers have more time at their hands. *Stalin* (1992) starring Robert Duvall would be an example of an expansiveness that television can incorporate in the hands of talented writers and filmmakers.

2. EVER-DECREASING ATTENTION SPANS

Television is largely responsible for this, especially MTV with its zip-zap *montage* editing that *manipulates the viewer so that he or she has little chance to observe, consider, enjoy a character working or not working things out*. But the mind-numbing editing is itself a product in part of the need to try and hit the audience with enough stimulation so that viewers won't press the remote control switch at random taking in ten seconds of this show and five seconds of that one. Alan Parker said that while he was shooting *Angel Heart* (1987) the opening encounter between Mickey Rourke and Robert De Niro was shot as a "wonderful ten-minute scene with no cuts" (Parker 1987). As it plays in the final cut of the film now, it is long, but Parker felt he could not use the full ten minutes simply because "producers don't feel audiences will sit still that long."

3. NINTENDO NIRVANA

Marsha Kinder has perceptively observed the impact of kids' shows such as *Teenage Mutant Ninja Turtles*, but especially of Nintendo and video games on our nation's youth in *Playing with Power in Movies, Tele-*

vision, and Video Games. Such sound and light stimulation and digital interaction may be great fun. And they certainly do a lot for hand-eye coordination—and thus to that degree they are active rather than passive media, which, as Kinder explores, evolve their own "interactive narratives" (1991, 4). They do not, however, prepare or invite individuals to delve further into the mysteries and mazes of the human character, for they are, ultimately, dialogues between the machine and the player rather than between individuals.

4. THE GENERAL SPEED AND FRAGMENTATION OF LIFE TODAY

Fragmentation appears to be the pattern of our lives today. Precious little time for talk, for a walk, for undirected play, or for daydreaming. In short, no real time to take in, reflect, respond, to BE. Thus the plot-heavy scripts in some way mirror the schedule-heavy lives of the viewers! I think this in part explains why so many of the recent character-centered scripts such as *Driving Miss Daisy* (1989), *Rambling Rose*, *Fried Green Tomatoes*, and *Man in the Moon* (all from 1991) are set in the past and, in the case of the last three, the rural past (and what are we to make of the fact that they are all about the South?): these films build on a sense of nostalgia, of course, for a more *leisurely* time. But the past makes it seem *natural* that people would talk more, interact more, take their time about things in a way that doesn't often occur in contemporary stories; stories set in the present often have difficulty pulling off more dialogue, more interaction because of the pace, fragmentation, and overstimulation of our lives today. French filmmaker Jean-Luc Godard caught such a feeling for life today in his 1966 film *Masculine-Feminine* when the young male protagonist proposes to his girlfriend in a noisy café complete with street noise outside and pinball machine noise inside. Instead of answering him, she states that she is late for an appointment and will talk to him later and rushes out. With wry irony Godard suggests that even the most emotional moments of our lives get "crowded out" these days.

Industry Specific

5. SCREENWRITERS AND PRODUCERS WHO ADMIRE HEAVILY PLOT-ORIENTED FORMULAS AND SCRIPTWRITING BOOKS THAT CHAMPION PLOT OVER CHARACTER

Many structure-oriented books (and seminars) such as the ever-popular *Screenplay* by Syd Field, or more recently, Christopher Vogler's *The Writer's Journey: Mythic Structure for Storytellers and Screenwriters*, have had a profoundly negative effect on the quality of American screenwriting in the past decade. The point is simply that an emphasis on structure and plot without a clear understanding of the nature and working of character often leads to a lifeless script. Character and action are inextricably intertwined. Aristotle said it, and we still need to remember: "Men are better or worse, according to their moral bent; but they become happy or miserable in their actual deeds" (1947, 24). And it's ironic to note how Aristotle anticipated Hollywood's plot-heavy/character-light scripts when he went on to comment that it is possible to have dramas without strong characters, but not possible to have dramas without action, ending with the observation: "In fact, the works of most of the modern tragic poets, from the time of Euripides on, *are lacking in the element of character*" (24, emphasis my own).

Seymour Chatman (1978) goes beyond Aristotle's comment to point out how little has really been written on a theory of character. Furthermore, in the centuries-old debate over action versus character, Chatman remarks, "There seems no self-evident reason to argue the primacy of action as a source of traits, nor for that matter, the other way around" (110). Given Chatman's perspective, *the danger of plot- and structure-oriented script books is that, as Chatman says about formalist and structuralist critics, they see character as a PRODUCT of plot and thus as "participants rather than as PERSONAGES"* (111).

Finally, few if any of these books truly suggest to the would-be screenwriter the possible European and independent options above/beyond/in addition to "Hollywood."

Veteran Hollywood and television scriptwriter Michael Elias (whose credits list hundreds of television shows including "Head of the Class," "All in the Family," and "The Mary Tyler Moore Show" as well as films such as *The Frisco Kid* and *The Jerk*) recently complained that the kind of "formula" writing championed by the host of scriptwriting books around and the equal number of screenwriting seminars and weekend workshops is "nightmarish" (1991). He complained that too many studio heads are MBAs under twenty-five who have taken these "quickie" courses or only read one or two of these "how to" books; even the writers themselves tend also to be under twenty-five and raised on MTV and the same books and courses. "No wonder so much garbage gets made, recycled, remade!" Elias complained.

Producer/director Gilbert Cates, presently Dean of the School of Drama, Film, and Television at University of California, Los Angeles (UCLA), made much the same observation, adding an often-heard complaint among those who care: "Too many of our students have only studied other films and television. They know NOTHING about life and real characters, therefore what they write winds up sounding like the TV shows and films they've seen" (1991). He concluded that at UCLA, "What we need really are fewer students and especially students who have lived more fully and read more widely."

Cates was even more specific: UCLA and other American film schools should pay closer attention to the model seen in several European schools, especially the famous FAMU school in Prague, which produced Milos Forman, Emir Kusturica, and other well-known directors. At FAMU, students had to study drama and literature as well as film. The director I have worked most closely with, Srdjan Karanovic of the former Yugoslavia, was educated at FAMU and fondly remembers having to take a course called "The Contemporary European Novel" from no less an authority than Milan Kundera, the author of *The Unbearable Lightness of Being* (which was a memorable script in 1988 by Jean-Claude Carriere and Philip Kaufman) and other novels. "How can you write a good screenplay if you haven't read some of the best plays and some of the best literature?" Cates questions. To write screenplays with only a knowledge of John Ford, Alfred Hitchcock, and Shane Black, he suggests, is to impoverish the potential of the craft.

The master Japanese writer-director, Akira Kurosawa, is even more emphatic: *"In order to write scripts, you must first study the great novels and dramas of the world. You must consider why they are great. Where does the emotion come from that you feel as you read them?"* (1982, 193, emphasis my own).

"Cinema has not yet been invented," the French critic Andre Bazin used to like to say. And of course his seriously playful words were meant to challenge us: "Cinema has been too reduced and too limited in its short history" might be a literal reading of Bazin's words. This "European" view of a broader training and background for the screenwriter is one, as I shall point out, that I have been fortunate enough to share in as an American screenwriter sometimes working abroad.

Some persons in key positions share Cates and Elias's feelings on the matter. David Bruskin is a head reader at Columbia Pictures who says that of the ten or so scripts he reads and reviews per week, he passes (says no) to almost all. "If I recommend ONE script a year without reservations, it's a good year," he comments, citing the same formula-ridden construction as the problem infecting most of the material turned in. The problem therefore appears to be this: not that people don't know how to write a script, but that far too many writers are turning out the same cookie cutter/microwave instant script.

6. THE HOLLYWOOD BLOCKBUSTER MENTALITY

The larger the budget, the fewer the chances taken by everyone involved. This is a cliche in Hollywood, but it is still true. It affects us for the purposes of this book, *for, as we have noted above, to take chances is to begin to develop a character-centered script.* A character-centered script does not HAVE to be low budget. After all, so much of a budget depends on stars' salaries. But we are saying that many of these scripts can be made quiet simply and inexpensively—*sex, lies and videotape* and *Time of the Gypsies* at around $2 million are examples—because it is character rather than special effects and exotic locations that hold us, involve us, move us.

No book can really teach anyone to write a best-selling blockbuster or an Academy Award–winning film, let alone a Significant Novel, Poem, or Play. But it is my hope that the analysis, commentary, advice, encouragement, and information presented here should at least create a *climate* within which you may find your own voice, direction, and inspiration to write a script that you truly care about. This is not to say that I am acting as a sideline coach on how to write scripts that WON'T sell. Far from it: the closing section is dedicated to getting your script on the screen, and each professional script discussed has made money as well as won awards.

But what I am stressing here is that worrying about how many thousands of dollars you will get for your first draft from a major studio should not be your concern. None of the scripts analyzed here, from *Boyz N the Hood* to *The Silence of The Lambs*, were written with ambitions of pushing *E.T.* and other megahits off their perch as leading box office hits. Rather, let us return to our first film, *Cinema Paradiso*. Who can forget this tale about a middle-aged man recalling his youth in a small town, especially as it intertwines with the films and people in his life. The film only pulled in about $10 million in the United States as opposed to the hundreds of millions of dollars of a *Home Alone* (John Hughes 1990) or *Terminator 2* (James Cameron and William Wisher 1991). Then again, note from the beginning, *Cinema Paradiso* did not cost $85 million or more to make. Think also of *Boyz N the Hood* or *Straight Out of Brooklyn* (written and directed by Matty Rich, 1991), each made by young African-Americans with vision rather than large pocketbooks, yet each creating films that have drawn strong critical praise and national as well as international attention for their honest depiction of the tough contemporary situation of the urban black American family. Both are strongly character-centered films, and each *in terms of percentage of cost to make to box office receipts* outsold *Terminator 2*.

This book is, I emphasize, the product of practical experience with both American and European filmmaking. I have written, been commissioned to write, optioned, and sold commercial feature films and have had features produced. In fact, I believe that what I have most to offer is perhaps that I am aware both of Hollywood and what I call the "European model" as well as the "independent" film approach. What I write about, therefore, I have been through, from A to Z, both writing scripts and seeing them through to the final cut and on to distribution. And I also have found that over a decade of teaching has helped clarify much of my thinking about the craft. (I should add that, as in any teaching, my students often have had much to offer that has influenced me over the years.)

Part 1 provides a broad context for the character-centered script by examining various conceptions of character; it also provides a look in some detail at the characters in our five selected scripts: *Boyz N the Hood, Thelma & Louise,* and *The Silence of the Lambs* from the United States, *Time of the Gypsies* from abroad, and "Northern Exposure" from television. My emphasis is squarely on recent works as opposed to classical films (which I do allude to) because of my feeling that we need to better understand the trends and possibilities of our own screenwriting environment, worldwide. *I also feel there is a need for a separate text describing and analyzing a variety of classical screenplays.* Each of the five films discussed in this study was chosen to help illustrate a different dimension of contemporary filmmaking: *Boyz N the Hood* is an example of minority filmmaking done through a major studio; *Thelma & Louise* is written and produced by women working in a "man's genre," the road film (of course it helped that a director of Ridley Scott's reputation wished to make the film); *The Silence of the Lambs* is an example of adaptation from fiction to film, and of an effort to take a popular genre—the horror/crime film—and make something more of it (remember that Dostoevsky's *Crime and Punishment* was based on a newspaper murder story). And finally, *Time of the Gypsies* deserves study because it is a "foreign" film even though it was produced through Columbia Pictures; furthermore, it is a foreign film with a world audience.

Part 2 goes into the narrative and structure of character-centered scripts within the context of Western narrative since the time of the Homeric oral epics. A review of the "classical Hollywood narrative" becomes the basis for exploring variations to this "standard" narrative structure that has varied little since its codification in Hollywood as early as 1917.

Part 3 focuses on the practical needs of writing such a script, based on exercises for a fourteen-week "character building" schedule and a fourteen-week feature script schedule, which should see you through the writing of a screenplay from concept and treatment to finished work.

And the final section is a guide to computer software, how to enter your script in contests, or apply for fellowships, or possibly work with foreign filmmakers and even produce your script yourself. Concerning this last subject, I would suggest that I have tried to provide an insider's look at the importance of film festivals and independent productions as well as screenplay competitions and specialized screenplay programs across the country and abroad.

The appendix contains samples of "coverage" (one-page script summary/analysis exercises), and also added are examples of self-critiques and recommended books and scripts for your personal library and information on where to find almost any video you wish at a reasonable price.

> I may be crazy, but I'm nobody's fool.
> Bessie Smith

The Greek word for poet is *poietes*, which translates as "one who makes." From the ancient Greek perspective, a poet did not WRITE a poem or play. Rather, he or she MADE it.

I feel this approach is helpful for us as we face the screenplay, especially the character-centered script. For "making" suggests there is a craft to be learned (furniture making, weaving, architecture) which involves materials to be shaped through skill, talent, experience, *and inspiration*.

You will be asked to *make* characters and then *make them into a narrative script that we hope will become a movie.*

After all, we DO say we "make" movies, just as we say we make love.

This book is about making scripts. And it is about the very real *pleasures* of screenwriting. I have long felt that screenwriting gives me more pleasure than just about anything else I can think of. I simply like to make scripts. And I enjoy seeing the pleasure begin to set in with beginning screenwriters who break through the frustration and pain barriers that go with the first stages of writing.

This book is also about developing the courage to take risks, stretch your imagination, travel to uncharted regions, and report back to yourself.

Seymour Chatman put it well: "A viable theory of character should preserve *openness* and treat characters as autonomous beings, not as mere plot functions" (1978, 119).

Enjoy the odyssey, the open road. And remember the advice of wise screenwriters everywhere: more important than watching movies and television for the process of writing scripts is to live fully and read deeply.

REVIEW: CHARACTER-CENTERED CHECKLIST

1. The character-centered script portrays character not as a static state of being but as a dynamic process of becoming which we

will call the carnivalesque: in brief, the carnivalesque describes an ongoing, ever-changing state in which character is recognized as being made up of many "voices" within us, each with its own history, needs, flavor, limitations, joys, and rhythms.

2. The character-centered script takes chances.

3. In the character-centered script, we and the characters are confronted with difficult and often contradictory moral choices.

4. The character-centered script often breaks some or many of the so-called "rules" of Hollywood scriptwriting.

5. The character-centered script is aware that the characters' lives are strongly affected by core characteristics and experiences that the audience and the characters themselves may or may not come to identify and understand.

6. The character-centered script suggests that beyond core characteristics and experiences, there is mystery and a realm of the unresolved—that area which we cannot fully or totally know, understand, embrace.

Works Cited in Introduction

Aristotle. *On The Art of Poetry.* Trans. Lane Cooper. Ithaca: Cornell University Press, 1947. [Originally published 1913]

Bakhtin, Mikhail. *The Dialogic Imagination.* Ed. Michael Holquist, trans. Caryl Emerson and Michael Holquist. Austin: University of Texas Press, 1981.

Bettelheim, Bruno. *The Uses of Enchantment: The Meaning and Importance of Fairy Tales.* New York: Vintage Books, 1989.

Buñuel, Luis. *My Last Sigh: The Autobiography of Luis Buñuel.* Trans. Abigail Israel. New York: Alfred A. Knopf, 1983.

Cates, Gilbert. Directors Guild of America workshop, Los Angeles, August 1991.

Chatman, Seymour. *Story and Discourse: Narrative Structure in Fiction and Film.* Ithaca: Cornell University Press, 1978.

Collin, Richard, and Rima Collin. *The New Orleans Cookbook.* New York: Knopf, 1989.

Egri, Lajos. *The Art of Dramatic Writing.* New York: Simon & Schuster, 1949.

Elias, Michael. Directors Guild of America workshop, Los Angeles, August 1991.

Frolov, Diane. "Interview." In William Froug's *The New Screenwriter*

Looks at the New Screenwriter. Los Angeles: Silman-James Press, 1992.

Goldman, William. *Adventures in the Screen Trade.* New York: Warner Books, 1983.

Goodell, Jeffrey. "Hollywood's Hard Times." *Premiere,* January 1992: 29–36.

Hill, George Roy. Personal interview, New Orleans, 1991.

Hinson, Hal. "Yarns That Don't Connect." *Washington Post,* 23 November 1990, sec. C, p. 7.

Horton, Andrew. "The 'How to Write the Best Ever Screenplay' Book Biz." *Cineaste* 19, nos. 2–3 (Winter 1992–1993): 12–14.

Khouri, Callie. Symposium on *Thelma & Louise,* Writers Guild of America West, November 1991.

Kinder, Marsha. *Playing with Power in Movies, Television and Video Games.* Berkeley, Los Angeles, London: University of California Press, 1991.

Kshetarpal, Amit. "Civilization and Its Discontents Revisited." Speech delivered at the New Orleans Psychoanalytic Society, December 1988.

Kurosawa, Akira. *Something Like an Autobiography.* Trans. Audie E. Bock. New York: Alfred A. Knopf, 1982.

Lipsitz, George. "Mardi Gras Indians: Carnival and Counter-Narrative in Black New Orleans." In *Time Passages: Collective Memory and American Popular Culture.* Minneapolis: University of Minnesota Press, 1990, 233–256.

Lucey, Paul. "Story Sense." Unpublished manuscript.

McMurtry, Larry. "Character, the Tube, and the Death of the Movies." In *Film Flam: Essays on Hollywood.* New York: Touchstone, 1987.

Nicolaides, Steve. Personal interview, Directors Guild of America, August 1991.

O'Connor, Flannery. "The Grotesque in Southern Fiction." In *Mystery and Manners.* New York: Farrar Straus, 1969.

Parker, Alan. Personal interview, New Orleans, April 1987.

Pond, Steve. "The Year in Revenue." *The Washington Post,* 27 December 1991, p. C-7.

Schneider, Wolf. "Playing It Safe." *American Film,* December 1991: 2.

Soderbergh, Steven. *sex, lies and videotape.* New York: Harper & Row, 1990.

Swain, Dwight V. *Creating Characters.* Cincinnati: Writers' Digest Books, 1990.

Taylor, John. "Woody in Wonderland." *New York,* 30 September 1991, 21–24.

Thomson, David. *Overexposures.* New York: William Morrow, 1981.

Todorov, Tzvetan. *The Poetics of Narrative*. Ithaca: Cornell University Press, 1977.

Vogler, Christopher. *The Writer's Journey: Mythic Structure for Storytellers and Screenwriters*. Los Angeles: Michael Wise Productions, 1992.

PART I

CHARACTER

Life's too slippery for books, Clarice. Typhoid and swans come from the same God.

Hannibal Lecter, in *The Silence of The Lambs*

The horizons of personality always recede before us.

Seymour Chatman, *Story and Discourse*

CHAPTER ONE

THE FEAST OF BECOMING: CARNIVAL AND CHARACTER

> What is going on in these pictures in my mind?
>
> Joan Didion, "Why I Write"

A PROCESS THEORY OF CHARACTER

Novelist William H. Gass writes, "A character, first of all, is the *noise of his name*, and all the sounds and rhythms that proceed from him" (1988, 272, emphasis my own). Seymour Chatman, on page 23, takes note of the endlessly receding nature of such "noise." For we all feel we KNOW what character is until we try to explain it. Yes, character is somehow everything that makes us *who we are as individuals*.

But what is that? And what is the difference between the way we see ourselves and how we are perceived by others? As the twentieth century winds down, perhaps we are too self-conscious in that we in the West have come to think of character (thus our "selves") in basically Freudian and post-Freudian psychological and psychoanalytic terms as opposed to other models (religious, historical, cultural). Yet in posing a question about the nature of character, I wish to go beyond the usual psychological labels and categories to offer a more open-ended view of character as *process* and *discourse* rather than product.

Roland Barthes (1974) comments that "character is a product of combinations" (67). As such, he continues, character is an ever-changing "adjective" rather than a thing or "noun": "Even though the connotation may be clear, the nomination of its [character] signified is uncertain, approximate, unstable" (190). Translation: character is never complete, set, finished but always glimpsed in motion from a certain perspective. "What is character?" thus leads to "Who is asking, how, why, when?"

Barthes is speaking of characters in written fiction. But his observations help start our investigation into the theory of character *as we perceive it in "life"* and as we create it on the page while imagining it for its final destination: the screen. What we should focus on in Barthes's approach is his centering of character not in *psychology* per se, but in interactive *language* processes. "Characters are types of discourse," he adds (179). With such a basis, he builds his theory of character on the *seme*, the smallest unit of linguistic meaning, observing that a single seme is not complete in itself but is "only a *departure*, an avenue of meaning" (191). A complete character, therefore, is, in Barthes's view, "no more than a collection of *semes*."

Anthropologist and cultural theorist Claude Lévi-Strauss takes us a step farther. His study of myth suggests implications for a process theory of character as well. He points, like Barthes, to an ongoing, open-ended view of culture, personality, and narrative myth. "The evidence is never complete," writes Lévi-Strauss (1969, 5). The "deep structure" he has sought in myth and culture and the "core characteristics" we have discussed in the introduction must be viewed against an ever-shifting context:

> There is no real end to mythological analysis, no hidden unity to
> be grasped once the breaking down process has been completed.
> Themes can be split up *ad infinitum*. The unity of the myth is never
> more than tendential and projective. (5)

Such thoughts may seem very far from the actual work of writing a *Raiders of the Lost Ark* action/adventure movie under contract or even an off-Hollywood independent feature such as *Just Another Girl on the IRT* (written and directed by Leslie Harris, 1993).

But in actuality, the emphasis on process and discourse—the interaction of voices and languages through history and cultures—that both Barthes and Lévi-Strauss suggest, should prove useful for all screenwriters. The message is clear: treat character as a complex network of "discourse" or "myths" that cannot be totally explored, explained, examined. The rub is to be able to create characters who have such resonance, even in what may appear to be a stereotypic genre film (western, musical, thriller) or a campy comedy, that they break out of any limiting stereotypes we are used to. Take one simple example: why does the Clint Eastwood figure in *Unforgiven* (screenplay by David Webb Peoples) leave his children, home, and farm and, after so many years of the "straight life," take up his guns again to become a hired gunman? No simple answer can be given. "For the money," "for the adventure," "because his life has become too boring," "for the cause of justice," "because a woman has been wronged and he remembers his own dear departed wife," and so forth. The motivation is perhaps all of these processes and discourses and more. But *it doesn't matter*. As created by screenwriter David Webb Peoples, the "evidence" of this film, which won four Oscars, is "never complete" to quote Lévi-Strauss once more. We thus have a double experience as audience members; first we enjoy the *genre*—western—with all its "set" codes, formulas, cliches. And then Peoples expands the experience by opening up his characters beyond what we have seen in traditional westerns. It is this very incompleteness that makes People's western what *Premiere* editor Peter Biskind called the only 1992 Hollywood film that "deserves to stand with the other great movies of the past" (1993, 51).

The sense of character as process leads us to the concept of the *carnivalesque* and to Mikhail Bakhtin's description of it. But it is not carnival per se that the Russian theoretician Bakhtin was initially concerned with. Thus we must look at Bakhtin's view of language and character. Years before Barthes and others were writing about character as discourse and process, Bakhtin (1981) wrote:

> My voice gives the illusion of unity to what I say; I am, in fact, constantly expressing a plentitude of meanings, some intended, others of which I am unaware. (88)

This point is driven home even more clearly by Bakhtin in his elaboration of the "polyphonic." Bakhtin best explained his term in his discussion of Dostoyevsky's novels. He pointed out that what really distinguishes Dostoyevsky not only as a great novelist but as the father of the modern novel is the unresolved nature of his characters. Bakhtin (1984) puts it this way:

> In none of Dostoyevsky's novels is there any evolution of a unified spirit. . . . Each novel presents an opposition which is never canceled out dialectically, *of many consciousnesses*, and they do not merge in the unity of an evolving spirit, just as souls and spirits do not merge in the formally polyphonic world of Dante. (26, emphasis my own)

What Bakhtin suggests is that the polyphonic character and thus the polyphonic novel is one in which the hero is not a "fixed image, but *the sum total of his consciousness and self-consciousness*" (1984, 48). The novel itself and Dostoyevsky's novels in particular, Bakhtin held, allowed for a polyphonic viewpoint and form because, unlike poetry and drama, it was the literary form that was most "formless" and thus more plastic, more capable of incorporating "a particular point of view on the world and on oneself" (47).

Bakhtin's comments are useful on a number of levels. His focus on the novel, for instance, helps us to move beyond the mindset of *drama* which has so thoroughly dominated the classical Hollywood script and those industry-oriented books about screenwriting that emphasize an Aristotelian, cause and effect, plot-driven form of writing. Yes, a film is like a drama in that it uses actors and is limited to what the audience will endure within a two- to three-hour framework. But *film resembles the novel in its ability to transcend time and space (film editing) and present a truly POLYPHONIC universe.* In this sense far too much film and television is composed of an unimaginative use of the medium. On the one hand, much of what we see in either medium in terms of narrative programming consists of "talking heads": characters in medium close-up talking. On the other hand, we are aware that other programs and films focus much more on special effects and fast editing (montage) at the expense of character development.

But cinema and television have so much more potential to render character, action, human experience that we should feel free to explore. Of course when Hollywood moved from silent films to sound, playwrights were hired by the dozen to write for the screen with the result that many of those early talkies were quite "stagey." But the best of these East Coast dramatists, such as Preston Sturges and others, quickly saw the polyphonic possibilities of the medium which far exceeded the boundaries of theater both in terms of character and plot. Linda Seger (1990) underscores this sense of polyphony in her book, *Creating Unforgettable Characters*, when she notes that "the defining of character is a back-and-forth process" (22). We could add more: *defining character is an always unfinalized process because character itself is never finalized—except by death itself, which merely wraps the mystery rather than exposes it.*

Character as defined by Bakhtin involves the crossing of multiple traits/voices with a process that is one of becoming rather than that of stasis or "being." This calls to mind the notion of carnival. For it is carnival itself, Bakhtin points out, that is just such a festive embodiment or heightening of such a description.

Carnival is process—becoming—in its purest form. It is the time when no rules hold or rather when one can become whatever he or she wishes. This is the true "feast of becoming." Nobody is stuck, static, passive within the world of carnival. There are only participants, Bakhtin notes, and all participants win because they can do and be anything, anybody. Bakhtin writes: "During carnival time life is subject only to its laws, that is, the laws of its own freedom. It has a universal spirit; it is a special condition of the entire world, of the world's revival and renewal, in which all take part" (1968, 7).

By extension, beyond a literal sense of carnival as a real event located in time and space (Bakhtin was especially interested in the thousand-year-old tradition of European carnival before the Industrial Revolution), the concept of the "carnivalesque" has several implications for a theory of character:

- Character as process (state of becoming)
- Character as polyphony (multiple voices interacting in different ways at different times)
- Character as a social discourse that belongs to and interacts with a culture and its many voices

By this latter comment, we suggest that although each of us is an "individual," there can be no completely "unique" character, for the languages within us have come down to us through time and from the culture in which we participate. Nevertheless, the nature of language and experience guarantees that no two people are exactly alike. Caryl Emerson, in writing on Bakhtin, puts it this way: "Because no two individuals ever entirely coincide in their experience or belong to precisely the same set of social groups, every act of understanding involves an act of translation and a negotiation of values" (1984, 24).

The embracing of the carnivalesque in creating characters could involve literal festivity and plot development centered on carefree actions. It is important to John Sayles's *Passion Fish* (1992) that the resolution of the relationships the two main women—May-Alice (Mary McDonnell) the crippled soap opera star and Chantelle (Alfre Woodard), her black nurse—reach with their men takes place at a Cajun festival. The open air festivity of Louisiana blacks and whites mingling happily as they dance, laugh, feast, and sing literally embodies the sense of the carnivalesque each woman has needed in her life.

But the term as I will use it throughout the text is meant to embody the sense of both *potentiality* and of the *unfinalizedness* which carnival evokes for characters whether they are in a "festive" atmosphere/event/location or not. And I employ the carnivalesque both as a description of the free play and fantasy needed to actually write a script and as the end result of the characters finally placed on the page in all of their "unfinalized" glory.

A sense of the carnivalesque becomes even clearer if one understands the difference Bakhtin sees between the traditions of the Epic and that of the Novel.

As I mentioned earlier, Bakhtin saw Dostoevsky as taking advantage of the open-endedness of the novel as a form to create polyphonic characters. In his essay "Epic and Novel," Bakhtin goes further. The point of epics such as those of Homer is that they are completed and set. "We encounter the epic," he writes, "as a genre that has not only long since completed its development, but one that is already antiquated" (1981, 49).

The novel, however, Bakhtin argues, is still a genre without a canon, without a defined form. "The novel parodies other genres," he notes, because of its freedom to incorporate any material in any style/manner/language through any characters imagined. The strength of the novel is, therefore, a sense of the carnivalesque: "The novel inserts into other genres an indeterminacy, a certain semantic open-endedness, a living contact with unfinished, still-evolving *contemporary reality* (the open-ended present)" (53, emphasis my own).

The character-centered screenplay reflects the same capacity and potential for cinema that the novel holds for Bakhtin. And, as used in this text, "the carnivalesque" is the term we shall use to embody this sense of open-ended, multivoiced discourse and potential for character and for narrative. As Bakhtin writes, "The novel is, by its very nature, not canonic. It is plasticity itself."

Of course a sense of the carnivalesque—of plasticity itself—may have its set limitations depending on the genre. George Lucas's *Star Wars* trilogy comes much closer to the realm of the epic as described by Bakhtin. But it is our premise that any script, no matter the genre, can develop more fully realized characters that break out of stereotypic genre patterns by making use of some of the advice and exercises suggested in this text.

In terms of the carnivalesque embracing "plasticity itself"—that is, of a free play of the imagination, I do not mean to suggest that you will create characters that change radically from moment to moment dressed in carnival masks. What I do suggest, however, is that *your characters must constantly be capable of surprising you even when you think you know them well because they and we are made up of so many voices that often do not have the chance or means to be expressed.* Our opening quotation from the great Spanish surrealist filmmaker, Luis Buñuel, celebrates *personality/character trait contradictions that are not resolved.* It is the spirit of carnival, as incorporated in your writing and attitude, that can free you to celebrate and thus explore a wider range of character possibilities that lie outside the realm of the clearly motivated script. *This is not to suggest that you should do away with all motivation*: rather it is to say that you should not be a slave to simple/obvious motivations. Woody Allen ends *Husbands and Wives* (1992) with the tellingly appropriate line as he himself faces the "documentary camera" and says "the human heart does not know from reason."

Finally our other term—core characteristic or core experience—needs further clarification. Such a description is not meant to suggest that any one characteristic or experience "determines" or sums up a character.

Far from it. But within an individual's experience of many voices constantly in the process of expressing themselves (or in the process of being repressed), *there are those experiences, painful or pleasurable, and characteristics which tend to be repeated or which gain importance because they offer further insight into the complexity of a character.* One such core experience for Louise in *Thelma & Louise* is whatever happened to her in Texas that was so extreme (and we assume it was a rape experience) that it had a direct bearing on her pulling the trigger when Thelma was being raped. That experience in and of itself (never named in the script or film) did not "determine" all. But the hint of it throughout the film suggests its strong influence on all of the "voices" within Louise.

These terms—core experience and core characteristics—are not meant to be reductive in any simple psychological way. Rather, they are meant to suggest certain patterns of behavior and traits that help us "center" our understanding of that character.

· · ·

How do you create or find such characters? Once again, start with those who come to you, those you can't forget, can't get out of your mind. Ask yourself why, what makes them tick, why are you drawn to them (as in the case of Hannibal Lecter, the draw might be a mixed one of sympathy and fear!). *We don't understand ourselves, so why should we be able to understand our characters?*

Beyond this capacity for growth and surprise, your character should be *engaging*. This does not mean that he or she is necessarily a "good" person with a winning personality. I choose "engaging" rather than "sympathetic," for if we consider Hannibal Lecter again, we see that what engages us is not covered by the concept of "sympathy." *We are interested in him despite our better (conscious) judgment.* Thus I suggest our characters, either by being honestly ordinary or arrestingly unusual, must pull us into their worlds.

Certainly part of the engaging element is *vulnerability*. Even in *Henry, Portrait of a Serial Killer* (John McNaughton and Richard Fire 1990), we see that Henry turns off the snuff video his partner has made because it is clearly "too much" even for a serial killer. If a character is 100 percent invulnerable, he or she is closed off, complete, DEAD. What makes even *Terminator 2* more than just the plot-centered script it might otherwise be is the fact that the Terminator becomes fully "human" in his character and emotions. *As a machine, the Terminator becomes increasingly vulnerable as he comes to love, share, care for those around him.*

His last act is one of sacrifice—his life (or is "existence" more accurate?!) given for that of a woman and son—an act of self-lessness we do not expect from a mere machine.

We should note that vulnerability does not equal "weakness." Vulnerability rather means your character is open to experience—at whatever level—and that even if he or she does exhibit self-confidence, she can be put in situations that test that confidence and which *open new levels of awareness and response.*

The concept of the carnivalesque is the best way I can think of to remind us that *much of the time when a script is not working, the blame falls on the writer for not knowing more than one or two "voices" within his/her characters.*

Let us express the carnivalesque one other way: what you see is not necessarily what you get. Rick in *Casablanca* seems a hardened, strong, silent type: he's not. He's a sensitive talker who has been wounded in love. The "core experience" that has strongly shaped his adult life is that sense of hurt he still bears. His challenge, which he meets, is to overcome his hurt, let go, and accept love on a higher level. We are not speaking of scientific formulas here, but there is a goodly percentage of character in any frame of the character-centered script which is *outside the frame* simply because of that sense of mystery and surprise that awaits us. If we do not feel that, we become bored in life as in film. *Think how dull our own lives would be if we knew exactly what we would do and when in every circumstance.* We could not stand life on these terms.

The crossing of the three "C"s—character/circumstance/chance—allows for an endless range of "voices" to speak and express themselves, both verbally and visually. This is the realm of the carnivalesque. That which is totally known or known completely in advance is routine! Simply for the point of emphasis, if we can say that in a typical scene in a traditional Hollywood film, maybe (rough guess) 25 percent of what is going on is unknown to us (and thus a surprise), in the character-centered script, that can often approach 50 percent or more. This is particularly true, I think, in a production like *Time of the Gypsies*, since both the characters and plot seem very "foreign" (and thus exotic) to us. But it is also true of seemingly simple projects such as Jim Jarmusch's minimalist films including *Night on Earth* (1992), which is a series of five taxi rides in five cities of the world—Los Angeles/New York/Paris/Rome/Helsinki. We are given so little to go on in each "ride" that at least 50 percent of what is going on is a delightful mystery to us to puzzle over and enjoy.

The dance between the two—between the known and the unknown—gives us character, that ongoing, never-ending feast of possibility and becoming, that carnival which is truly what human character is.

It is up to you to hear those voices, identify those traits, and place them, through this process, on paper. But begin with a question rather than a statement.

Creating the character-centered script means asking a continuous set of questions to and of yourself and others. Joan Didion, who writes screenplays as well as novels and essays, notes: "I write entirely to find out what I'm thinking, what I'm looking at, what I see, and what it means" (1976). Instead of *imposing* a structure or a set of characters, she begins with "pictures in my mind" which are "images that shimmer around the edges." She allows, therefore, the characters and story to *become*: this is, a true sense of the *carnivalesque*. The images in her mind have a resonance, a texture, a meaning that cannot be easily pinned down or identified. But the existence of the strong impression (in her mind) is the clue that there is an echo that cannot be ignored or forgotten, even if it is difficult to express.

WHO'S CARRYING A FROG IN HIS POCKET? REALITY AS CARNIVAL

No one has ever created a more carnivalesque form of cinema than Yugoslav director Dusan Makavejev. In films ranging from *Loves of a Switchboard Operator* (1964), *Innocence Unprotected* (1966), *W. R.: Mysteries of the Organism* (1971), and *Sweet Movie* (1974), Makavejev celebrates the seemingly endless potential of cinema and life to be whatever it/they would want to be. Only partially scripted, his films became carnival in every sense, especially in the destruction of traditional narrative and psychological character "logic."

But Makavejev began as a documentary filmmaker and has always claimed that reality is stranger than any fiction (1989). His sense of the mystery of human character is likewise strong. In a recent speech in Holland, he illustrated this capacity for CHARACTER to outstrip even our wildest imagination with this tale:

> While working on my first feature film, *Man Is Not a Bird* (1961), I wanted to have a man who eats snakes in the travelling circus scene. I found him actually performing for miners in the mine where we were shooting the film. We agreed to talk about him taking part in the film on Wednesday morning. He arrived for breakfast, impeccably dressed: white shirt and tie. In the middle of our breakfast it dawns on me that he must be keeping his beasts in his room. "What if the cleaning maid bumps into them?" I asked him. "Oh, no," he says, "they need a warm place. They sleep during the day." Then he

unbuttoned his shirt and there they were, two snakes sleeping under his armpit. I don't dare to ask the people in this hall if there is any-body who carries a frog in his pocket. Or a bomb. We have no way of knowing and we don't want to learn about it. Please don't throw out this frog. *We are passionate about movies, because we are passionate about life.* (1991, 33)

The character-centered script knows that each of us carries *something* under our shirt!

"Reality is there: why change it?" Vittorio De Sica, the Italian director who championed "neorealism" used to say.

Fiction grows out of the real world we each come to know in our own way. Thus the need in creating character to start with life, with the *documentary self.* Obvious? Perhaps, but as *Washington Post* critic Hal Hinson notes, "With rare exceptions, the lives we see portrayed on the screen are dim reflections of the lives we live. We sit in the dark hoping to see ourselves, our conflicts, our ecstasies, to see the true facts of our relationships and our struggles revealed. And we depart the cinemas in despair" (1992, G1).

Consider this scene:

Dan, a pudgy, middle-aged man with a moustache and a balding head in blue jeans and a sweatshirt, shoots baskets outside a Mental Health Clinic in Flint, Michigan in the slanting sunlight of a late afternoon winter day.

He pauses, looks at us, holds his pack of cigarettes, and begins to talk about why he went a bit crazy after being laid off five times in five years from the General Motors plant in Flint:

DAN

I just couldn't take it any more, so I told the guy next to me on the assembly line to tell the boss I was sick to my stomach—I just didn't give a shit any more, and I flew out the door, pushed past the guard, jumped into my car and got onto Bristol Road and went back to my apartment, turned on the radio thinking that might cheer me up because I had like TEARS coming out of my eyes, and I strike into the middle of "Wouldn't It Be Nice" by The Beach Boys, and I think to myself, "What a horrible song to hear in the midst of this panic attack and I try to sing along . . . "Wouldn't it be nice if we were older . . .", and I have this apple in my throat as I try to sing.

There is an engaging, boyish twinkle in his eyes, which also have the lines of troubled times around them.

The scene is not a monologue in an Elia Kazan *On The Waterfront* dramatic saga. Rather, it's one of the many memorable moments in the most popular American documentary ever, Michael Moore's *Roger & Me* (1990), a funny and sad subjective look at what is happening to many of our cities as big industries such as General Motors pull out and begin to set up factories abroad. Moore and those who worked with him for three years to put this homegrown film together learned an important fact about character: *real people are every bit as fascinating to us as fictional figures, if not more.* Who could script a more telling, more moving auto worker than Dan himself? Look at how much character comes through in his speech alone: his sense of being able to construct a narrative out of his own pain, his colorful use of verbs that personalize his speech such as "strike into," or the slightly archaic "in the midst of," together with his otherwise very informal speech. His feel for telling details, especially the Beach Boys tune. He MOVES us with his pain as he recounts it.

And Michael Moore succeeds in his mission as filmmaker because he has *allowed characters to speak for themselves, to be their own witnesses within the framework of his purpose*: to document the disaster that Flint has become in large part at the hands of a large American corporation.

Every writer of fiction scripts would do well to begin with documentaries. Note that this is the approach I suggest in part 4 in the series of character exercises offered.

For *Roger & Me* also brings out another major point we should all remember: *the line between documentary (that is, "real life") and fiction is always a thin one, a shifting one, a complex one.* A book that is definitely useful in helping a writer understand how to draw honest fiction from real life is Erving Polster's *Every Person's Life Is Worth a Novel.* Polster notes, "All people start with a journey through the uterine canal to enter a foreign world" (1987, 3). That journey, that life, guarantees, as he remarks, that "no one can escape *being* interesting" even if people do "*ignore* the profusion of influences" on them. According to Polster:

> Whether realizing it at the time or not, each person is recurrently party to mystery, violence, suspense, sex, ambition, and the uncertainty of personal resolutions. And eventually, there is death for all! Like a mountain stream that carves out a river bed, these and many other experiences cut through people's lives, engraving character. (3)

Thus the call to the writer to live fully, observe accurately, to discover more than impose shapes, shades, gestures, actions, meaning itself.

"A film is a documentary fairy tale," says director Srdjan Karanovic with whom I have worked on a number of projects, "and that goes double for my films: begin with something very real and move out." *Virgina*, the 1991 film we had worked on together, started with Karanovic's fascination for an old custom in parts of the former Yugoslavia where villagers could raise a girl as a boy if they had too many daughters. It's not hard to come up with a fictional story given this strange a reality!

Documentary fairy tale. Karanovic's phrase suggests the double effect of narrative: on one hand, as writers and as viewers/readers, we enjoy the pleasure of fiction—that is, make believe. On the other hand, narratives that move us to tears or laughter or deep involvement do so because they connect with elements or characters we recognize as "real." We know that deer don't speak. But we recognize that part of the "documentary" power of a children's film such as *Bambi* is that it treats the very real pain of losing a mother at an early age. In this sense, "documentary" suggests not just newspaper/CNN and a photographic reality but *emotional* truth. But I emphasize that the importance of the "documentary" in creative writing is not an attempt to minimalize the significance of the imagination. It is rather to say that in an age in which so many filmmakers/writers recycle previous narratives from television and film rather than from personal life experiences, there is clearly a danger of screenplays being produced that fail to involve us beyond a surface plot level.

Of course the documentary glance begins or ends or both with a closer look at yourself, whether you feel you are writing highly autobiographical projects or not. Shakespeare did not leave a very detailed record of his personal life, but it doesn't matter. The richly drawn carnival of characters he created is the testimony to a self that documented a wide spectrum of human existence. Those characters did not come from imagination alone. They come from life deeply observed, felt, transformed.

Charlie Chaplin felt this strongly, too. He knew that most comedy comes from pain and that the pain he portrayed is based on his experience and observation. His Tramp became popular when millions were (as they still are) homeless. He often said he would spend days observing people—drunks, crazies, high society types, street people—before making a film, and the enduring quality of his work testifies that he lived life fully and observed it accurately. Note that it is the distillation of the real that reveals the deep structure, the motivations and details upon which you can more successfully construct character.

Chaplin is not remembered so much for particular bits of slapstick, comic moments, farcical routines as he is for being the Tramp. He knew that the close-up he so often employed with those sad eyes and boyish smile expressed the Tramp's deep structural need: the need to be loved, embraced, taken in, respected. He needs these things because the Tramp is the eternal Outsider. Thus the ending of most Chaplin films: the Tramp alone, back to camera, going down the road doing his awkward, funny walk.

What Chaplin knew how to do was to bring out the "truth" of the reality around him. A recent article by Constance Brown Kuriyama (1992) points out how much of Chaplin's response to his real life actually wound up in his films, especially his manic-depressive response to his alcoholic father and his at times insane mother.

It is this process, this locating of the deep structure within reality that the screenwriter must do as well. Critic Hal Hinson points this out in his 1992 essay on "Screening Out Life: How the Movies Lost Their Grip on Reality" when he concludes, "Facts aren't enough, as even the garishly authentic court cases of William Kennedy Smith and Jeffrey Dahmer numbingly proved. Issues and facts, without the designing hand of the artist, are only part of the story. The artist provides the essential context, the emotions behind the facts; without them, the truth in these 'true' stories is without meaning, a mere sketch without dimension or resonance" (G-5).

CHARACTER AND CONTEXT

Consider the degree to which character is influenced and determined by context: by the times and places in which we live. An example:

A plain twelve-year-old girl holds her eight-year-old brother's hand. They stand by a deserted highway in the rainy mist hitchhiking. The way they are framed, they are engulfed by the immensity of the misty sky that surrounds them. They are the main figures in the Oscar-nominated film by Greek director Theo Angelopoulos, *Landscape in the Mist* (1990). And even if you did not know that the film concerns their running away from their mother to undertake a fruitless search for a father "who doesn't exist," Angelopoulos's use of place would suggest all the "character" you need to understand his film.

We are all "children of accident," as Luis Buñuel has said (1983, 170). We are a crossroad of inherited, biological traits and psychological potentialities, but also of environmental "voices" of PLACE AND TIME mixed by CHANCE.

Place and time—CONTEXT—have much to do with determining character. We begin our investigation of character by recognizing this power.

Your script will concern characters and actions. But your script takes place somewhere, at some time, either specific to history or purposely ahistorical and mythic. Orson Welles's *Citizen Kane* (script by Welles & Herman J. Mankiewitz 1939) is defined to a large extent by the foreboding castle framed in the opening shot by the threatening fence with the sign "NO TRESPASSING." We are not meant to identify any specific time, but we do feel this space is one that is quite removed from our world and full of darkness and gloom. Think how much of the dying Kane's character is set by this use of place. It would not be the same film had Welles begun with the scene of Kane dropping the snow-filled paperweight and muttering "Rosebud," for we would have missed the "character" established through the opening "trespassing" shot.

To create characters for the screen is to search for individual voices to whom you wish to give life. But we begin with a realization that such individuality is centered in a particular location, society, era. This goes for films with a studio look as well as those that strike us in their realism. *Casablanca* is a Hollywood creation of North Africa during the war, but its psychological "place" is very much of the times, of an America that was turning from noninvolvement to a full commitment to fighting. To see Rick and his café merely as movie entertainment is to miss the resonance and deeper structure the film conveys.

In contrast, some scripts make it clear that place and time are really central characters: *Boyz N the Hood* with its focus on black Los Angeles, *Time of the Gypsies* and its world of Yugoslav gypsies, *Thelma & Louise* and its celebration of the landscape of the Southwest all lead us to *feel* as well as think of how time and place reflect, act upon, shape character.

I am speaking of individual shots/scenes as well as a dominant sense of a whole script/film. Writer-director Alan Pakula likes to speak about the "architecture" of his films. Both *The Parallax View* (Lorenzo Semple 1974) and *Presumed Innocent* (Frank Pierson & Alan J. Pakula 1990) open and close with shots of courtrooms, using a slow tracking forward for the openings and a slow tracking back for the closing shots. Of course such a framing establishes the world of the law as the main protagonists of these narratives. In *The Parallax View* it is the paranoid world of injustice as a Kennedy-styled assassination is hushed up in court, and in *Presumed Innocent* we encounter a personal story of a lawyer who is himself caught up in a web of murder and deceit. The empty courtroom used in *Presumed Innocent* becomes the space filled with characters. But even in its empty state, it presents itself as a force to be considered.

Knowing the place and times makes knowing the character much easier.

CORE CHARACTERISTICS AND CHARACTER

You should know your characters well enough to know *to what level you can know no more.* Luis Buñuel put it this way: "All this compulsion to *understand* everything fills me with horror" (1983, 175). You should not oversimplify your presentation of character. If you are, as director Robert Bresson says, discovering only what can be explained, then your characters will not resonate as they will if you can suggest what cannot be totally shown, explained, captured. Take an action genre film such as Walter Hill's directorial debut, *Hard Times* (1975), starring Charles Bronson as Jean, a tough street boxer who passes through New Orleans during the Depression. What we do know is that Jean is an unbeatable boxer who is tough but fair in all his relationships with those around him. And we also learn that, finally, he is not in the ring for the money as he at first says he is, for by film's end, he gives away all the prize money and walks off into the dark from whence he came at the beginning of the narrative. Thus what we never come to know is where he came from, where he is going, and why he is the way he is. *Hill deepens the effect of his film by not explaining away Jean's behavior with some simplistic flashback to a troubled past or a direct discussion of some specific wrong done that accounts for his character.*

Robert Bresson has always been a particular purist in his films to the degree that he preferred to work with nonprofessionals in order to capture a nontheatrical level of character. In one of his most affecting films, *Mouchette* (1966, based on the novel by Georges Bernanos), he used a fourteen-year-old French village girl (Nadine Nortier) to play a French village girl who "expresses" little and experiences more in terms of gestures of rejection and abuse than anyone should experience. She does not *tell* us what she is thinking and, in fact, we come to feel she most likely could not or at least would not articulate exactly what it is and how she feels. In part, her inability to express herself and her lack of anyone to turn to is the point of the film.

Thus the ending when, in what looks like a simple childish game of rolling down a hill into a pond, she finally falls into the water and fails to surface, becomes both a shock and a nonshock. On the immediate level her suicide is totally unexpected. And yet the "aftershock" we the audience feel is one of realizing what Bresson has prepared us for all along: that Mouchette's *core characteristic* is one of a deep inner strength that does not want to compromise and live in a world as cruel as the only world she knows: provincial patriarchal French society. Bresson's character centeredness is further seen in his remark, "Your imagination will aim less at events than at feelings while wanting these latter to be as *documentary* as possible" (1977, 8).

Actions and the visible, in other words, lead us to that deeper level of character and feeling that can be glimpsed without being explained away. Without that, we have a cinema of surfaces only. This is true to a large degree of many Hollywood films that are motivated on a simple psychological level that can be explained. *Batman Returns* (Daniel Waters 1992) failed to satisfy many beyond the level of spectacle in part because the psychology offered is explained far too well. The Penguin (Danny De Vito) is the way he is, we are blatantly made to know, because his parents threw him into a stream, rejecting him because of his deformity (he was born with webbed hands and feet). *A core experience so clearly set forth is not deep structure at all.* It is more a plot device than a character trait.

Think of Shakespeare's Iago in *Othello*. Iago is one of the purest examples of evil ever to walk the stage. "I am not what I am," (I,i,62) he says in full awareness of his complete duplicity. But why is he out to destroy Othello? We are given an immediate reason: Cassio was chosen over Iago to be Othello's lieutenant. But this action is not sufficient to explain Iago's core need to destroy. Thus by the tragedy's end, just when you might expect some explanation in a lesser work, Iago is carried off without saying a word. Shakespeare leaves us haunted by this man who is captured but not defeated, exposed but not explained. A large part of the effect of *Othello* is Shakespeare's ability to create a character who so totally understands human nature that he can manipulate those around him at his pleasure. *And yet he himself never reveals his innermost feelings and motivations.* We are thus left with a sense of evil and ill will which cannot be explained away. What we can name, we can deal with. But the Iagos of the world are so dangerous precisely because they are not what they are.

. . .

We can think of character as including both personal (inner) and interpersonal (social, public, professional) elements. We should also be aware that there is the level of self-consciousness that the character himself or herself possesses and there is the viewer's/reader's level of awareness which is most often greater than that of the characters. *Traditionally in the classical Hollywood narrative, the viewer has a "privileged position" and thus knows more than the characters involved.* Rick in *Casablanca* does not see all that we see in the opening montage sequence as the various characters with their particular problems begin to gravitate toward Rick's Café. Similarly, the opening crosscutting between

Thelma and Louise in *Thelma & Louise* allows us to know what each character is doing, a point of view that Thelma and Louise do not share.

All characters have inner needs and goals, as well as interpersonal desires (romance, friendship, and so forth), and professional ambitions that help characterize them and impose their own requirements, restrictions, and privileges. To what degree the personal, public, and professional blend, separate, and are accented is up to you and your particular concept of that character.

Note, however, that there may be a large difference between a character's concept of himself/herself and a true deep structural reality. As writers, we deal not with certainties, but with pregnant ambiguities. Too much certainty and we are in danger of falling into clichés once again. Too much ambiguity, of course, can lead in the opposite direction: chaos and boredom. In the middle is the writer as mediator between such opposites.

COMEDY, CARICATURE, AND CHARACTER

CHARLES
Men, that is lots of men, are more careful in choosing a tailor than they are in choosing a wife.

THE LADY EVE
That's probably why they look so funny.

from Preston Sturges's *The Lady Eve* (1941)

Comedy in all of its variations offers the fullest opportunity for carnival and thus for as many voices as possible to have their playful say.

Creating comic characters is a particular talent. The veteran television writer Milt Josefsberg has written most revealingly about the subject in his practical *Comedy Writing*: "Successful comedy is built around solid characters interacting in humorous situations, not just jokes" (1987, 20). He is a firm believer that in comedy as in other genres, we must be able to identify in some way with the characters: "The jokes have been fitted specifically to the person, which helps you identify with the character."

The writer of comedy should begin with the realization that there is nothing inherently funny, sad, tragic, or farcical. It is all a matter of context and perspective (Horton 1991, 3). It is one of the marvels of "Northern Exposure," for instance, that topics that many would consider quite "serious" are treated with wry sympathetic humor: race relations, lesbianism, democracy, death, and aging to mention but a few.

Comedy may well be America's strong suit in cinema. French critic Andre Bazin was fond of saying so whenever he discussed Chaplin, Keaton, Capra, Sturges, Hawks, and many more filmmakers and entertainers who have made the world laugh since the silent period. Yes, comedy can be simply pie-throwing farce on one hand. But as George McFadden has noted, "The great works of comic writing [and we can add 'film'] have extended the range of our feelings" (1982, 243). Put another way, Hollywood of course entertains through comedy, but comedy may also be the way we say some of the most important things we want to say.

In terms of characterization, the writer of comedy most often treads a particular line between stereotypes and fully drawn characters, that is, between caricatures and realistic characters. The secret is to make sure you have written your figures so that the audience has no trouble in distinguishing on what level to take your world of comedy. In *Naked Gun 2½* (David Zucker & Pat Proff 1991), for instance, we open with a scene in which a very dotty "Barbara Bush" winds up hanging from a White House balcony in her bra. A case for a libel suit from the President's lawyers? Not at all. Because even though this was one of the strongest uses of political humor in recent American cinema, Zucker has clearly (and boldly!) set up the Barbara character as a *caricature*: there is no way we are asked to take her seriously or as a copy of the real person. Remember that caricatures are purposeful distortions of character. *By nature the art of caricature is one of being "unfair" to the people being caricatured.*

There are two main divisions of film comedy: the anarchistic, which embraces the satirical in particular, and the romantic. Anarchistic comedy has to do with determining characters with a crazy urge/desire/idea who try to act out that desire with or without success. It is important that they do not compromise themselves. Included under this heading would be all the works of Aristophanes down to the Marx Brothers, Monty Python, "Saturday Night Live," standup comedians and comediennes, and even *Home Alone* and *Sister Act* (1992). Note that real romance has nothing to do with the world of anarchistic comedy, though sex is often central.

Romantic comedy involves a coming together of lovers to form a new partnership after overcoming obstacles. At the center of such comedy is the need to compromise one's own impulses in order to fit in harmony with those of another. Romantic comedy is thus usually prosocial because it suggests a sense of continuity with no basic threats to society. In Freudian terms, you can think of anarchistic comedy as "pre-Oedipal" since it is about a stage of development when the individual is all appetite and no compromise. Romantic comedy, however, is "Oedipal" for it recognizes the need to sublimate one's own desires to work together with those of your partner. The tradition from Roman comedy to Shakespeare and down to our own *screwball comedy* tradition of the 1930s and 1940s lives on in altered contemporary versions such as *Pretty Woman* (J. F. Lawton 1990) and *All of Me* (1984). And although anarchistic comedy tends toward caricature, romantic comedy has always embodied a fuller view of character because of the emotions evoked in romance.

There are, of course, in-between narratives as seen especially in "Northern Exposure." The hints of romance are everywhere, but the characters are also very much their own individuals, leery of compromising at all, and thus happy to be citizens of Cicely, Alaska.

Impostors, Innocents, and Ironic Figures

The two basic divisions of comedy also mean that characters tend to fall into three types: the Impostor, called the *alazon* in ancient Greece; the "innocent," naive figure who, like Buster Keaton in his persona, learns to weather and triumph over adversity; and the "ironic," worldly, and manipulative figure, called the *eiron* in Greek. *Twins* (Herschel Weigrod, Timothy Harris, William J. Davies, and William Osborne 1988) assumes that Danny DeVito and Arnold Schwarzenegger were twins separated at birth. It is classic in its comic structure and characterization as DeVito plays the *eiron* and Schwarzenegger the innocent, "good-hearted" figure at odds with a cynical world. And in Preston Sturges's classic comedy, *The Lady Eve*, it is the Lady Eve (Barbara Stanwyck) who is both *eiron* and imposter out to "get" Charles (Henry Fonda), one of the richest and most naive men in America who has spent years in the jungle hunting snakes.

Of course much of film comedy is built around comedians who have their own personas ranging from Woody Allen, Groucho Marx, Richard Pryor, and Steve Martin on one hand and Goldie Hawn, Mae West, Bette Midler, and Whoopie Goldberg on the other. *Note that the most common main character in American comedy is an eiron: a worldly wise, cynical on the outside, soft in the center kind of character.* It is less common to construct a film around an innocent, a victim, a blank page, as was so successfully done in *Being There* (1979, based on the book and screenplay by Jerzy Kosinski), as Peter Sellers plays a total innocent who has no experience of "the world" other than through allusions to the two areas he does know: television and gardening.

Or, in the spirit of the carnivalesque, there may be any combination of these figures. Woody Allen builds on both traditions and, though he is most often at heart a romantic, trying to find THE woman, even that urge is often undercut by an anarchistic element. Remember that the conclusion of *Bananas* (1971) is that he does indeed marry Louise Lasser. But instead of fading out with the wedding, we go to their first night of the honeymoon in which their bedroom activities are broadcast live on television with Howard Cosel as the sportscaster giving a "blow by blow" account.

A final note: *Since the borders between comedy and drama often cross over and break down, part of thinking of character from a carnivalesque perspective is to think of its "comic" dimensions, even if you are writing a drama.* Think how often these days we describe a film as a comic drama or a dramatic comedy. Is *War of the Roses* (Michael Leeson 1989) really a comedy as all the paperback reference books on movies say it is? And despite the overall seriousness of *The Silence of the Lambs*, don't we delight in Lecter's devilish humor as he plays, in comic terms, a deadly *eiron* to Clarice's naive figure? *Thelma & Louise* seems to mix both comedy and drama equally but with the overall effect centering on drama since the jokes mask or express deeper needs that are serious and, finally, deadly at the same time that they are life affirming.

CHAPTER TWO

VARIETIES OF VOICES WITHIN CHARACTER

> Self-consciousness, as the artistic dominant in the construction of
> the hero's image, is by itself sufficient to break down the monologic
> unity of an artistic world—but only on condition that the hero, as
> self-consciousness, is really represented and not merely expressed,
> that is, does not fuse with the author, does not become the mouth-
> piece for his voice.
>
> Mikhail Bakhtin,
> *Problems of Dostoevsky's Poetics*

Carnival embraces all voices, all characters.

But what kinds of voices exist? To what extent do particular voices
speak through your character at any given time? What follows in this
chapter is meant to be a suggestive overview of a variety of approaches
to character, helping you explore the carnivalesque potential of your
own work. In this sense, do not take any of these descriptions as static,
set, limiting but only as areas of focus that may be useful as you develop
your own scripts.

GENDER/RACE/ETHNICITY

We live in an increasingly pluralistic and diverse culture. And yet that
fact is far too infrequently apparent in our film and television narratives.
At issue here is the number and kinds of characters presented. But it is
also, as we shall remark, about allowing more women and minorities the
chance to write, produce, and direct films and television shows. *For not
only is it likely that women and racial/ethnic minorities have a different
perspective on character, but they are also likely to have a different slant
on narrative, that is, storytelling itself.*

A telling example comes from the history of the novel. Many schol-
arly books on the history of the novel begin with England in the eigh-
teenth century with such figures as Defoe, Richardson, and other white

male writers. But what are we to make of the Japanese "novel," *The Tale of Genji*, by a woman, Murasaki Shikibu, written in the eleventh century? Seven full centuries before *Robinson Crusoe*, *Tom Jones*, and *Candide*, a highly sophisticated woman author in another culture was weaving a complex tale of love and loss, ambition, and human limitations. Furthermore, her method of narration, involving not only large amounts of poetry and nonlinear associative narrative strands but also woodblock prints as illustrations, make a reading of Murasaki's work an experience quite unlike that of any Western novel.

In terms of screenplays, therefore, we are touching on two important topics: on the one hand, the inclusion of women and racial and ethnic minority characters within a "classical" narrative form (see the discussion of the "classical Hollywood cinema" in the next section) which may or may not be *written by women and minority writers*; and, on the other hand, *scripts definitely written by women and minority writers which incorporate narrative voices and modes of narration that differ from classical Hollywood standards.*

In discussing types we have already said a great deal about gender. Certainly all three topics—gender, race, and ethnicity—have become issues we are much more conscious of in the 1990s than in the past. That few important roles have gone to women, blacks, and other minorities and ethnic groups need hardly be repeated. But we must emphasize that writing scripts today means to be particularly conscious of the nuances of character choice. We do not mean for anyone to make a superficial "politically correct" bow toward tokenism in each direction. Rather, we speak of a need today to think through narratives that do not consciously or even inadvertently belittle, insult, or exploit one group as opposed to the other.

Much more needs to be done to allow minority and women's voices to be heard. Of course it was a positive step for actress Jody Foster to take on a director's role and turn out Scott Frank's *Little Man Tate* (1991) as a sensitive nod toward single motherhood, but, in many ways, it was an even bigger surprise to see a film such as *Daughters of the Dust* (1992) written and directed by Julie Dash, a black female filmmaker, get made and distributed. Here is a film close to being a historical dream-poem about blacks living on the islands off the coast of the Carolinas at the turn of the century. Even more surprising in some ways than simply having a black narrative is the way in which the film unfolds: we follow a whole group of characters as our attention is shifted constantly from one character to the other, interweaving one story with another to create an overall feeling for the texture of life on that isolated Carolina island. And we can also point to *Mississippi Masala* (1992), which brought Southern black culture and Indian culture from India via Africa to the screen with an interracial romance filmed by Mira Nair, the talented Indian woman director whose impressive debut film was *Salaam Bombay* (Sooni Taraporevala 1989). We should point out, however, that many Indians who see Nair's films do not feel her style and sensibility is very "Indian" in terms of the traditions of Indian cinema. Clearly, Nair has opted not to present four-hour epics structured in set ways as is traditional in Indian films. Rather, as an Indian woman educated at Harvard, she has chosen to present Indian concerns in narratives that move at the pace and have the shape of more Western models.

Of our group of films we can note that *Boyz N the Hood* represents a promising debut by a young black director, that *Thelma & Louise* is a debut script by a woman, and that *Time of the Gypsies* concerns one minority group—gypsies—depicted by a Yugoslav (Bosnian) director financed through an American studio. *The Silence of the Lambs* places a white female lead within a basically male world. "Northern Exposure" has done much to bring more Native American culture to view for millions of Americans (Marilyn, the American Indian secretary for Dr. Fleischman, played by Elaine Miles, has become something of a national institution in her monosyllabic wise manner!), while also providing some stereotype-shattering images of older characters—Ruth Ann, Holling, and Maurice in particular—and strong roles for women, especially Maggie O'Connell.

The question is not "have you added a quota of minorities and women to your script?" You do, however, need to be sure that the racial and ethnic groups represented are not treated as simple stereotypes, and of course such advice goes for the depiction of women as well. Clearly, if you do include minorities, you should be careful to have done enough research to have your characteristics and details and dialogue as accurate as possible. You might also consider working with an "advisor" or a co-writer to bring out that dimension of your script if it is important enough to you.

We clearly have a long way to go in this area before we can feel that justice has been done on the screen. Even a film such as Michael Blake's *Dances with Wolves* can be faulted for not going far enough. For all of its attention to American Indian life on the plains over a hundred years ago, the core narrative is still one of a white man in love with a white woman! It is ironic that a film made in Russia the same year, *Brown Dog Running Along the Seashore* (written and directed by Kevin Gevorkian 1990) was shot with native tribes along the coast opposite Alaska with no whites, no symphonic orchestra on the soundtrack, and no language other than that of the native peoples. Furthermore, instead of being branded simply an unusual experiment, the film was voted the Best Film at the 1991 International Moscow Film Festival.

Despite Academy Awards for such films as *Gandhi*, we still have a long way to go in screenwriting and in filmmaking before such a completely minority project may be so honored.

We realize that Hollywood continues to be an industry controlled by white males. It is, as we have noted, no wonder that so many of the characters and stories are white male centered. Thus any other stories in which women, blacks, or other minority characters figure prominently is "pushing" the boundaries of what gets made to one degree or another. Most scripts, however, continue to play it safe. The *Lethal Weapon* (1987, 1989, 1992) series, conceived originally by screenwriter Shane Black, took a chance on a "salt and pepper" cop formula that has paid off handsomely as Danny Glover plays the black sidekick to Mel Gibson's leading role. But Shane Black is careful not to make "race" a central issue in their relationship: rather, the balance is between Glover's responsible family man character and Gibson's Dionysian craziness. The same mixed analysis has often been made of a television show such as "The Cosby Show," which many feel lasted as long as it did because, as one Louisiana black teacher told me, "There's nothing African-American about the show!"

The challenge to create character-centered scripts with more fully drawn, more accurate figures of all kinds remains.

CHARACTER TENDENCIES

Part of our effort to emphasize the carnivalesque in character is to get beyond facile labeling of character TYPES, as if any label "sums up" a person. Psychologists, mythologists, anthropologists, astrologers, theologians, psychiatrists, among others, all have their pet labels, divisions, types they use to carve up the carnival discourse of character, attaching significance to this trait or that. *But the character checklist offered at the end of this section subscribes to no ONE approach, Freudian, Lacanian, Jungian, or otherwise.* It is rather what I hope is a helpful—even PLAY-FUL—basic list of characteristics to consider.

No matter what kind of screenplay you are writing, it is important to keep such an open sense of character in mind. And it may be that you are best off simply drawing up your own character without worrying about the following list of character tendencies. But let us briefly explore a group of character TENDENCIES that have evolved from various discourses on character over the years.

Clinical psychologists David Keirsey and Marilyn Bates speak of the importance of *temperament* in looking at character. Their definition of temperament ties in well with our concept of the carnivalesque (polyphonic) in character, and it matches well with what television writers in particular like to call a "character arc": the projection of a character's overall development given his/her general character tendencies, background, core characteristics, and experiences. Keirsey and Bates (1984) write that temperament is "an overall coloration or a kind of thematization of the whole, a uniformity of the diverse" (27). In our view, temperament is directly related to core characteristics in character. Building on Carl Jung, Keirsey and Bates suggest we think about four pairs of preferences:

- Extroversion or introversion
- Intuition or sensation
- Thinking or feeling
- Judging or perceiving

They report that 75 percent of the population chooses extraversion and sensation, whereas the other two pairs of choices come up fifty/fifty (25). That's worth thinking about! On the basis of these tendencies, the dominant temperaments begin to become clear if we look at the characters we have discussed. There is no need to outline each film, but let us glance at the main carnival of characters in "Northern Exposure" according to these tendencies. A rough chart might look like the following, using as a simple key: ex = extrovert; int = introvert; intuit = intuition; sens = sensation; think = thinker; feel = feeling oriented; judge = judgment oriented; perceive = nonjudgmentally oriented.

Character	ex	int	sens	intuit	think	feel	judge	perceive
NORTHERN EXPOSURE:								
Fleischman		X	X		X		X	
O'Connell		X		X		X		X
Chris	X			X		X		X
Marilyn		X		X		X		X
Shelly	X		X			X		X
Holling		X		X		X		X
Maurice	X		X	X			X	
Ruth Anne		X		X		X		X
Ed	X		X			X		X
The Moose!	X			X		X		X

The purpose of this book is not to become rigid or diagrammatic, for the spirit of the carnivalesque is quite the contrary. But even a brief mapping of characters in "Northern Exposure" according to such a simple chart suggests more clearly what the creators of the show have in mind. To create a "nonjudgmental universe" means, in practical terms, *to present a galaxy of characters who are predominately extroverts who trust feelings over thought or whose thoughts are definitely tied to deeper feelings and who tend toward "perception" of those around them rather than judgments.* That Joel Fleischman as the New York Jewish doctor is quite the contrary sets the show in motion. Note too that Maurice is the character closest to Fleischman in this sense because he, like Fleischman, tends to IMPOSE his ideas/morals/plans on others more than he tends to simply accept, embrace, observe, enjoy those around him.

Thus we see, for instance, in *Thelma & Louise* that Louise is more of an introvert who tends toward thought and judgment (thus the "judgment" to kill the would-be rapist), whereas Thelma is quite the opposite: extrovert/feelings/perception.

Victims/Persecutors/Saviors

Clearly there are other "tendency" leanings we could map out beyond these we have mentioned. But let us merely consider three others for now: I am thinking of the tendency we all have—on a fluctuating, ever-shifting basis—of being saviors, victims, and/or persecutors. None of us is purely one or the other, but at any given time one of the three tendencies dominates. All is a matter of degree, of development, of a mixing of these voices in particular blends or polyphonies. Which of these three voices is dominant in your character? Why? Will he or she change to another? What particular blends of these three will your character undergo? Clarice in *The Silence of the Lambs* moves from being a victim of her own past to becoming a savior for herself and the senator's daughter who was literally about to be the next victim of the serial killer, Buffalo Bill. Perhan in *Time of the Gypsies* evolves from a young victim within his provincial gypsy village to becoming the "savior" of his sister and of himself only to become a godfather persecutor himself—and, we could add, a victim once more of gypsy mentality as he himself is finally gunned down.

We can be even more specific about each tendency.

VICTIMS

To be a victim is to let others control your life. Such a character obviously has low self-esteem together with a number of fears about himself/herself, others, the world. Such a person is clearly "passive" but may, of course, be passive-aggressive as well. Does your character make things happen, or do things happen to her or him? Rick in *Casablanca* seems passive, but he's a lapsed savior. By film's end, he is no victim of past love or Nazi terror, but rather he is a full-fledged savior as he sacrifices his own love interests for Ilysa's greater good and for the cause of freedom everywhere. Graham in *sex, lies and videotape* is clearly passive-aggressive in his taping of women speaking about their intimate concerns coupled with his inability to come close to them physically. He is thus a victim of his own fears until Ann ("savior") shakes him out of his frigidity.

PERSECUTORS

Clearly this label is most often used for the antagonist, for it is in the nature of the persecutor to bother others for any number of reasons. Such characters, on the surface at least, have a high opinion of themselves, a clear sense of what they think they want. Something more: these characters tend not to trust others (or, ultimately, themselves). *They work by suspicion.* Everyone is guilty until proven innocent, and that almost never happens from their perspective. Paranoia is the extreme trait of the persecutor: everyone is out to get them, so they must get others first. The persecutor takes rather than gives. He/she is a doer.

SAVIORS

The savior figure most often is at peace with himself or herself and therefore operates according to a *desire to nurture* self, relationships, others. The savior is thus the *preserver* of self and community. He or she may be a loner as in the traditional western, but the savior comes down on the side of growth, selfless giving, trust, love. Of course a traditional label for much of what makes up the savior is the "hero." Savior, however, more accurately defines the role of nurturing and preserving. It is interesting, for instance, to see the evolution of the "terminator" character from *Terminator* to *Terminator 2* as that from persecutor to savior as he (it?!) leaves us with his act of self-sacrifice and a life-affirming thumbs-up gesture.

• • •

The concept of the carnivalesque helps us to see that as individuals, we really have all of these "voices" within us and that these voices are constantly changing. At one time or another we all play the savior, the victim, the persecutor. Put another way, most of us may be extroverts at one time, introverts at another. Circumstance does count. As the great French director Jean Renoir liked to say, "I believe all of us are villains. And we are all of us good. It depends on the day, it depends on the way we slept during the night, on the quality of the coffee." A *tendency*, however, is exactly as we have described: a voice among many that tends, for whatever deep structural characteristics, to surface more frequently than others.

PARENT/CHILD PROCESSES

To create is not to deform or invent persons and things. It is to tie *new relationships* between persons and things which are, and *as they are*.

Robert Bresson, *Notes on Cinematography*

Character as process and discourse suggests an ongoing interaction with those around you. Of course the parent/child process is, for each of us, one of the strongest of discourses in our lives. Who your characters are is thus bound up with their family backgrounds, experiences, needs to a large degree. And although the spirit of the carnivalesque suggests that anything is potentially possible, we need to acknowledge specific patterns that do appear because of gender in the father/mother versus son/daughter development.

Fathers and Sons

Freud opened many doors to our understanding of character, but most of them, as his emphasis on the Oedipus legend suggests, were from the male point of view (this is, of course, ironic, as feminists have pointed out, since most of the important studies he did were the result of treating women). The Oedipus tendency therefore is one that centers on the SON and his rite of passage to manhood as he must come into conflict with the father and learn to separate his affection for his mother from that for other women.

Note that Hollywood has traditionally been a male-centered industry in which the majority of tales told have centered on Oedipal tendencies. The father-son paradigm in particular is at the heart of the *Star Wars* trilogy and the *Indiana Jones* trilogy of both George Lucas and Steven Spielberg. Luke Skywalker (the son) must reconcile the fact that Darth Vader is his father and Indiana Jones (the son) must deal with Sean Connery, James Bond himself, as his dad. Of course these films have been enjoyed by millions and made millions, too. But in terms of our interests *Premiere* editor Peter Biskind has pointed out the danger of the *false sense of character* projected by these particular narratives:

> Narrative became hostage not to stars' wars, but to special effects. And just as Lucas's and Spielberg's insistence on infantilization had an unanticipated result—the rise of a new patriarchy inimical to many of the values the directors thought they believe in—so their attempt to restore traditional narration had an unintended effect—the creation of spectacle that annihilated story. (1993, 147)

Biskind focuses on how Lucas's and Spielberg's narratives by forefronting narrative over character ironically tended to render even plot ineffective. Expressed in terms of character, we see that the process of "sanitizing" character that both engage in—for example, in the desexualized world of *Star Wars*—leads to an unsatisfactory sense of character. Many may say, "So what? They are only entertainment movies." But our answer is once again that of Bruno Bettelheim: movies like fairy tales are *by nature value-encoded narratives*, and to avoid the honest sense of character inherent in the material is to rob viewers—of whatever age—of what narratives *should* offer.

The Passing of the Blessing

Peter Blos (1985) has written about what the father-son relationship suggests beyond the level of conflict emphasized by Freud. Suggesting that too much attention has been placed on the role of the father as the "punishing father under whose threat of retaliation the little boy abandons his competitive strivings" (10), Blos refocuses our understanding of the relationship to highlight the need for a father-son reconciliation. This later-stage bonding is accomplished at the end of adolescence (real or psychological) when the son receives the "blessing" of the father. The "blessing" is vital for a male to become a man. This blessing, Blos tells us, is "transmitted by the father's general bearing and responsive presence (not necessarily verbalized)" (11).

Thus Peter Biskind's analysis of Lucas and Spielberg as males who delayed their own and—figuratively—our (speaking collectively of males only!) passage into manhood until Luke finally accepts Darth Vader as his father and—"the blessing"—and Indiana Jones receives Sean Connery's blessing in the third and final episode is useful.

The importance of the passing of the blessing or the opposite, the lack of a blessing, becomes central to the character development of so many males in screenplays as in life. *Boyz N the Hood* is almost completely a father-son tale that preaches the need for a father to "bless" his son with his own example and with his nurturing acceptance of his son. We have emphasized that, statistically, such an image of a black family is more the exception than the rule, but that is Singleton's pitch and wish: more fathers and more blessings passed on are needed if the "hood" is to survive.

And we have pointed out how *Time of the Gypsies* is very much the flip side of Singleton's film. There is no father and no blessing passed in Kusturica's gypsy world. There are only father substitutes—Grandma and the gypsy godfather figure, neither of whom is complete or nurturing enough. Thus Perhan's doomed voyage through life.

Note also that Homer's *Odyssey*, one of the first works in Western literature, is at heart a father-son tale. It is significant that long before we meet Odysseus, we are introduced to his son, Telemachus, who sets out on a double journey to find his father and thus to find himself as a person and as a boy turned man. In a real sense the climax of Homer's tale is not the slaughter of the many suitors who have been camping for years in Odysseus' palace hoping to win Penelope's hand and Odysseus' estate. In terms of core characteristics, the tale is complete when father and son are reunited, introduced, and accept each other in an *embrace*. The embrace is the passing of the blessing from Odysseus to Telemachus, thus completing his son's passage to manhood. It follows these words in which Odysseus responds to Telemachus' charge that he, Odysseus, appears to be more like a god than a man:

ODYSSEUS

No, I am not a god. Why liken me to the immortals? But I am your father, for whose sake you are always grieving as you look for violence from others, and endure hardships. (Homer 1968, 245)

Father and son are able to move on thereafter as one to complete the task at hand: the freeing of the palace of the suitors.

In recent American film, we can point to *A River Runs Through It* (1992), based on the autobiographical novel by Norman Maclean (screenplay by Richard Friedenberg), to find a satisfyingly honest portrayal of the father-son passage toward maturity. Set in Montana in the first part of the twentieth century, this simple tale of a family, made up of a minister father, a supportive mother, and two sons, traces the boys' development without sentimentality, sensationalism, or special effects. What we get is a straightforward, honest depiction of the growth and change of the family members over time.

Mothers and Daughters

Post-Freudian psychologists and feminists have been quick to suggest what should have been obvious: that the Oedipal triangle is male-centered. It goes without saying that in writing scripts today, one needs to be aware of the limitations that have existed in the cinematic (especially Hollywood's) representation of women. Clearly a strong sense of the carnivalesque—freedom, fantasy, imagination—is needed in conceiving and developing female characters for the screen. As Teresa de Lauretis (1987) states, "The problem is the notion of sexual differences(s), its conservative force limiting and working against the effort to rethink its very representations" (17).

Part of the spirit of the carnivalesque in breaking through traditional categories would be to more clearly acknowledge the importance of the mother-daughter relationship. Yes, daughters too need blessings. Yet the carnivalesque approach to character forces us to explore not only core experiences that shape our characters, but the multivoiced possibilities of development beyond the limits of sexual difference as we have noted above.

MINOR CHARACTERS

Think how much minor characters add to any imaginative narrative work. What is Sophocles' *Oedipus Rex* without the shepherd, *Hamlet* minus the grave diggers, *The World According to Garp* without Roberta, the former linebacker, and *Psycho* without the highway patrolman behind his sunglasses? And what about the bartender in director John Ford's *My Darling Clementine* (script by Samuel G. Engel & Winston Miller) when Henry Fonda near the end looks up with no one else around and says, "Clarence, have you ever been in love?" And Clarence who has said almost nothing the whole film replies with a deadpan expression, "No, sir. I've been a bartender all my life." Suddenly a very minor almost invisible character takes center stage for a brief second and we never forget him! That one line does it: nine words make us laugh and then reflect, however briefly, on a world of silent bartenders leading their own quiet, lonely lives. And who can forget the bartender in *The Crying Game*!

To say that the focus of our work is on the character-centered narrative is not the same as meaning that the main protagonist has to be in the spotlight the entire time. Character-centered applies to all the characters in such a script. The point is that each character in such a narrative stands out for his or her own traits as well as for the plot function served.

Each minor character exists in her/his own right but acts as a means of further defining/expanding/exploring the main determining character. They thus enrich and complicate the main narrative.

Messengers/Mediators/Muddlers

Minor characters tend to fulfill three basic roles: messengers, mediators, and muddlers. Either they bring us new information of one sort or another, or they try to help out in one way or another, or they make it more difficult for the main protagonist, either consciously or unconsciously. *The degree to which your minor characters stand out as individuals is a strong gauge of the texture/resonance/density of your script.*

The more screenwriting I do, the more affection I have for and the more attention I pay to these folk in my scripts. Almost everybody in the movie audience in *Cinema Paradiso* is a character we remember, often drawn with simple brush strokes of characteristics, a line of dialogue, a mannerism. Similarly, who can forget the social worker in *My Left Foot* (Christy Sheridan and Shane Connaughton 1989), who surprises us not only with her efforts to mediate in behalf of our crippled protagonist, but who can match him four-letter word for four-letter word. Or in *The Silence of the Lambs*, the latest female victim of Buffalo Bill, the senator's daughter, is seen only briefly, but we come to know her whole personality in those few fleeting scenes in which she appears, and we feel both her similarities and contrasts to Clarice.

It may well be that your minor characters will grow/change/develop greatly in the rewrite. You may be so wrapped up in getting the first draft done that the minor characters may just spill out to fulfill the roles needed to get the story told. But if you haven't rethought them before writing, during the rewrite you can examine each character carefully. What if the judge in your script were an African-American? What if the pizza delivery boy was actually a Vietnam vet? And what if the hockey coach were a woman? *Minor characters give you the perfect opportunity to bring in issues/themes/conflicts that matter to you or to our culture and to do so without being heavy-handed.* Think again of the importance of what people wear (we are, after all, a t-shirt culture!), eat, drive, drink, say, or don't say. Be careful, however, not to add minority groups only as a token nod to those groups.

Beware of three dangers: don't create a minor character so well that he or she steals the film from your main protagonist! The gypsy grandmother is such a strong character in *Time of the Gypsies* that she almost walks off with the whole film (the Italian sections without her seem flat in comparison with the energy and resonance she creates in her scenes). And Martin Short as the nutty wedding coordinator in the Steve Martin remake of *Father of the Bride* (1991) comes very close to walking off with all of the memorable scenes.

A second danger is to be wary of creating too many minor characters. The number needed depends entirely on the nature of your script. *sex, lies and videotape* clearly set out to be a chamber piece and thus to *exclude* as many characters as possible in order to focus on the four in the forefront. *Boyz N the Hood*, however, is about Los Angeles street culture, so there is a need to introduce us to a variety of types and figures. Finally, don't do with two characters what you can do with one. Part of the skill of the rewrite (actual or as you proceed with your rough draft!) is the ability to realize that you can tighten your script and create a more vibrant minor character by giving him/her double duty. Robert Bresson put it well when he advised "not to use two violins when one is enough" (1977, 8).

CHARACTERS YOUNG AND OLD

The very young and those over sixty have not been in general well served by Hollywood in the past. From Shirley Temple and the Our Gang crowd down to Macaulay Culkin's cartoonish performance in *Home Alone*, kids on the American screen have appeared more as "cute" miniature adults than as the children they might have been. Similarly, the aging either have been absent from most of Hollywood's youthful dreammaking process, or they have been presented in one degrading stereotype after another.

Foreign filmmakers have a much better track record in allowing children to be children and the aging to share their true character on screen as we shall mention. But we should also note that American cinema has improved a lot in recent years in attempting scripts and films that are more honest, more true to the character of the young and the aging.

Consider some of the more encouraging images of older characters. Henry Fonda and Katharine Hepburn in *On Golden Pond* (Ernest Thompson 1981) began something of a new wave of intelligent films about mature characters living fully in the carnival of the twilight years. Then there is David Berry's quietly affecting portrait of two aging sisters beautifully portrayed by Lillian Gish and Bette Davis in *The Whales of August* (1987). And on a more commercial level, we can speak of Art Carney in *Harry and Tonto* (written by Paul Mazursky 1974) and Ruth Gordon in the wildly irreverent *Harold and Maude* (Colin Higgins 1971) as breaking new territory for the aging in American film.

Abroad in cultures less youth oriented, the aging have been the focus of many important character-centered films. Think of Ingmar Bergman's strong portrait of an aging male egotist who learns at long last to love more selflessly in *Wild Strawberries* (1957). Vittorio De Sica and Cesare Zavattini captured the loneliness of old age with sensitivity in *Umberto D* (1955). And Francesco Rosi and Tonino Guerra masterfully brought old age and the very young together in his *Three Brothers* (1980), a film about three Italian brothers returning home to their village when their mother dies. In one scene typical of Rosi's feel and respect for characters young and aging, we see a five-year-old granddaughter afraid of sleeping alone in her room. She goes into her grandfather's room, climbs on the bed next to her grandfather who lies on the bed fully clothed, and with a face full of the grief he feels for his departed wife. The girl nuzzles up next to her grandfather taking up the place in bed, of course, that had in the past been that of his wife. No words are spoken, but the camera holds for just long enough for us to feel the fears and sorrow each character has as well as the comfort being next to each other has given them.

The same is true, of course, when we speak of images of youth on film. European and other foreign filmmakers have created many strong films that are brutally but sympathetically honest about young characters whose innocence is often shattered by the cold realities of their environments. Nagisa Oshima's *Boy* (1969), for instance, traces the hard life of a Japanese street boy who is forced to support his family by throwing himself in front of oncoming cars in order to collect personal injury money from the drivers. Luis Buñuel's *Los Olvidados* (1950) strips the glamour from street gang life by capturing, in almost documentary detail, the life of a Mexico City gang. And the recent Soviet film, *Freedom Is Paradise* (written by Sergei Bodrov 1989), follows with direct simplicity the odyssey of a thirteen-year-old boy who escapes from reform school to hitchhike to Siberia and to break *into* a maximum security prison to meet, for the first time, his criminal father.

Here in the United States, we do see signs of a more accurate portrayal of the young in some films. John Hughes's *The Breakfast Club* (1985), for instance, sent millions of American teenagers to the cinemas again and again to listen to razor-sharp dialogue that obviously struck home in this clearly structured character study of five teens, each with different needs. Rob Reiner etched a sensitive rite of passage film with *Stand by Me* (1986), based on a Stephen King autobiographical story. And in *The Man in the Moon*, one of the best films of 1991, Jenny Wingfield follows the lives of two young sisters in the rural South in the 1950s with 100 percent accuracy of character, dialogue, atmosphere.

The message is obvious. In writing character-centered scripts that involve the young and the aging, we need to be sensitive to the stereotypes of the past that should be shattered and replaced with more open, more honest, and more carnivalesque portraits.

ANIMATION AND THE CARNIVALESQUE

If Mickey Mouse is not the most seen, most used, most loved image of the twentieth century in the world, he is very close to the top. Certainly the cartoon image created by Walt Disney over fifty years ago has been seen on the screen and on everything from t-shirts to training potties and watches everywhere. That guarantees that Mickey is way ahead of other "images" that have had much currency during our century including Elvis, Marilyn Monroe, Hitler, Stalin, the Beatles, Gandhi, and Kennedy.

To salute such a universal cultural power is to say much about the craft and art of animation as well as about Disney's particular vision.

Cartoons open up the ultimate world of the carnivalesque. 'Toons need obey no laws of logic, physics, time, and space. They represent the process of metamorphosis in its purest state. The animated film can be a pure representation of freedom, even the freedom from form and narrative itself as experimental animators have long shown us—there are many examples in animated films of pure color and nonnarrative movement of nonrepresentational shapes across the screen. It is worth noting that, influenced by American animation, animation in East European countries including Hungary, Poland, the former Czechoslovakia, the former Yugoslavia, and the former Soviet Union developed into a particularly powerful medium of humanistic expression, often without the need for verbal language.

And though the history of animation is a long and varied one, we can certainly say that the potential for animation has not yet been fully realized. The popularity not only of Disney's empire and television kid's shows from "Ninja Turtles" to "Beetlejuice" and "The Muppet Babies" have pointed the way to the remarkable popularity of "The Simpsons" and "Beavis and Butthead," and of adult cult films such as Ralph Bakshi's *Fritz the Cat* (1972). Finally there have been the imaginative and enjoyable mixtures of animation and real life action as in the Gene Kelly dance with Jerry the mouse in *Anchors Aweigh* (Isobel Lennart 1946) and wacky *Who Framed Roger Rabbit?* (Jeffrey Price and Peter Seaman 1988).

Think of how easily animated characters can enchant us and hold our attention if they are given a clear sense of character. Disney's *Snow White and the Seven Dwarfs* (1937) establishes sharply defined characters for each of the seven dwarfs. I suggest it is because their characters are so clear and so different from each other that Disney was able to build a carnivalesque sense of even the smallest narrative gesture. Before Snow

White will serve her little friends supper on her first night in their home, she requires them to wash their hands. The handwashing scene seems to slip by very quickly but it actually takes up ten minutes of screen time! The riffing possibilities of mixing seven characters (and, by the way, a wonderful touch of one little insect caught up in a soap bubble as well) for each phase of washing multiply mathematically to our delight. In summary, the very real freedom of animation in tandem with Disney's strong emphasis with character allowed his animators to maximize the power of his films.

One last observation might be worth making. Screenwriters today need to be aware of how many live-action films and television shows are conceived of either directly or indirectly as "cartoonlike" in characterization and narrative. Thus we have our "Superman" series, *The Adams Family*, the *Batman* films, and much more. The writers of such shows and films need to tread a particularly difficult line between the simplified world of 'toons and a more sophisticated world that maintains enough of a human scale that we do not simply dismiss what we see as pure fantasy.

Animal and Nonhuman Characters

Mickey is not human, and neither are the Muppet Babies or a large percentage of animated figures. Certainly the worlds of animals and other living creatures from dinosaurs to monsters as well as of inanimate objects brought to life and animation are perfect for each other. Such an anthropomorphizing process relates directly to our deep needs to mythologize and to create fantasies that need to be expressed. The Disney Studios pleased everyone in 1991 with its familiar magic by releasing *Beauty and the Beast*. What kids remember most are dancing and singing tea cups and candlesticks. Of course what we come to discover is that such animated inanimate objects are actually humans transformed. Beauty's love for the Beast not only releases the Prince inside but also transforms his staff once again into their original human form. In writing such characters, you obviously need to know that the deep structure of the very British tea kettle is that of an actual British maid held captive inside her transformed shape!

From Animation to Special Effects

Is there anyone who saw *Alien* (1979) who can forget the creature that pops out of one of the unfortunate humans lost in space? On the one hand the specifics of such a creature depend on the budget and the talent of the special effects teams hired. But some *concept of the creature and "its" character must be provided by the screenwriter*. In the case of *Alien*, Dan O'Bannon, who has suffered from stomach trouble most of his life, had no trouble projecting his personal pain into the kind of demon he must often feel inhabits his own being. E.T., on the other hand, was designed, like Mickey, to be a nonthreatening creature, purposely meant to be gender nonspecific, but being the size of a small child and having the features of an old person.

Once again, within the world of special effects (and large budgets) the screenwriter may indulge in many of the same freedoms that the animated narrative allows for. Yet also once again, there is the need to come to terms with what degree of the narrative—surface and deep structure— is to be taken as pure fantasy and what degree is there to further the human growth and narrative. The "Star Trek" television series and the films as well have opted for human characters and concerns over special effects and have done well with faithful audiences in their bid for this territory. George Lucas and Steven Spielberg, however, have chosen the plot-driven route in which character development takes a back seat to action and special effects in their respective trilogies (*Star Wars/Indiana Jones*). *Jurassic Park* (Michael Crichton and David Koepp, 1993) is another, more recent, example.

Animals Who Do Not Speak

Beyond animation and special effects, we sometimes encounter films using real animals who are allowed not to speak human talk! The two *Benji* films, for instance (1974, 1987), build on old tried-and-true formulas formerly acted out by Lassie and Rin Tin Tin to bring canine delight to millions of kids everywhere. In terms of screenwriting, these films are still within the plot-driven realm, for what we are treated to is not an exploration of how dogs might act in any given situation, but rather we see how clever the editing of the filmmaker and the special training of the well-paid animals work together to produce a narrative.

Films like *Gorillas in the Mist* (1988) are another matter. Screenwriter Anna Hamilton Phelan had, of course, protagonist Dian Fossey's own book of the same title from which to work. Thus Phelan's "character research" was, in a real sense, done for her. But think of the very real pleasure the scenes with the gorillas afforded audiences as the "documentary selves" of real animals came through. Here we were not in the fantasy world of talking mice and battling, pizza-chomping turtles, but in the presence of animals allowed to be themselves.

Of course the ever popular "Animal Kingdom" kind of documentary fulfills part of our need for such contact with animals we don't meet personally. And certainly Hollywood feature films centered on nonspeaking animals are not likely to become a new wave of summer hits in the near future. But one should not discount the possibility of constructing effective scripts about animals, either for children or for adults, which insult neither us nor the subjects. For further enlightenment, I refer those interested to the engaging study, *How Monkeys See the World: Inside the Mind of Another Species* by Dorothy L. Cheney and Robert M. Seyfarth (1990).

CHAPTER THREE

FIVE NOT-SO-EASY PIECES:
ANALYSIS OF CHARACTER-CENTERED SCRIPTS

Before going further let us take our first glance at the characters in our four sample films, *The Silence of the Lambs*, *Thelma & Louise*, *Boyz N the Hood*, and *Time of the Gypsies*. Let us also analyze "Northern Exposure" as a character-centered television series that challenges and entertains audiences everywhere.

The brief overviews of each script in this chapter are offered in the spirit that hand in hand with the process of learning to write a script is the need to study scripts and films to learn how they *work*. Obviously the analysis presented here is not the only way of reading these scripts, for such analysis necessarily suggests a crossing of film studies and creative writing interests—and as such reflects the particular interests of the person doing the analysis. But these comments should at least help open up these texts for further discussion and more detailed analysis.

First, let us make some general observations of these films, which were made between 1989 and 1991, before considering each film by itself. All of them challenge traditional Hollywood notions of either character or plot or both. In this light, note that two of the five present women as the main characters: Clarice in *The Silence of the Lambs*, and Thelma and Louise of course. Given that Hollywood has traditionally been male centered and male dominated, the popularity of films such as these suggests a shift in sensibility throughout the United States and thus throughout the film industry. However, the two male-centered scripts, *Boyz N the Hood* and *Time of the Gypsies*, are both male coming of age stories that track a child to the brink of manhood (*Boyz*) and all the way through manhood to death (*Time of the Gypsies*). Both of the women-centered films deal with women who are learning to grow and gain control of their own lives, even if the payoff is death, as in *Thelma & Louise*.

In terms of social class, it is worth noting that all offer us primary characters from the lower or lower middle class or, in the case of Clarice, a "rube" from the countryside, that is, West Virginia. The gypsies in

Time of the Gypsies are farthest away from mainline society, of course, since they live *outside* all elements of acceptable society.

And in terms of genre, each of these character-centered scripts "plays" with a recognized film genre. *Thelma & Louise* is a female version of the male buddy road movie. *The Silence of the Lambs* is an updated film noir with contemporary turns, whereas *Boyz N the Hood* builds on teenage gang films and director John Singleton's favorite coming of age film, *Stand by Me*. *Time of the Gypsies* is consciously, on one level, patterned on *The Godfather* and thus on a family-crime/gangster narrative.

"Northern Exposure" mixes all of the above. This mythical Alaskan town founded by two lesbians embraces all social classes, races (remember that Chris has a "twin" brother who is black), including, of course, American Indian, and it seems fairly evenly divided on a gender line. The all-embracing nature of the show is reflected in the across the country popularity of this offbeat series. According to William Coveny III, the former Director of Current Programming for CBS, "The show is just as popular in urban as rural areas and in the South as in the North" (1992).

This is also the place to mention what should be obvious in speaking of character-centered scripts: We need to acknowledge the major influence of *performance* and thus the actors in bringing the script to the screen. Humphrey Bogart IS Rick in *Casablanca*, just as much as Jody Foster IS Clarice in *The Silence of the Lambs*. In fact the performance (and the direction and production values including cinematography/lighting/locations, and so forth) make it difficult for us to turn back to films already completed to try and appreciate individual screenplays as the original artistic blueprints.

"NORTHERN EXPOSURE"

"This place has given us the freedom to be what we want to be," says Cicely, the lesbian cofounder of the small Alaskan town before she dies in 1905. This line in the final episode of the Spring 1992 season captures a core characteristic for all the strongly etched characters who inhabit "Northern Exposure." From the very beginning, we see how different this show is: founded by two lesbians who tamed the "wild west" in this one town which becomes something of the semi-utopian society they dreamed of, Cicely and the show reflect a *matriarchal view of culture!* Given the extreme patriarchy of our own culture, the overall orientation of "Northern Exposure" is definitely refreshing fare for prime-time viewers.

• • •

We begin our closer look at character-centered scripts with "Northern Exposure" for two reasons: this "sleeper" show that suddenly took off nationally in the summer of 1991 and has been building a wide audience everywhere ever since is almost literally a weekly dose of the carnival-esque in every sense. And secondly, there is a growing feeling among writers that television, once earmarked as a wasteland for quality writing, is now in many ways on the cutting edge of excitement, opportunity, and quality. Says Diane Frolov, supervising producer and one of the four staff writers of "Northern Exposure," who writes with co-executive producer husband Andy Schneider, "I think a writer's best position right now is in television as a writer-producer" (Froug 1992, 265).

What executives sitting in Los Angeles ever expected a show about Cicely, a mythical small town in Alaska (filmed in Rosalyn, Washington, near the site of the *Twin Peaks* set some eighty miles east of Seattle), founded by two lesbians and inhabited by an odd menagerie of characters ranging from Maurice, a retired astronaut, to Marilyn, a monosyllabic but very wise Native American working as a medical assistant, would take the country by storm?

Again writer Diane Frolov expresses how unusual this show is: "We never write down to our audience. I think that's exciting. We touch on everything from quantum physics to Franz Kafka. Sometimes the network thinks we over-intellectualize, but we believe our audience appreciates it . . . It's what creator Josh Brand calls a nonjudgmental universe. There are no bad guys in Cicely" (Froug 1992, 266). *Realize immediately that this means there are no true negative characters in the show: everyone is an embracing figure to one degree or another!*

Andy Schneider is even more specific: "One viewer put it well when he told Diane and myself that all our lives we are presented with a certain fictional standard of behavior in America. But in the world of "Northern Exposure" we see things can be different, that there are other models for behavior" (1992).

If American television comedy has tended to fall between two camps— the status quo–oriented family sit-coms and the much more radical stand-up shows such as "Saturday Night Live"—"Northern Exposure," even more so than "M*A*S*H" or "Cheers" is a hybrid: a character-centered comedy that definitely has radical tendencies that weekly challenge the status quo of mid-American values.

The concept of a "nonjudgmental universe" describes the spirit of carnival: a feast of becoming in which just about anything can—and does—happen. Cicely is wonderfully "upside down" compared to the lives most of us live in urban areas with strict timetables and a multitude of fears, problems, restrictions, limitations, dangers. It is too small to have a police force or a stop light, and until an episode in 1992, "Democracy," they had never had an election because everyone just, well, got along! And the radio station is so small that D.J. Chris can play whatever eclectic music he wants to while reading and quoting from all of Western literature/philosophy/history: "Why can't real radio be more like KBHR radio?" muses *The New York Times* (Pareles 1992, H-29). Meanwhile relationships are definitely "upside down," too, as Holling, the sixty-seven-year-old owner/operator of the café-bar in town has a twenty-something girlfriend, Shelly, who is just wild about this man old enough to be her . . . grandfather. Meanwhile Ruth Ann, the seventysomething owner/operator of the post office/general store/library is followed by Ed, the young Native American would-be filmmaker.

But the central characters in this ensemble show are Dr. Joel Fleischman, the New York Jewish doctor "condemned" to spending two years (renewed to five!) in Cicely to pay off the medical school loan the town provided him, and Maggie O'Connell, the bush pilot from Grosse Pointe, Michigan, whose boyfriends all die violent deaths. This offkey duo turn the notion of screwball comedy upside down as they never quite seem to get together either because of his Jewish hangups or her 1990s existential fears (in "Ill Wind," the February 15, 1993 episode, they *do* finally make love, but the consequences throw both into shock).

"I always find myself surprised with the scripts that come to me," says William Coveny III, formerly of CBS (1992). Take the "Spring Break" episode written by David Assael. The theme is what the coming of spring does to everyone in terms of turning their own lives upside down. Ex-con, D.J. Chris Stevens is the voice and conscience of Cicely as he glosses every activity with his rambling but erudite voice over the air. Halfway through the "Spring Break" episode, as everyone is waiting for the "ice to break" so that life will return to normal, Chris breaks into this monologue after reading from *Where the Wild Things Are*:

CHRIS

Thank you, Mr. Sendak, for reminding us that we should never lose touch with the wild and untameable spirit within us all. Mayhem has gotten a bad rap and chaos has taken it on the chin in these pathologically normal and rational times. Even up here in Alaska, we're turning our back on the beast. We've opted for the zoo where lion can't eat you, instead of the jungle where he can. Quelle dommage—what a drag.

Chris puts on "Wild Thing"

VOICE

"Wild thing, you make my heart sing/ you make everything . . . oh, baby, Wild Thing . . ."

What is important to realize is that the show is organized around theme and character with plot/narrative in a clearly third-place status. The pleasure is in following this galaxy of unique characters as they drift in and out of each other's lives. And of course paradoxes that have no final solution are set up simply by the nature of each character being who she or he is. The creators make it clear, for instance, that the initial idea was simply a Jewish doctor in an Alaskan town. That premise alone is good for many episodes as Fleischman's New York–bred character "fights" his provincial surroundings.

In "Spring Break" that conflict is resolved in a truly carnivalesque ending in which every man in Cicely gets to be what he wants to be: a part of the group of men who celebrate spring and their manhood by running naked down the main street of Cicely as the women cheer them on. We see them all (carefully cropped for national television, of course, but apparently naked in real life during the shoot!) running—the fat and the thin, the old and the young, the white and the Indian—joined, at last, by Fleischman, puffing and pumping to catch up with the group as the screen fades out.

Finally, I wish to suggest that the carnivalesque in this show can be seen in the way that documentary blends with fiction so effectively. When Elaine Miles, the Native American who plays Marilyn, came to New Orleans with her mother, Armenia, who originally tried out for "Marilyn's" role, over four hundred showed up on campus to see, speak with, and listen to them (Loyola University, March 12, 1992). Everyone agreed they enjoyed the other characters and the actors who play them as well, but the point was that Elaine Miles, a "nonactress" who has fallen into the role, interests the audience members very strongly *because of her natural ease and sincerity on the show.* Marilyn was not "scripted" originally, at least not to the degree she has become loved by millions, because she herself has become a presence, a character (and a warmly embracing one at that) by being herself. She is a splendid example of how a powerful real character can "take over" a show *because she is so real.*

It is to the credit of the creators and writers of "Northern Exposure" that they recognize and build on such strengths to create a truly carnivalesque world for fifty minutes once a week.

Final note: How do you keep a show that demands the writing of twenty-five one-hour shows a season, fresh? The third season, for instance, did, by most viewers' feelings, take a few dips from the high levels established during the first two seasons. Andy Schneider (1992) once more focuses on character in his response: "We keep exploring new facets of character. Freshness has to do with surprise which is at the heart of the show. We must be *surprising but logical.* We surprise, yet when we think about what the character has done, it actually makes sense."

THE SILENCE OF THE LAMBS

The Silence of the Lambs was one of the most successful box office films of 1991, pulling in over $140 million for a work made by screenwriter Ted Tally, director Jonathan Demme, actress Jody Foster, and actor Anthony Hopkins. The film also garnered much critical acclaim including four Oscars: best picture, best adapted screenplay, best actress, and best actor.

Clarice Starling is the main protagonist.

Think how telling names can be: she is like Clear-ice and is struggling to be a less common bird than a "starling." Clarice is an Old World name that has a prim and Victorian ring to it. As the determining character in Ted Tally's Oscar-winning script from Thomas Harris's novel, Clarice is, in Lecter's words in their first interview:

> . . . A well-scrubbed, hustling rube with a little taste . . . Good nutrition has given you some length of bone, but you're not more than one generation away from poor white trash, are you—*Officer* Starling . . . ? That accent you're trying so desperately to shed—pure West Virginia. What was your father, dear? Was he a coal miner? Did he stink of the lamp . . . ? And oh, how quickly the boys found *you!* All those tedious, sticky fumblings, in the back seats of cars, while you could only dream of getting out. Getting anywhere—yes? Getting all the way—to the F . . . B . . . I. (Tally 1989, 13)

Tally then comments in the script: "His every word has struck her like a tiny, precise dart. But she squares her jaw and won't give ground."

Lecter (called Dr. Quinn in the first draft of the script for copyright reasons) knows *character*. And in these first, telling lines with her, he announces that he has her pinpointed almost exactly based on his first impressions.

In fact, we learn, he almost has everything, including some core experiences, but not quite. Clarice WANTS to be an FBI agent, but her NEED is to come to grips with the murder of her father when she was still a very young girl. Also, as we have mentioned previously, an even deeper need not developed is the death of her mother when she was two.

Her life and much of her character are strongly shaped by the shock of her father's murder in the line of duty as a sheriff. On a simplistic level, her desire to become a law enforcement officer is her outward attempt to right that wrong, to follow in her father's footsteps, to grow up. In a larger sense, however, we see what Clarice must learn is how to become herself in a heavily male-dominated world in which her role models and the "bad guys" are men and in which women are the victims.

Hannibal Lecter plays the role of antagonist, for he himself is an unrepentant murderer who is withholding information that will lead to the capture of Buffalo Bill, the serial killer of women who is on the loose. But he can also be seen as an embracing figure, one who helps out the main character. He does finally help Clarice deal with her deep need using the tools of his trade: psychotherapy. The seeming diametrical contradiction within his character between his super-refined taste and knowledge—remember he is truly something of a Renaissance Man Gone Wrong for even his walls hold drawings of Florence, the center of the Renaissance—and his cold-blooded ability to murder without guilt or apparent remorse.

The complex blending of these roles in one character whose own *core characteristics* we never come to discover makes *The Silence of the Lambs* much more than another standard studio horror/thriller. In psychological terms, however, it is clear that he is fixated at an oral (infantile) phase: look at the emphasis on *biting* and the desire to control in particular.

We shall return to the structure of the film in more detail later. But we see that Clarice's desire—to become an FBI agent—is fueled by her inner need—to reconcile her father's death and thus the loss of both her parents since her mother had already died—and that in between these two is the immediate goal of solving the case of Buffalo Bill. This plot line becomes the means of resolving both her desire and need.

Let us add that her core need has helped determine that she is basically an introvert rather than an extrovert and that *she has no romantic interest in men.* In fact, we will comment more about the fact that she is positively surrounded by father figures. One of them is her boss at the FBI, Campbell, whose relationship is complicated in that he is old enough to be her father, but has vaguely romantic leanings since, in the original script, we are told his wife is ill and incapable of giving him the affection he craves (this was cut from the final film). Other father figures include the country sheriff, Brigham (her marksmanship instructor), and Dr. Prentiss, who becomes a dividing character as he tries to use Lecter to further his career especially when Clarice repels his advances.

The sense of unresolved tensions and contradictions that underlie the character-centered screenplay are clearly drawn in Tally's script. We can notice, for instance, the tension between the following elements in the script which help to give it both character and *texture*:

male	female
father	daughter
teacher	student
psychotherapist	patient
the law	the illegal
country	city
physical force	psychological force
rationality	the irrational
articulate	silent
the professional	the personal
refined manners	vulgarity
the West	the East Coast and Europe
age	youth
self-esteem	self-hate

These elements interact in pleasing and troubling ways, and in fact, we sense a rhythm of pairing and contrasting of these elements throughout.

Buffalo Bill's victim, for instance, is Catherine, a name not unlike Clarice, and her last name is Martin, the name of another species of bird, but a more delicate one (think of the fun that Hitchcock had playing with the bird motif in *Psycho* [1960] as Marion Crane was the victim of Anthony Perkins, a taxidermist by hobby!). Ironically, however, whereas Catherine is a senator's daughter, she seems to have less "class" than Clarice who is the "rube with taste."

Note once again how unusual it is in a major motion picture NOT to have a romantic plot or subplot. Note also that Clarice is even denied the strong role of a nurturing "sidekick" as in many police/thriller films (her black roommate has a slightly larger role in the first draft of the script but plays a minimal role in the final film).

The polyphonic or carnivalesque nature of these characters is clear both in the contradictory "voices" offered us and, in the case of Lecter, *withheld* from us as well. Remember that what is finally unsettling about the film is that Lecter is on the loose (of course we are set up for a sequel!). It would be quite a different film if it ended with Clarice receiving her FBI badge, even if we knew Lecter was on the loose. But the ending with Lecter walking into the crowd throws the narrative *off center* compared to the "typical" Hollywood narrative we will discuss in part 2. We are left not with our main character, but with the dividing/embracing figure, Lecter, alone and yet, paradoxically, in a crowd, ready to strike again.

THELMA & LOUISE

Few American films have sparked such an immediate strong reaction—for and against—as Callie Khouri's *Thelma & Louise,* directed by Ridley Scott. It was praised, damned, placed on the cover of *Time,* debated, dissected, championed, and awarded an Oscar for best original screenplay.

To talk about *Thelma & Louise* is to begin with Callie Khouri. She and John Singleton of our group under study share the distinction of getting their first projects onto the screen with critical and popular acclaim. Khouri's background? Five years of working on MTV shorts. "I learned more about screenwriting by doing something that had nothing to do with screenwriting," she has commented.

Khouri definitely fits our emphasis on scriptwriting more as discovery than as an act of imposing structure on character and narrative. "The story for *Thelma & Louise* discovered me," she stated at a Writers Guild of America Symposium on the film (1991). "Two women go on a crime spree: the idea came with the velocity of a sixteen-ton weight hitting me. It hit me that hard. I just knew this would change my life. I really had that feeling. It was then a question of discovering/exploring who these two women were and how they came to go on a crime binge."

The rest is well documented—and often controversial—history. A studio reader who "green lighted" the script remarked it was the first script in eight years he said an unqualified "YES" to. "There's nothing wrong with it," he said, "and part of what makes these characters work is that you can't figure them out completely. There's something a little off." Others connected with the project said much the same: in terms of characterization, "there's something to play that's not in the lines," added Christopher McDonald who plays Darryl, Thelma's irate and bewildered husband.

Of course even the title itself *suggests* a female "makeover" of the male buddy film from *Butch Cassidy and the Sundance Kid* (William Goldman 1969) and *Thunderbolt and Lightfoot* (Michael Cimino 1974) to *Smokey and the Bandit* (James Lee Barrett, Alan Mandel, and Charles Shyer 1977) or a 1990s retake on *Bonnie and Clyde* (David Newman and Robert Benton 1967). But as critic Jack Kroll noted, Thelma and Louise as characters "create a friendship that goes way beyond the Butch-Sundance syndrome in warmth and complexity" (1991).

We have already quoted Khouri in our introduction as having purposely set out to take chances with this script—thus the ending that she always held her ground on and which Ridley Scott told her from the beginning would be the one point they would never change. Perhaps it is worth beginning our discussion of the characterizations of Thelma and

Louise by taking on the ending. Because Butch and Sundance have been mentioned in so many reviews of *Thelma & Louise*, we should underline the differences between the endings of the two. In William Goldman's script and George Roy Hill's film, it is never made entirely clear whether Butch and Sundance know they are rushing to their deaths as they charge out into the open to meet the Bolivian army. They certainly never mention it, and their innocence in other matters in the film suggests that here too, at the end, they might once again not be quite bright enough to get the total picture.

But Thelma and Louise make a conscious pact as we have quoted in the introduction. Louise's "Go?" becomes Thelma's "Go." And the shared soulful smile at the end between them is clearly a conscious bonding of the two women before plunging into the abyss. Thelma and Louise thus grow a lot more as individuals than Butch and Sundance. "They have to die," says psychotherapist Dr. Amit Kshetarpal, "because they've broken all the rules and there are no appropriate males to form any real relationships with" (1992).

...

Do we have two main characters? Of course in the overall sense we do, as the title announces. But it is important for those interested in developing character-centered scripts to look more closely. I cannot think of a buddy script in which two characters are equal protagonists: certainly Butch *determines* what the duo will do in *Butch Cassidy and the Sundance Kid*: "Keep thinkin', Butch. That's what you're good at," remarks Sundance throughout the film. Thus Sundance is the major embracing buddy figure who sticks it out according to the groundwork laid out by Butch (note that the film begins with Butch and that he is favored in a number of important scenes including the New York city montage sequence).

Thelma & Louise is similar. We begin with Louise, and we quickly realize she's the one who takes charge and then, at the key point, it is she who commits the murder of the would-be rapist. She is, finally, the one too who, besides doing the driving, says, "We're not giving up, Thelma." Thelma *embraces* Louise's lead throughout the first half of the film. Not to realize this is to misunderstand the writing and development of these two unlikely casual friends who become something much more. The pattern can actually be seen as one of, as we shall discuss, mother and daughter as well as two female friends, as Louise "mothers" her friend Thelma. Louise plays the accepting, nurturing, protective "mother" to Thelma's innocent, unprotected "daughter"-like character.

But Thelma grows. Midway through the script is the long motel sequence. Thelma finally has a grand sexual encounter with the Hitchhiker (Brad Pitt) who then walks off with Louise's life savings. From that point on, Thelma begins to take charge of her own life and turns her back on her former life. Character as process: she always had the *potential* to enjoy herself and lead her own life. She just simply had not had the opportunity while living with Darryl.

Men in this film are clearly antagonists. Harlan is the would-be rapist who is murdered early on. Darryl is the redneck husband Thelma wishes to escape from, and J. D. becomes a complex mixture of both antagonist and embracing figure for Thelma as he brings out her strong pleasure in sexuality but also walks off with all of Louise's cash.

But two men help balance the spectrum of male characters offered by Khouri. Jimmy, Louise's boyfriend, is sympathetic as a guy who wants to embrace even when he doesn't understand Louise or their relationship. When he shows up at the motel while Thelma and Louise are on the run, he asks Louise to marry him:

LOUISE

Jimmy, we've gone all these years . . . we never made it work. We're not gonna be able to just . . . I'm not . . . What kind of job, honey? Can you see it. I can't.

Jimmy doesn't answer right away. He's trying to see it.

JIMMY

I'm the one . . . I never made it work. I just . . . It's not that I don't love you. It's not that. I just never thought I'd be thirty-six years old and I never thought . . . I don't know what I thought. What do you want, darlin'. What do you want me to do.

LOUISE

I don't know. It doesn't even matter anymore. I just want you to be happy . . . It's not that I don't love you either. But Jimmy, your timing couldn't be worse.

Jimmy does not really understand why this is happening.

JIMMY

Are you just doin' this to punish me?

LOUISE

Believe me, the last thing I want is for you to get punished. (60–61)

Harlan's brutality toward Thelma in the beginning of the film is clear enough. But the kind of *character shading/texturing* that occurs in the above scene keeps *Thelma & Louise* from becoming a simplistic feminist or antimale tract. Jimmy is drawn here with a number of voices, including those of being vulnerable ("Are you doin' this just to punish me?"), sensitive ("What do you want me to do"), and yet not very bright ("I never thought I'd be thirty-six years old and I never thought . . .").

Likewise the Harvey Keitel cop figure, Hal, proves to be an unusually sensitive law officer, torn between duty and his sympathy for Thelma and Louise:

HAL

I swear, Louise, I almost feel like I know you.

LOUISE (V.O.)

Well. You don't.

HAL

You're gettin' in deeper every moment you're gone.

LOUISE (V.O.)

Would you believe me if I told you this whole thing is an accident?

HAL

I do believe you. That's what I want everybody to believe. Trouble is, it doesn't look like an accident and you're not here to tell me about it . . . I need you to help me here. (107)

As police officer, his job makes him an oppositional figure, out to get the women on the run. But his talk and motivation seem genuinely to embrace their situation and to help them escape *with their lives*. In terms of character portrayal, Khouri is shading Hal as an officer with an inner life of his own, with alternative voices that are expressed. And yet part of that complexity of character development is that none of these men acts fully as a male. Jimmy in particular takes on a kind of maternal role in bringing the money Louise needs and in trying to accept and understand Louise. Yet Jimmy's "nonmacho" behavior is more one of impotence rather than of a newly gained sensitivity.

• • •

The carnivalesque in the characterization of both Thelma and Louise is clear. They are not summed up by what they appear to be—a waitress in a small town café and a lower-middle-class housewife. This is especially true of Louise whom we never get to know through flashbacks of childhood problems as in *The Silence of the Lambs* or through dream/fantasies as in *Time of the Gypsies* or through straightforward childhood plotting as in *Boyz N the Hood*. We just don't clearly know what happened in the past to make Louise who and what she is: the mystery remains (of course what is strongly hinted at is a core rape experience in Texas years ago). What we do know is that a film that looks like a light-hearted romp at first turns suddenly dark when unsuspected depths in Louise's character are revealed. It is Thelma's gun that Louise holds on Harlan as she comes to Thelma's rescue:

HARLAN
Now, calm down. We were just havin' a little fun.

Louise glances at Thelma. Thelma shakes her head no.

LOUISE
Looks like you've got a real fucked-up idea of fun. Now turn around.

Louise starts to back away, but the gun is still close to his face. His pants are undone in the front. She is still backing away with the gun raised. Thelma is inching away as well.

LOUISE
Just for the future, when a woman's crying like that, she's not having any fun.

HARLAN
(pulling up his pants)
Bitch. I should have gone ahead and fucked her.

Louise stops in her tracks.

LOUISE
What did you say?

HARLAN
I said suck my cock.

Louise takes two long strides back toward him, raises the gun and FIRES a bullet into his face. (18–19)

We don't expect Louise's action given what we have seen so far. What does this mean? That we don't know all that there is to know about Louise. Part of Khouri's talent in this script is to *play with the audience by manipulating stereotypes for fresh, nonstereotyped results.* Critic Roy Grundmann puts it well when he notes that the film constantly asks us, "Is their reaction to the assault, their decision not to report the crime, and their subsequent rampage, 'appropriate'" (1991, 35). Did Thelma and then Louise bring their end upon themselves? Grundmann concludes, correctly I think, by saying, "What is not mentioned is that, in a case of sexual harassment, the subject of appropriate reaction and self-induced guilt are false issues to begin with. A woman cannot bring rape upon herself. How can appropriateness of action be an issue in an assault situation of that type?"

It has been argued that Thelma's character never goes much beyond that of the stereotypic bimbo. "Thelma becomes poor Thelma, a fugitive version of Lucille Ball in *I Love Lucy*," quips critic Alice Cross (1991, 33). You decide. But Khouri definitely wishes us to see Thelma as a much less complicated person than Louise. Thelma is an extrovert who is contrasted to Louise, an introvert, a repressed individual.

The ending, as we have discussed in the introduction, tests our sense of "appropriate behavior" once more. There can be no doubt, however, given the carnivalesque nature of Louise's personality, that no other choice is possible. The endless debates about the ending when the film was released simply help to underline the fact that even though we get to know Louise well, *we still don't know her core characteristics completely.* She goes to her death as a mystery.

BOYZ N THE HOOD

Only 1.5 percent of the members of the Writers Guild of America are black (F.Y.I. 1992). This statistic alone helps emphasize the phenomenal success of John Singleton, a twenty-three-year-old black graduate of USC film school who landed a three-film contract with Columbia Pictures beginning with *Boyz N the Hood* (1991).

That the film, especially after the April/May 1992 Los Angeles riots, has become an American "event" more than a movie, is known to all. But let us look beyond the debates and the violence surrounding the film, the popularity and the Oscars won and nominations made, to the script and the characters themselves. Surely credit should be given to other young black filmmakers, especially Spike Lee, whose *Do the Right Thing* (1989) in particular pointed the way for a "cinema of reality" that faced social ills and issues straight on. *Malcolm X* (1992) clearly signaled Lee's power and importance in the eyes of Hollywood as well as within American culture as he made an epic about the greatly misunderstood Black Muslim leader. Interested readers would do well to get hold of Phyllis Rauch Klotman's edited collection of six scripts in *Screenplays of the African-American Experience* (1991) for a further appreciation of the accomplishment of independent black filmmakers such as Charles Lane, Charles Burnett, Bill Gun, Kathleen Collins, and Julie Dash.

Within that context, *Boyz N the Hood*, released the same summer as *Terminator 2*, was the more explosive work—even though "increase the peace" was the basic message—because it contains the ring of TRUTH. Singleton was writing about what he knew best: his neighborhood in South Central Los Angeles.

Ironically, even though the subject matter is much stronger than major studios would consider touching, the shape of the script is perhaps the most conventional of the scripts we are considering. Singleton's story is a straightforward coming of age story of a young black, Tre (Cuba Gooding, Jr.). The script sets up Tre's situation carefully in part 1, which is set in 1984 when his mother passes him on to his father (Larry Fishburne) so that she can pursue her own career. The second and third acts of the story jump to the present (1991) and follow Tre through his interaction with his father and his gang on the block headed up by Doughboy (Ice Cube) and Ricky (Morris Chestnut), the athlete of the group, and his black Catholic girlfriend. Almost like an urban western, the film builds to the shootout and then the swift resolution with a "happy ending": Tre will go to Morehouse College in Atlanta, and his girlfriend will be down the street at Spellman College.

Singleton manages a fine balancing act between such a conventional Hollywood narrative and his explosive, timely, contemporary subject matter. In all the discussions about the violence in the film, critics and audiences alike seem to have overlooked how absolutely *moral* the film is. In fact, some may see it as a fault that Tre becomes so positive, that his father is such a pillar of common sense, wisdom, patience, and support, and that the ending IS such a victory over the tragedy of the "hood." Statistically a majority of black American families are run by mothers, most often because there is no father around. And when they are, few are as loving, supportive, intelligent as Tre's dad. Clearly he is the key embracing or supportive figure.

But Singleton's film announces itself as one that portrays "the problem" and offers a solution: family support, strong fathers, and education outside the hood. As we shall see, such a moralistic vision is diametrically opposed to the approach taken by Emir Kusturica in another Columbia Pictures release, *Time of the Gypsies*, which offers no real hope for change and no way out of the downward spiral of gypsy life.

The moralistic tone is established even before we see the first scene. What we hear on the soundtrack is street talk from a gang, full of "nigger" and "fuck that shit" expressions with a police siren wailing in the background which continues over the Columbia Pictures logo (a wonderfully ironic touch, that!). Then two sentences appear on the screen, one after the other: "ONE OUT OF EVERY TWENTY-ONE BLACK AMERICAN MALES WILL BE MURDERED IN THEIR LIFETIME" and "MOST WILL DIE AT THE HANDS OF ANOTHER BLACK MALE."

We then fade in on a close-up of a STOP sign, itself a clever embodiment of Singleton's point of view: STOP the violence and increase the peace. (Not all critics appreciated the simplistic moralizing of the film: Thomas Doherty and Jacquie Jones observe that "for all its touted realism, Boyz is beset by labored symbolism, instructional monologues and unlikely behaviors" [1991, 19].)

Much of who we are is shaped by our environment, and in these few brush strokes, Singleton has already told us much of what we need to know. Within this framework, Tre, as a young boy, and then as a young man, becomes the central protagonist we sympathize with and follow. On the level of core experiences, he needs love and needs to work out his own identity and self-respect in a very difficult environment. Add to this, the breakup of his parents and the mother's (Angela Bassett's) giving away of her son, and his need to reconcile such a personal loss, is more than clear.

In a real sense, the major antagonist is the "hood" itself. Not just the street life, but even the cops, for we discover early on that a black cop on the beat works against helping other blacks. When he shows up with his more sympathetic white partner after a break-in at Tre's father's home, the black cop says with a sneer to Tre's dad, "Somethin' wrong?" Tre's dad stares at him and replies, "Somethin' wrong? Yeah. Somethin' is wrong. It's just too bad you don't know what it is."

In part 3 we will discuss structure further, but we should identify the basic story in Singleton's script as a father-son narrative in which the son comes of age because he receives the "blessing" of the father. The father guides Tre through each step of the way, speaking about sex ("Any fool with a dick can make a baby, but only a real man can raise his kids"), about business, about education, about his friends, even about the army (he is a Vietnam vet): "Don't ever go in the army. Black men ain't got no place in the army." And the father has even boiled down his philosophy to three principles which he has Tre repeat: "Always look someone in the eye, never be afraid to ask, and never respect anybody who doesn't respect you back."

Singleton depicts Tre's friends/gang as fulfilling a mixed dividing and embracing function. Doughboy is the leader, and we know at the end of act 1 that even as a kid, he is sent to prison for shoplifting. He is the true product of the hood who is unable to rise above it, and, in the end after "smoking" (murdering) those who murdered his brother Ricky, he in turn is murdered. Ricky, the athlete who wants to go to USC on a scholarship, becomes the sacrificial character: he wants a better life but doesn't make it. That Tre does get out in the end completes the spectrum of possibilities portrayed by Singleton. In this sense Ricky's death has not been in vain: it leads, along with Tre's father's strong guidance, to Tre's maturity and desire to go beyond the hood.

Part of Singleton's accomplishment is to bring out the character of each gang member. Doughboy is not just a "bad dude" on the street: we learn he has read much literature while in prison and he wonders about the larger issues. At one point he muses, "If there's a God, why do people get smoked every night?"

A final character note on *Boyz N the Hood*: the conventional Hollywood script does have a clearly marked antagonist over whom the central figure must triumph. Singleton's script is, as we have suggested, conventional in many ways, but he does not opt for a single "bad" character. That would be too simplistic. For the problem is, as the 1992 riots have shown us painfully, that the "evil" in the hood is complex and involves poverty, ignorance, racism, economics, and the breakup of the family. This absence of a single dividing character adds much to the realism of his script and film.

Think how much of the pervading sense of "something wrong" is conveyed in the film through the seemingly ever-present hovering police helicopters which we hear even when we don't see them.

TIME OF THE GYPSIES

"Joy includes everything: happiness and sorrow," Bosnian-Yugoslav director Emir Kusturica has said (Horton 1988, 64). His expression echoes the carnivalesque in the truest sense, and his films, coming from one of the most exciting and yet troubled areas of the contemporary world, mirror such a wide spectrum of human experience. Raised in Sarajevo, the predominately Moslem capital of Bosnia, Kusturica attended film school at the famous FAMU academy in Prague and joined a new wave of Yugoslav filmmakers in the 1970s and 1980s who managed to make films that were entertaining and challenging at the same time. His first film, *Do You Remember Dolly Bell?* (Abdulah Sidran 1981) was a coming of age story of a young teenage boy in Sarajevo who falls in and out of love as he starts up a rock group sponsored by the local Communist

Party. And his second film, *When Father Was Away on Business* (Abdulah Sidran 1985), which won the Best Picture award that year at the Cannes Film Festival, is a touching study of a Bosnian family during the troubled 1950s when a "father" is sent to prison accused of being a Stalinist.

Time of the Gypsies (1989), written by Goran Mihic and directed by Kusturica, has the unusual distinction of being a Hollywood-produced film (Columbia Pictures) shot in Yugoslavia and Italy in the Romany language! It is a coming of age tale of a young Yugoslav gypsy who lives fully and dies young as a kind of gypsy godfather. On a structural level, the film consciously echoes Coppola and Puzo's *The Godfather* to the degree that, as the determining character, Perhan (Davor Dujmovic), grows to maturity, he looks more and more like Al Pacino in Coppola's film.

Part of the carnivalesque concept of the film, therefore, is that Kusturica and Mihic take us into a world we know little about—the real world of East European gypsies today—but they provide, on a second narrative level, "cinematic" clues from Coppola and many other filmmakers including, finally, Chaplin, not only to add texture to the film, but to anchor it in the familiar: that shared world culture of the movies that we all have lifetime subscriptions to.

Unlike *Boyz N the Hood*, which we have suggested is basically quite conventional in its characterization and narrative drive, *Time of the Gypsies* creates a greater air of mystery and the carnivalesque: this is accomplished first of all by the strangeness to us of gypsy life. At this level we are really speaking of a kind of documentary satisfaction the film provides: How do gypsies live? The film helps us learn. And on another level, Kusturica and Mihic (one of the very best Yugoslav screenwriters responsible for a large number of the most important films from that area in the past twenty years) make use of a kind of "magic realism" that *grows out* of a kind of black magic-gypsy folk culture: things happen that we can't rationally explain. We might best describe the style and nature of the film as, using Srdjan Karanovic's term, "documentary fairy tale." *Time* said of this mixture, "Kusturica knows that magic realism finds its perfect home in the movies, and in this story . . . the film neither romanticizes nor flinches from the popular image of Gypsies as a primitive, stealthy people" (Corliss 1990, 82).

Let us take a closer look at what is happening in this most unusual film.

Whereas Tre in Singleton's film is "explained" almost too much, Perhan's origins and background are wrapped in mystery. We meet him as an awkward, goofy-looking teenager who is just beginning to learn about love, sex, life. His deep structure is that he never knew his parents and therefore has a need to be loved and to come into his own without parental love. But though he lacks parents, he does have a grandmother who is the true matriarch of the family, beautifully played by a large engaging walrus of a gypsy woman, Ljubica Adzovic. She is the major embracing figure who has to stand in for both parents, and thus is the one who must raise and nurture and bless her young.

What we do learn early on is that Perhan has the power to "move" things: he has telekinetic powers. Cans move along platforms, spoons climb walls, and so forth as he wills them to do so. This extra dimension—never explained—ultimately becomes his means of destroying the "godfather" he had trusted "like a father" who betrays him (I do not wish to give away the ending for those who have not seen it: let it suffice to say that a flying fork plays a highly original role!).

I return to Perhan and his character. We sense the powerful contradictions that have no apparent resolutions early on. He is deeply in love with the girl next door, Azra (Sinolicka Trpkova), but is rejected by her parents, and he knows he loves his grandmother, but he has no living parents of his own. "Was my mother beautiful?" he asks her one night and she spins a loving tale of his mother's beauty and his "Slovenian soldier" father who was strong and handsome. This comforts him and leads him into one of the most lyrical dream sequences in recent cinema as he fantasizes his sexual initiation during the important feast of St. George's Day by a river.

To delve into this one sequence is to see how many levels Kusturica and Mihic work on simultaneously:

1. Perhan has been wounded in first love and has tried to commit suicide in a tragicomic scene in which he hangs himself from the bell rope in a ruined church. But the scene has even deep implications for with no real father figure to resist or symbolically "kill" in an Oedipal sense, he must either attempt suicide, which he does, or kill another father figure, which, in the end, he also does.

2. This leads him at night to ask his grandmother about his parents (his growing need to know his own identity/roots).

3. Grandma tells him of his parents, but we soon become aware (if we do not already sense it) that we may never know if anyone is telling the truth in the gypsy world of myth and storytelling where truth and fiction blend in unusual ways. Grandma is a nurturing, embracing figure, but this does not necessarily mean she is telling the truth! This matter of trust/betrayal becomes a central theme later when Perhan, now married to Azra, refuses to believe that the son she carries and gives birth to is his. Clearly that deep ambiguity about trust goes back to his deep structural need to know what he can never really know or recover: his parents. This deep contradiction of an all-embracing grandmother's love but

a total lack of parental love/existence is never resolved except . . . in Perhan's death.

4. But the comforting words of Grandma lead him into sleep and into the fantasy/dream of his sexual initiation with Azra in a river (suggesting a kind of "baptism" into sexuality!): it occurs during a strangely beautiful ritual gathering of hundreds of gypsies carrying lighted torches along the river for St. George's Day as a haunting melody is played/sung on the soundtrack. Humor and pathos and mystery mix in this scene as well as "magic," for Perhan enters the scene floating through the air clutching his beloved pet: a turkey given him by his grandmother.

5. The dream ends with the grandmother weeping. It is an odd but deeply affecting moment. Is she crying because she knows what will happen to Perhan? Is she crying for his lost innocence? Because she knows what really happened to his parents will happen to him? And furthermore, where is she? Is Perhan dreaming of her crying within his own dream?

I do not suggest that the audience asks all of these questions or consciously articulates the complexity of such a sequence. But I do wish to emphasize that this mixture of personal dream, family reality, and cultural ritual is as pure an example of the carnivalesque in cinema as can be imagined. Kusturica and Mihic have constructed Perhan's character with such complexity but with *deceptive ease*. We "get it" without understanding everything. In fact, being "locked" inside a gypsy universe for several hours, we are forced to enter the realm of the truly carnivalesque and touch both mystery and horror, divided and embraced by those we encounter.

As in *Boyz N the Hood* we could say the main antagonist is the society we are shown itself. As mentioned earlier, Kusturica is not moralistic or optimistic like Singleton: Perhan dies, the godfather dies, Azra dies, and the son—if it is his son—steals the coins from his father's eyes (note: placing coins on the eyes of the deceased is an old custom in a number of cultures). Clearly the godfather, Aimed (Boa Todorovic), pretends to embrace his protégé but actually works against him, cheating him on his promise to take care of his sick sister (Elvira Sali). And his philandering Uncle Merdzan (Husnija Hasimovic) is a dividing figure within the family and may, in fact, be the father of Azra's child.

But it is to Kusturica and Mihic's credit that everyone is given his/her "reasons" for behaving as they do and thus no easy blame can be cast. The grandmother does favor Perhan over her own son, Merdzan. And despite his trickster-like behavior, Merdzan is portrayed as a Chaplinesque figure. Before the dream sequence described above, he consciously dresses and acts out a Chaplin routine to get the family to laugh, and in the final image of the film, he leaves Perhan's funeral having witnessed the son's stealing of the coins. As he walks through the rain and mud, back to the camera, dark ragged suit clutched to him, cane and hat in place, feet at angles, he becomes once more Chaplin, walking down the road alone as he did at the end of almost every film.

Thus we end not with the depressing death of Perhan but with the transcending continuity of the living gypsy echoing Chaplin, the Tramp, the outsider who didn't fit in to any society but made us all laugh. In that sense Merdzan the dividing figure is transformed into Chaplin the embracing character who is never embraced himself.

Joy becomes happiness and sorrow through cinema.

A CHARACTER CHECKLIST

Trust your gut reactions as to which characters you choose to develop, what they are like, and how they came to be that way. Writing character is not a scientific or computerized exercise in doing case studies.

But in *refining* and further *defining* them, you may wish to consider the following checklist. Clearly you do not need to be scientific or mechanistic about using this list. Nor would you need to apply it to every minor character. Yet you should consider many or most of these points for your main characters, your antagonists, and your embracing (friend or lover) figures.

    I. Background
        A. Place and time
        B. Parent's profile including race/ethnicity/socioeconomic level, habits
        C. Brothers/sisters/significant-other relatives: same
        D. Family structure/life (important to be able to imagine)

    II. Basics (Background may answer a number of these)
        A. Gender: male/female
        B. Physical abilities/limitations
        C. Race/ethnic background and religion
        D. Socioeconomic class/standing
        E. Location—is your character from the area in which your story takes place or not? What influence of environment?

    III. Personality traits/tendencies
        A. A main protagonist or antagonist?
        B. Introvert or extrovert?
        C. Intuition or sensation?

D. Judging or perceiving orientation?
E. More thinking or feeling?
F. Life/career/personal goals?
G. What do you see is your character's core characteristic?
H. What do you see is the biggest contradiction(s) your character lives out?
I. Father or son? Daughter or mother?
J. Tends to be victim/persecutor/savior?
K. Tends to be innocent/imposter/ironic figure?
L. Mostly self-centered? Selfish? Selfless?

IV. Personal/individualizing habits/tastes
A. Personal appearance/physical stature
B. Clothes (think how much can be done with this one!)
C. Favorite and hated foods/drinks
D. Education (not just school and degrees but perhaps the importance of being "streetwise," etc.)
E. Hobbies
F. Fears (for instance, attitude toward death)
G. Most hated activities
H. Most enjoyed activities
I. Deepest secret or wildest fantasy
J. Closest friend(s)
K. Attitudes toward self, others, friendship, sex, love, family, marriage, country, the world, religion
L. Sense (or lack!) of humor: what makes your character laugh?

V. Professional/public life
A. Job/career/occupation
B. Accomplishments in "society's eyes"
C. Clubs/organizations belonged to
D. Public causes supported/protested

VI. Now for more telling details/likes/dislikes
A. Would you consider your character conservative/traditional or liberal or radical or something else?
B. What kind of cause beyond self would your character care about?
C. Which figure in history would your character most admire?
D. How much would it take for your character to do something seemingly contradictory or out of character (and thus indicative of a deeper level of character!)?

E. Vegetarian or meat and potatoes or lean cuisine?

F. Alcoholic or drug user or son/daughter of one or the other?

G. Is your character the right person at the right time in the right place? Or the wrong person at the wrong time in the wrong place or any combination of the above?

H. What would your character become during a New Orleans Mardi Gras?

I. What should you write on your character's tombstone?

J. A loner? Family oriented? Couple oriented?

K. Favorite music or group/favorite TV shows or films

L. Which photo in the family album best captures "everything" about your character (note: I've met people who have absolutely no photos of themselves; this too is an option!)

M. How would your character tend to react to:
- Inheriting $1 million
- The death of a loved one
- Two weeks on a Greek island
- A natural disaster: hurricane/earthquake, etc.
- Being fired
- Meeting an old friend or enemy not seen for years
- A blind date
- Children: having them/raising them
- Being raped/mugged/violated in some way
- An unexpected kindness or compliment
- A serious illness such as aids or cancer
- A flat tire on the expressway
- An unexpected day off
- An interracial relationship
- Five minutes on local or national TV

You make up the rest of your list!

WORKS CITED IN PART I

Bakhtin, Mikhail. *Rabelais and His World*. Trans. Helene Iswolsky. Boston: M.I.T. Press, 1968.

———. *The Dialogic Imagination*. Ed. Michael Holquist, trans. Caryl Emerson and Michael Holquist. Austin: University of Texas Press, 1981.

———. *Problems of Dostoyevsky's Poetics*. Ed. and trans. Caryl Emerson. Minneapolis: University of Minnesota Press, 1984.

Barthes, Roland. *S/Z: An Essay*. Trans. Richard Miller. New York: Hill and Wang, 1974.

Biskind, Peter. "Blockbuster: The Last Crusade." In *Seeing Through Movies*, ed. Mark Crispin Miller. New York: Pantheon, 1990, 112–140.

———. "Dead Zone." *Premiere* 6, no. 8 (April 1993): 51.

Blos, Peter. *Son and Father: Before and Beyond the Oedipus Complex*. New York: The Free Press, 1985.

Bresson, Robert. *Notes on Cinematography*. Trans. Jonathan Griffin. New York: Urizen Books, 1977.

Buñuel, Luis. *My Last Sigh: The Autobiography of Luis Buñuel*. Trans. Abigail Israel. New York: Alfred A. Knopf, 1983.

Campbell, Joseph. *The Hero with a Thousand Faces*. Princeton: Princeton University Press, 1968.

Cheney, Dorothy L., and Robert M. Seyfarth. *How Monkeys See the World: Inside the Mind of Another Species*. Chicago: University of Chicago Press, 1990.

Corliss, Richard. "A People Cursed with Magic." *Time* (February 19, 1990): 82.

Coveny, William, III. Personal interview, New Orleans, March 1992.

Cross, Alice. "The Bimbo and the Mystery Woman." *Cineaste* 18, no. 4 (December 1991): 32–34.

de Lauretis, Teresa. *Technologies of Gender*. Bloomington: Indiana University Press, 1987.

Didion, Joan. "Why I Write." *The New York Times Book Review Section*, 8 October 1967, p. 5.

Doherty, Thomas, and Jacquie Jones. "Two Takes on *Boyz N the Hood*." *Cineaste* 18, no. 4 (December 1991): 16–19.

Emerson, Caryl. "The Outer Word and Inner Speech: Bakhtin, Vygotsky, and the Internalization of Language." In *Bakhtin: Essays and Dialogues on His Work*, ed. Gary Saul Morson. Chicago: University of Chicago Press, 1984, 21–41.

Freud, Sigmund. *Jokes and Their Relationship to the Unconscious*. Trans. A. A. Brill. New York: Random House, 1938.

Froug, William, ed. *The New Screenwriter Looks at the New Screenwriter*. Los Angeles: Silman-James Press, 1992.

"F.Y.I." *Premiere*, January 1992: 4.

Gass, William H. "The Concept of Character in Fiction." In *Essentials of the Theory of Fiction*. Ed. Michael Hoffman and Patrick Murphy. Durham: Duke University Press, 1988, 267–276.

Gerzon, Mark. *A Choice of Heroes: The Changing Face of American Manhood*. Boston: Houghton Mifflin, 1982.

Gilligan, Carol. *In a Different Voice*. Cambridge, Mass.: Harvard University Press, 1982.

Grundmann, Roy. "Hollywood Sets the Terms of the Debate." *Cineaste* 18, no. 4 (December 1991): 35–36.

Hanlon, Lindley. "The Future of an Illusion: *sex, lies and video tape.*" Lecture delivered at Loyola University, New Orleans, April 1992.

Hinson, Hal. "Screening Out Life: How the Movies Lost Their Grip on Reality." *The Washington Post*, 8 March 1992, pp. G-1, G-5.

Homer. *The Odyssey of Homer*. Trans. Richmond Lattimore. New York: Harper & Row, 1957. Reprinted 1968.

Horton, Andrew. "Oedipus Unresolved: Covert and Overt Narrative Discourse in Emir Kusturica's *When Father Was Away on Business.*" *Cinema Journal* 27, no. 4 (Summer 1988): 64–81.

———. *Comedy/Cinema/Theory*. Berkeley, Los Angeles, London: University of California Press, 1991.

Josefsberg, Milt. *Comedy Writing*. New York: Harper & Row, 1987.

Keirsey, David, and Marilyn Bates. *Please Understand Me*. Del Mar, Calif.: Prometheus Nemesis, 1984.

Kempley, Rita. "*Videotape*: Lusty Splice of Life." *The Washington Post*, 11 August 1989, pp. C-1, C-7.

Khouri, Callie. *Thelma & Louise*. Final Shooting Script, June 5, 1990.

———. "A Symposium on *Thelma & Louise*." Writers Guild of America West, led by Richard Walter of UCLA, November 1991.

Klotman, Phyllis Rauch, ed. *Screenplays of the African-American Experience*. Bloomington: Indiana University Press, 1991.

Kroll, Jack. "Back on the Road Again." *Newsweek*, 27 May 1991, p. 59.

Kshetarpal, Amit. Personal interview, New Orleans, May 1992.

Kuriyama, Constance Brown. "Chaplin's Impure Comedy: The Art of Survival." *Film Quarterly* 45, no. 3 (Spring 1992): 26–38.

Lévi-Strauss, Claude. *The Raw and the Cooked*, vol. 1. Trans. John and Doreen Weightman. New York: Harper & Row, 1969.

Makavejev, Dusan. Personal interview, Moscow, July 1989.

———. "You Never Know Who Carries the Frog in His Pocket." In *Dusan Makavejev, Alexei Gherman, Henning Carlsen: The Cinema Militans Lectures, 1989–91*. Utrecht: Dutch Film Days Foundation, 19–34.

Maltin, Leonard. *Of Mice and Magic: A History of American Animated Cartoons*. New York: New American Library, 1980.

McFadden, George. *Discovering the Comic*. Princeton: Princeton University Press, 1982.

Pareles, Jon. "Radio Days in Cicely, Alaska." *The New York Times* 2 May 1992, p. H-29.

Pelton, Robert D. *The Trickster in West Africa*. Berkeley, Los Angeles, London: University of California Press, 1980.

Polster, Erving. *Every Person's Life Is Worth a Novel*. New York: W. W. Norton, 1987.

Schneider, Andrew. Personal interview, Los Angeles, December 1992.

Seger, Linda. *Creating Unforgettable Characters*. New York: Henry Holt, 1990.

Stone, Merlin. *When God Was a Woman*. New York: Dorset Press, 1976.

Szomjas, Gyorgy. Personal interview, Budapest, June 1992.

Tally, Ted. *The Silence of the Lambs*. Screenplay from the novel by Thomas Harris. First draft: June 6, 1989 (unpublished).

"Thelma & Louise: A Critical Symposium." *Cineaste* 18, no. 4 (December 1991): 28–36.

PART II

NARRATIVE AND STRUCTURE

It's a wrong situation. It's gettin' so a businessman can't expect no return from a fixed fight. Now, if you can't trust a fix, what *can* you trust? For a good return you gotta go bettin' on chance, and then you're back with anarchy.

> Caspar, in the Coen Brothers'
> *Miller's Crossing*

The Yekuana, like the Warao and the Yupa, say that to weave is to conquer death.

> David Guss, commenting on South American
> Indian basketweavers in *To Weave and Sing:
> Art, Symbol, and Narrative in the South
> American Rain Forest*

CHAPTER FOUR

BEYOND THE CLASSICAL HOLLYWOOD STRUCTURE

SCREENWRITING AND WEAVING

Man is a storytelling animal. Why? Because stories, myths, narratives answer deep needs in us all. We cannot exist without narrative. And narrative cinema is an important twentieth-century part of that deep-seated need. Frank Kermode (1979) put it well when he said that there is definitely what he calls a "radiant obscurity of narrative and a secrecy in all narrative" (53) which beckons us all to enter, follow, play with, weave, and interpret for ourselves.

The idea of weaving helps us understand character as a polyphony of voices and an intersection of core traits. It also helps us realize the *craft*, perspective, and attitude that shape character through narrative. When David M. Guss speaks of the Yekuana Indians of Venezuela as conquering death through their weaving, he is speaking of the power of human narrative to transcend limitations of time, place, chance, nature and touch a deeper "radiant obscurity," to use Kermode's term. Guss's remarks on the Yekuana weavers apply to all of us as screenwriters as well:

> Through the integration of forms achieved in the baskets, the *to-wanajoni* (weaver) announces the successful resolution of these same oppositions, whether they are defined as culture and nature, edible and toxic, being and non-being, or invisible and visible. Like the shaman or healer, he too has the power to make things whole. Yet instead of traveling into other worlds to do so, he simply weaves it with his hands. It is for this reason that the Yekuana, like the Warao and the Upa, say that to weave is to conquer death. (1990, 125)

The Coen Brothers' small-town hood, Caspar, speaks about the breakdown of such "weaving": a state in which pure chance takes over, "and then you're back with anarchy."

Part 2 is about setting your characters within a narrative structure even if they themselves tend toward the anarchy of pure carnival.

THE CLASSICAL HOLLYWOOD NARRATIVE

We should ask what the classical Hollywood movie is before we suggest variations that character-centered scripts often embrace.

Many point to Syd Field and his book *Screenplay: The Foundations of Screenwriting* (1982, reprinted in 1984) as perhaps the best-selling example of a text that has suggested to hundreds of thousands of screenwriting candidates the need to follow a script structure based on a tightly woven three-act narrative (turning points on page 30 and 90 for a total of 120 pages). Field, who came to film as a reader rather than a writer, makes it clear that his ideas are based on reading hundreds of scripts. What Field does not provide, however, is a broader context based on both the history of the Hollywood script and much of the fine research that has been done on the "classical Hollywood movie" in the past ten years.

We can, in fact, go back to 1920 and Francis Patterson's *Cinema Craftsmanship* and read a description of what makes an American script tick—which sounds every bit like Field's book: "Emphasis must be laid upon causality and the action and reaction of the human will" (5). More recently film scholars and historians David Bordwell, Janet Staiger, and Kristin Thompson (1985) have well described in *The Classical Hollywood Cinema: Film Style and Mode of Production to 1960* how little the American narrative film has changed since 1917 in terms of structure, story sense, ambiance, thrust. Bordwell, Staiger, and Thompson describe Hollywood films as an "excessively obvious cinema" made up of a linear cause-effect narrative built around a central protagonist, and demonstrating consistency of character, and the need for a successful resolution (read: usually "happy" ending). From William S. Hart's 1917 western *The Narrow Trail* to Michael Blake's *Dances with Wolves*, the classical Hollywood narrative has not shown any great variations.

Repeat: the basic American screenplay has been the same in terms of *structure* and *narrative modes* from 1917 to the present. What has changed is technology (William S. Hart didn't have Dolby sound, color, and a steady cam camera) and nuances of content and style. Thus the cause-effect, highly motivated, tightly structured three-act narrative structure suggested by most of the screenwriting works on the market led by Syd Field's book actually echo Patterson's 1920 directives.

Each of our four films, however, could be considered "off Hollywood." None of these films completely shatters such a classical model as does, for example, Dusan Makavejev's films such as *W. R.: Mysteries of the Organism* (1971) and *Sweet Movie* (1974); in these films, wild juxtapositions between three or four competing narrative strands create a "cinema of collage" rather than a psychological cinema as Hollywood may be described. But each of our four films and one television show "plays" with narrative possibilities beyond the realm of the traditional Hollywood film.

The Silence of the Lambs actually appears the most traditional in terms of a fairly strong "plot": a killer is on the loose and must be brought in by the good cop, in this case a fledgling female FBI candidate. But, as our analysis of *The Silence of the Lambs*'s structure will show, there is much that is quite different from a traditional "classical" narrative including the lack of a romantic subplot and the lack of a resolution for Hannibal Lecter who is still on the loose.

Thelma & Louise is also seemingly traditional for a well set up "buddy film" crossed with a "road movie" until the ending, which forces us to replay the whole narrative in our minds according to the nontraditional ending.

Boyz N the Hood is set up like a Hollywood gang film but it plays with the genre codes and structure by pulling the opposite effect than that offered by *Thelma & Louise*. Singleton opts for a happy ending, thus breaking the cycle of hopelessness suggested by so many gang films.

Time of the Gypsies has something of a Hollywood "epic" quality to its structure and narrative as it offers us a sweeping view of a whole culture through the eyes of a single determining character. And yet the magic realism and bizarre narrative twists pull us out of Hollywood and into a kind of "Balkan narrative" world!

ARISTOTLE ON STRUCTURE: PLOT/CHARACTER/SPECTACLE NARRATIVES

Aristotle identifies four types of tragedy in *The Poetics* depending on which is the most central effect: plot, suffering, character, and spectacle (1947, 60). For our purposes we can substitute "narrative" for tragedy, which is a particular dramatic form of narrative, and we come up with the same four with the substitution of "strong emotional effect either comic or tragic" for "suffering."

Aristotle's observations help us in dealing with film narratives. For we realize that each film has a specific thrust that can be assigned one of these four general headings. Take *Batman Returns* (Daniel Waters 1992), for instance. It would be ludicrous to look to Burton's sound and light show for a character-centered narrative. And, as it turns out, it is equally ludicrous to see in this film a "plot-centered" script as in, say, the *Star Wars* trilogy or the *Indiana Jones* trilogy (critic Tom Shales of NPR, for instance, said that the plot was so badly worked out that the only thing worse than watching the film a second time would be learning that the 1992 presidential campaign might be extended another year!). Critics were almost unanimous in finding the plot a complete mess. But plot and character are not what *Batman Returns* reveals itself to be about. Rather, I would suggest in Aristotle's terms, it is a narrative centered on "spectacle." The film is loud, flashy, and full of imaginative set and costume design. Whether this is enough to make for a satisfying movie experience is a matter of one's personal critical judgment. But in design and marketing strategy, *Batman Returns* announces itself as focusing on sizzle rather than narrative or character substance. And the box office rewards suggest that beyond the mountains of negative reviews from critics, the producers could lay claim to having fulfilled their ambitions of producing a movie with a lot of bells and whistles that people "bought."

Of Aristotle's four divisions, that of "suffering" is perhaps the least clear since it would appear to be an effect of one or more of the other three divisions. "Suffering," in our terms since we are speaking of narrative in general and not just tragedy, can be considered to be an overall emotional effect or response.

But for our purposes, I believe we can collapse this division into the others, thus leaving us with narratives of plot, character, and spectacle. If we work with these three narrative divisions, *we can see more clearly that our task in this section is to examine narrative structures that best serve to bring out the character-centeredness of your script.* Those writers who are more interested in plot-centered or spectacle-centered projects may find elements of this book useful. But once more we announce that our goal is one of carving out the *difference* between the character-centered narrative and that of the other two divisions. The narrative structures of *Time of the Gypsies, Boyz N the Hood,* "Northern Exposure," *Thelma & Louise,* and *The Silence of the Lambs* all lead us to focus on character, though each makes use of plotting and spectacle to varying degrees.

With such a tripartite division of narrative, we might say, for instance, that *Time of the Gypsies* with its use of magic realism as well as the "exotic" realism of contemporary gypsy life as it is makes the most use of spectacle of our sample group of projects. In terms of the evocation of "suffering" that Aristotle talks about, clearly *The Silence of the Lambs* is the most consistently emotionally wrenching narrative of the lot. And so on. The point, however, is that once again the varying narrative structures serve to highlight the characters presented.

NARRATIVE:
PLACEMENT/DISPLACEMENT/REPLACEMENT

A film should have a beginning, middle and end, but not necessarily
in that order.

> Jean Luc Godard

The traditional model for the screenplay is that of the three-act structure. Syd Field as we have mentioned has set forth a paradigm based on
the model of a 120-page script in which act 1 (pages 1–30) is the set up,
act 2 (pages 30–90) is the confrontation, and act 3 (the rest of the script)
is the resolution. And more scripts than one can count have been influenced by this tight formula. In fact, it is easy to clock most Hollywood
plot-driven films by how religiously they switch from one act to the next
at almost exactly those points as translated into minutes: act 2 begins
after the first half hour and act 3 clicks in after roughly an hour and a
half. In general, an awareness of a three-act structure can be helpful for
screenwriters. But you should note: *A character-centered script may or
often may not adhere closely to such a set paradigm.*

What is perhaps more important to understand in writing your script
is that a narrative is composed of variations of placement, displacement,
and replacement of narrative elements. You *place* your various characters in motion, and then something or some combination of events/
actions occurs to *displace* that equilibrium established in the beginning.
Finally there is a *replacement* that creates a new equilibrium that may or
may not resemble the opening condition. Yes, you can loosely see placement as "the set up," displacement as "conflict," and replacement as
"resolution." But such a reading out of narrative suggests more. Beyond
any vague or specific sense of the traditional three acts, the focus on
placement, displacement, replacement allows you to see that these three
forces are at work constantly within a moment inside a scene, within a
whole scene, and within a sequence, and between sequences. Put another
way, like Homer's Penelope, a narrative constantly presents characters,
"unweaves" them, and presents us once again with a new combination
that is both familiar but different. On an even more simple level, we can
say that as a storyteller you need to create a tension between what is
familiar (repetition) and new (conflict/reversal/surprise) and to finally
present some form of closure, even if your ending is an "open" one: life
goes on.

Narrative theoretician Gerard Genette (1990) has identified a slightly
different trilogy of elements that make up any narrative whether for film,
drama, or the printed page. He speaks of narrative as being composed of
order, duration, and frequency (32). The ordering has to do with place-

ment as we have described above. And frequency concerns replacement and repetition, whereas duration is Genette's more specific description of what happens in displacement in a broader sense than that mentioned above. Duration for Genette means that your narrative can be constructed in one of five manners:

1. Compressed time: Narrative can be constructed in compressed, summarized form in which much is covered in far less time than it would take to actually occur. Think of the voice-over "documentary" narration that opens *Casablanca*, for instance, which summarizes much of World War II focusing on how it affects North Africa. In more recent films, more common is a *montage sequence* (swiftly edited short shots strung together as in MTV music videos) set to music, for instance, to show the passage of time and events. Note how often compressed time is a tool of the plot-driven script: you have a lot of story to tell and only 120 pages to do so!

Note that in the character-centered narrative, compressed time is often used to "cap" or bridge parts of the character's life. *Tootsie* (Larry Gilbert, Murray Schisgal, et al. 1982) caps Dustin Hoffman's success of becoming "Dorothy," a tough-mouthed soap opera star, with a fast-paced montage of "her" appearance on various magazine covers thus indicating her swift rise to national fame without the need to play out any separate scenes.

2. Ellipsis: Here we focus on what we leave OUT of a narrative. Clearly the art of placement is also the craft of what not to place. To tell all is to bore your audience. Narration has to do with selection, and often what is left out can both heighten a sense of mystery and suspense, and also it can speed up your narrative. One of the great examples of ellipsis in American cinema occurs in Buster Keaton's *Sherlock Jr.* (1924); Buster, a projectionist in a movie theater, finally gets his girl—in the projection booth—and, while watching the movie he is projecting, he gets cues as to how to behave, which results in him kissing his lady love and placing a ring on her finger. In the final few shots, he looks back to the screen to see that there is a big ellipsis from the ring on the finger to a shot of the movie lovers rocking babies on their knees. We end with Buster scratching his head as he considers either (1) exactly what happened between the shot of the ring and that of the babies and/or (2) whether or not he actually wants to go through with such a "scenario"!

Obviously ellipsis becomes an important necessity in character-centered scripts that attempt to cover many years in a character's life. Steve Tesich did an excellent job of taking on John Irving's popular novel, *The World According to Garp* and turning it into what became a memorable film directed by George Roy Hill. Since the novel covers Garp's life from beginning (and earlier if we include his mother's background!) to end, Tesich had to figure out how to make ellipsis work *for* the script rather than *against* it. We should offer one dramatic example: a climatic moment in the novel is the "crash" scene in which Garp's reckless driving results in the death of one of his sons and in his wife's bizarre accident of biting off the penis of the young student with whom she has had an affair. Tesich with George Roy Hill's help took the wise decision to cut from a shot of Helen bending her head down toward the student's waist to one of Garp approaching the driveway, then to a freeze frame on Walt, the son who dies, at the moment of impact as we hear the crash. John Irving approved of the ellipsis of not showing a bitten-off penis: "You can't bleed just a little bit on screen; you BLEED!" he stated in acknowledging a major difference between screen and the printed page (Horton 1985, 162).

3. Screen time and narrative time are equal: what you see is exactly what you get in terms of duration. The emphasis on this form of presentation is on realism, a sense of the way life unfolds for us. *Clearly this is the dominant form of "duration" for character-centered films.* Much of the special rhythm of *sex, lies and videotape* has to do with the fact that the scenes are allowed to play themselves out without being chopped up, shortened, compressed. Soderbergh, in other words, savors the texture of the moment and allows us to do likewise. We sense, therefore, character being expressed, unfolding before us in a mostly *uninterrupted* manner. And think how much of the effect of *The Silence of the Lambs* depends on the unusually long scenes between Clarice and Lecter. The rhythm of the film has to do with the special feeling of these long uninterrupted scenes and the speeded-up urgency of the rest of the narrative in which many events are condensed, interrupted, edited. Similarly, *Thelma & Louise* alternates between long moments between Thelma and Louise themselves and more nervous, speeded-up montages of events as they interact with others.

4. Stretched time: Screen time stretches the actual time of the story beyond the bounds of the time it would take to unfold naturally. The Russian pioneer Sergei Eisenstein often used this technique of expanding reality for a particular effect through editing (montage). The "Odessa steps" sequence in Eisenstein's *Potemkin* (1925), for instance, expands through editing the time it would realistically have taken for citizens of Odessa to descend a long flight of steps while being fired upon by Czarist troops. Two other techniques, however, are in more common use for expanding actual narrative time: one is the "crosscut" between two or more actions happening simultaneously, and the other is the use of slow motion. Lawrence and Meg Kasdan expanded a few brief days in contemporary Los Angeles in *Grand Canyon* (1992) to give us a sense of what was happening in the lives of a group of characters *at that mo-*

ment. Clearly they set themselves the task of writing a kind of sequel to *The Big Chill* (1983), another strongly character-driven film, but in reverse: whereas *The Big Chill* builds on long scenes of a variety of characters assembled in one place, *Grand Canyon* focuses on characters scattered across a city and thus, figuratively, across a culture. Many felt, however, that with this later effort, the Kasdans became too diffuse so that such an expanded sense of the moment bordered on complete formlessness.

5. The pause or "zero" moment: A time-out from the narrative in which "nothing" happens. Genette writes about fiction, but in terms of cinema, we know exactly how such a zero moment can be created: the freeze frame. The troubled face of young Jean-Pierre Leaud at the end of Truffaut's *400 Blows* (1959), of Butch and Sundance rushing to their inevitable deaths in *Butch Cassidy and the Sundance Kid* (1969), of Jeff Bridges's battered and confused face as a down and out small-time boxer in John Huston's *Fat City* (1972), of Thelma and Louise about to go into the canyon, of a crowded street in the Caribbean in *The Silence of the Lambs*, as well as of Graham and Ann sitting in the rain at the end of *sex, lies and videotape*. And finally: the Charlie Chaplin pose of the uncle in *Time of the Gypsies* rushing, alone, through the mud and rain of Yugoslavia.

It's important to realize, however, that such a freezing of narrative does not freeze our perceptions. In fact, just the opposite. The freeze frame is a focusing technique. Because it does what cannot happen naturally in real life—an arresting of movement in time and space—such an "artistic" technique opens a space for us to examine, ponder, savor all that image evokes, both of the past (what we have just seen in the film) and the future (what lies ahead for these characters).

But a "zero moment" may be obtained through a scene as well. The bicycle scene played to "Raindrops Keep Falling on My Head" in *Butch Cassidy and the Sundance Kid* is often thought of as "time-out" from what goes before and after, a kind of transition from the American West to the beginning of Butch, Sundance, and Etta's wanderings to New York and subsequently to Latin America. And certainly it does serve this function as a bridge. Yet nothing is ever really zero, and that is especially true in this scene, which actually encapsulates many of the thematic strands of the film. Butch and Sundance are sympathetic bandits out of sync with the times. America is changing and they are not. Paul Newman riding *backwards* on a new invention—the bike—and crashing is both funny and emblematic of his downfall. It is also tied into romance, for he is performing for Etta, his best friend's woman.

Note that Genette's discussion of "duration" has to do with narrative duration and not with the specific length of a scene. To his investigation of these five areas of duration, we need to add the actual length of a scene. You don't need to be told that the average Hollywood film—influenced as it is these days by the ever-quickening pace of television shows—moves at a staccato pace. In most cases, this fact alone helps identify these films as plot-centered rather than character-driven. *And in most cases the character-centered script tends to go for longer scenes and a slower pace than that of plot-heavy narratives.* Boyz N the Hood does contain violence, but the bulk of the film is made up of scenes that are allowed to play themselves out in terms of dialogue and action between the characters at a pace slower than films that place violence at their center. In this sense, Singleton's film is constructed more like the classic western in which the narrative builds toward the showdown with very little violence before the brief, explosive moment when the gunfight actually takes place. The gunfight in John Ford's character-centered prototypic western *Stagecoach* (Dudley Nichols 1939) lasts no more than four seconds! The dialogue-driven scenes that make up the bulk of Ford's film, however, go on for minutes at a time.

Movies are sound and light shows of a certain duration.

Screenplays must manipulate time, space, sound, and light as well as character, dialogue, and action . . . on paper.

PLOT VERSUS CIRCUMSTANCE

The pursuit of becoming the best navy jet pilot (*Top Gun*) has to do with PLOT. How a whole African tribe is changed by a coke bottle falling from a jet into a small village (*The Gods Must Be Crazy* [1979]) has more to do with CIRCUMSTANCE. Thus let us follow through even more specifically with the issues discussed in the previous section.

Of course the circumstance generates actions from all characters involved. But I wish to point out that in the character-centered script a strong circumstance can provide the frame within which characters can react, interact, grow, transcend, and resolve problems. Think of the 1992 Oscar winner for Best Foreign Film: *Mediterraneo* (Gabriele Salvatores). An unlikely bunch of Italian soldiers (and one donkey!) are dropped off at the most distant Greek island that has absolutely "zero" military significance. And these soldiers are forgotten about for over three years from 1941 to 1944. That's their circumstance! Each has to deal with being on a sleepy Greek island where life is, well, damn near perfect! The result, as we shall mention later, is a very picaresque unfolding of a film that resembles Boccaccio's eye for comic detail and Homer's epic sweep of fact and fantasy, blended.

I choose "circumstance" rather than the buzz words "high concept" so popular in the 1980s in Hollywood. The saying then was that a really high concept should be expressed in two words with two to four syllables: *Top Gun, Home Alone, E.T.* (the ultimate, since the whole film becomes only two letters!), *Star Wars, Terminator, Basic Instinct,* and *Lethal Weapon.* High concept to Hollywood usually meant strong plot, but "high circumstance" varies in suggesting a strong framework within which a wide spectrum of possibilities exists. From this perspective, *E.T.* (Melissa Mathison) and *Mediterraneo* are both high on strong circumstances more than powerful plots: both are about "foreigners" who wish to get home when thrust into a "strange" environment (the so-called "fish out of water" narrative strand).

In terms of our sample films we could say that *Boyz N the Hood* and *Time of the Gypsies* depict characters in specific circumstances: black lower-class Los Angeles, and Yugoslav gypsy culture. The protagonists of these films must come to grips with his/her circumstance/environment/culture.

Thelma and Louise, on the other hand, begin by leaving their situations and striking out for "something else." Their narrative is picaresque, but it is one that is set up as a road adventure and thus as a plot in which we expect the unexpected along the road. Similarly, Clarice is such a strongly defined determining character that she has left her circumstances/environment far behind. She's turned her back on her West Virginia roots and struck out for Washington, D.C. and the FBI training program. Both *Thelma & Louise* and *The Silence of the Lambs,* therefore, feature characters who set their own narratives in motion outside their original circumstances.

CHAPTER FIVE

Developing a
Character-Centered Narrative

> As a narrative device, the ability to vary the distance between the
> camera and the object may be a small thing indeed, but it makes for
> a notable difference between cinema and oral or written narrative,
> in which the distance between language and image is always the same.
>
> Italo Calvino, *The Uses of Literature*

Getting Started:
Character or Narrative?

Do you start with character or with story?

Either way; it doesn't matter. Sometimes it is the character who comes
to mind first. And then again, it may be the story from which the narrative and characters develop. Callie Khouri began more with narrative
than character: "two women go on a crime spree." Crime is not so difficult to deal with, but who the two women were to become was where
Khouri really made her mark. Soderbergh, however, knew he was building a script based on his own life and experiences and needed a narrative
and structure that would become much more than autobiography in *sex,
lies and videotape*. The same could be said for John Singleton in shaping
Boyz N the Hood. Singleton clearly began with his own life experiences
and environment and worked toward finding a narrative and structure
that carried his experiences further.

Begin with either and work toward the other. Maybe you know a
"real character" but you need a "story" to bring him/her out more. Or
the opposite. A newspaper story about an ex-pro football player as a
homeless drug addict living under the interstate in a cardboard box captures your attention. *Time of the Gypsies* is such a newspaper story that
was turned into screen narrative by Kusturica and Mihic.

Character and story or, as we shall call it, narrative, are intimately
connected even if we can speak separately of each. We will follow the
current critical tradition that "narrative" is the wider term that includes

not only the events in time (story) but also the way in which they are told/presented/structured.

Since our focus is particularly on character, I will spend less time on narrative and structure, not because it is less important but simply because others have written well and at length on these twin areas of scriptwriting.

But perhaps it would be valuable to make one simple division between kinds of narrative structures: on the one hand there are *inner-driven* scripts and, on the other, scripts that appear motivated by external events/circumstances that set the frame within which characters must *react*. One does not exclude the other, of course. For characters caught up in an exterior circumstance such as a hurricane or nuclear war will still be motivated by their core-characteristic needs. But a film such as *On the Beach* (John Paxton from Nevil Shute's novel, 1959) places the exterior circumstance—nuclear war—in the forefront and then examines how a host of characters respond individually. *Boyz N the Hood* includes both categories: a coming of age story (inner motives) crosses with a strong external context—the tough Los Angeles neighborhood. *The Silence of the Lambs, Time of the Gypsies, sex, lies and videotape,* and *Thelma & Louise* are thus not only character-centered but inner-driven narratives: the characters want something and they set things in motion.

In developing your narrative, you must decide to what degree the inner and exterior narrative factors come into play.

WHERE SCREENPLAYS COME FROM

> I'm always taking: I never invent.
> Jean-Luc Godard

Screenplay ideas can come from anywhere.

Imagine trying to pitch *The Gods Must Be Crazy* (written and directed by Jamie Uys 1979) to a Hollywood producer: "Well, there's a coke bottle that falls out of a plane and a tribe of Africans think it is sent from heaven and meanwhile this shy white guy is in love with this woman and the two plots cross as . . ."

Consider these sources:

1. YOUR LIFE

I doubt that you would want to write a screenplay unless you feel you have been through some experiences you wish to explore and convey on the screen. Your life (including those of people you know or have met and can get to know better) is certainly the right place to begin, if for no other reason than it's the story you know best. Or do you? Obviously if you write a script based on your own experiences or your own family members' experiences, you will learn much in the process. One of the first things you'll catch on to is that your script is not your life, nor should you be limited by what *really happened*. Too often beginning screenwriters hand me autobiographical scripts and say, "Well, in real life my business went bankrupt in a year, not a month," or "As it really happened, the Stranger and I only made love twice, but I felt five times would make a better movie."

The point is nobody cares and certainly no one is checking. Thus start with what you know and explore, develop, go beyond. What you want is a good story, not a police report on your life. *Remember that autobiography is one of the biggest forms of fiction anyway!* Do you really think Ben Franklin is candid about his life in his much-read autobiography? Think again.

But of our example films, *Boyz N the Hood* definitely came out of John Singleton's life. He took his own experience and built on it, transforming it for the screen.

2. ADAPTATION

Don't feel you have to reinvent the wheel. I think a lot of beginning scriptwriters would be best off starting with a short story or novel and embellishing it for the screen. Adaptation is not an impersonal, mechanical craft. In fact, adaptations often surpass the originals, as Kurt Vonnegut (1981) has said about his novel *Slaughterhouse Five*: "George Roy Hill's film is better than my novel." Now Vonnegut was most certainly being modest, but there is truth in many cases in which a forgotten or lesser-known work has been turned into a great film. Almost nobody has read the American hard-boiled crime novel *Down There* by David Goodis that François Truffaut's *Shoot The Piano Player* (1960) is based on, but everyone agrees the film is great. And although a number of people did read Thomas Harris's novel, it is Ted Tally and Jonathan Demme's film of *The Silence of the Lambs* that is remembered.

Of course the traditional wisdom of Hollywood is to take a blockbuster bestseller (*Gone with the Wind* was the biggest selling novel in American history at the time) and make a blockbuster film. But, as usual, we suggest an alternative: take an unknown work and, most definitely, one that *no longer is covered by copyright protection* and rework it.

Think of the advantages: you have greater freedom to make changes because you are not being held to the common memory of the original, you do not have to pay anybody anything, and you don't have to invent everything: you can jump start a script and make it better.

That was what I did for my first script. I took Mark Twain's *Puddin'
Head Wilson* and wrote a script (it has since been turned into a TV
movie, but my script got there first, even if it wasn't used!). I loved the
circumstance of the story—a black boy and white boy with a common
mother, switched at birth so that the black child is raised white and vice
versa. But I felt Twain's ending fizzled out. Even more I was attracted to
Puddin' Head Wilson, the offbeat lawyer who had never practiced law
until he took on this case. His character in all its complexity made
Twain's story more than a clever cross-racial gimmick. I had fun making
changes, improvements so that the ending was far less sentimental and
coincidental.

I learned much—including that I couldn't sell my script even though
the book was in the public domain unless I said the script was "based on
a book by Samuel Clemens" and not "Mark Twain." Why? As it turns
out, Mark Twain is a trademarked name owned by the Mark Twain estate, and I would have had to pay royalties on the name.

Nevermind. I wrote my first script, never once suffered writer's block,
and learned more than I realized till much later.

One last piece of advice on adaptation: try taking a short story and
embellishing it into a feature film. Or, as noted in the exercises in part 3
and below under number 6, try a children's book that you transform
into a film: children's books are short, cinematic, imaginative! Either a
short story or a children's book is much easier than taking a novel and
trying to cut it back to a two-hour film. John Irving (1982) was asked
why he didn't write the script for *The World According to Garp*: "Hell, I
spent four years of my life writing the novel which is about 600 pages.
You think I'm going to cut it down to 120 pages! No! Never!" A wise
man. Screenwriter Steve Tesich, however, was able to face Irving's complicated novel and come up with a surprisingly effective script that main-
tained the integrity of Irving's original spirit.

3. THE NEWSPAPER/TV NEWS

It's a slow day when five good film stories are not in the daily paper. I'm
not speaking of the international news, but the local news, the personal
story. *Dog Day Afternoon* (Frank Pierson 1975) with Al Pacino, for
instance, is typical. Who could invent a more bizarre tale than that of
a Brooklyn married gay man who holds up a branch bank with his
lover so that they can get enough money for him to have a sex change
operation?

What made the script work was that such a strange case was made familiar, sympathetic. We cared about both characters and came to see
them not as pathetic but as trapped. That's good writing.

Yes, it is complicated legally to deal with real stories, and you will need a lawyer or agent or both to sort it out. But if you are learning the trade, no one is stopping you from having a crack at it.

I have a drawer full of clippings of ideas I'd like to get to sometime. And the advice is the same here as elsewhere: it is most likely that what you really need is to figure out how to bring at least two of these stories together to make one satisfactory film.

Time of the Gypsies came from Yugoslav newspaper stories about gypsies selling their own children into slavery in Italy. Emir Kusturica and screenwriter Goran Mihic simply brought out the potential in this horrific image.

4. HISTORY

Why is this area overlooked? Everyone praised *Glory* (Kevin Jarre 1989), the story of a black regiment in the Civil War. Of course the clichéd wisdom is that Hollywood won't touch historical productions because they are too expensive—but that's not really true. It's truer to say that unlike, say, France, there are just fewer good historical scripts written. *Dances with Wolves* is based on the history *of the times.* I emphasize this to separate a historical film from docudramas of famous people. It's certainly one kind of film to make something like John Ford's *Young Mr. Lincoln* (Lamar Trotti 1939) in which you are counting on the audience to recognize the character, and something quite different to simply set your film in a historical time period/event as happened in *The African Queen* (James Agee from the C. S. Forester novel, 1951) in which the authors have a much larger degree of freedom in creating characters who are true to the times but with whom we are not familiar as historical figures.

5. MOVIE GENRES/OTHER FILMS/REMAKES

If you set out with a particular genre in mind, the story will begin to shape itself. Say, you love gangster films, for instance, then, you need a gangster story. Or perhaps psychological horror is your beat. Then you are already half way to coming up with a story! *Thelma & Louise* is consciously a male buddy film like *Butch Cassidy and the Sundance Kid* done with women and with today's sensibilities. Part of the effect of the film, therefore, is that Callie Khouri counts on the audience knowing that there is a "film history" behind her story. *Boyz N the Hood* plays with the long tradition of teen gang films but goes beyond it in its realism and character development. *The Silence of the Lambs* is clearly modeled as a crime/investigation film with touches of the horror film as well, and *Time of the Gypsies* is a conscious Yugoslav "make-over" of Coppola and Puzo's *The Godfather* even down to the way in which Kusturica structures his film. Coppola and Puzo center *The Godfather* around

Catholic rituals beginning with a wedding, moving on to funerals, and closing with the famous baptism crosscut with the butchering of the opposition. Kusturica likewise uses a wedding at the beginning, in the middle, and at the end, followed by a funeral.

Genre films account for the greatest percentage of films in release, and more and more frequently the genres are mixed: comic adventure; romantic drama; comic crime adventure; horror melodrama; and so forth. But you should be sure you know your genres well. Do you understand, for instance, in writing a contemporary screwball romance that the tradition is for the lovers to be from differing socioeconomic backgrounds? In Frank Capra's *It Happened One Night* (Robert Riskin 1934), Clark Gable is a working journalist (middle class) and Claudette Colbert is the dizzy spoiled rich kid. Thus part of the thrust of screwball comedy is the triumph of democratic pluralism in a union of opposites within the American dream: the needy can get what they want and the spoiled can be enriched through a "marriage" with the working/middle classes. You may wish to "violate" these traditions, but you do so at your own risk. Many people seemed to enjoy Nora Ephron's *When Harry Met Sally* (1989), but for many others what felt like a screwball American romance was thrown off base by the fact that he (Billy Crystal) and she (Meg Ryan) were both privileged yuppies.

Remakes have also been a standard staple in Hollywood. There are, of course, plus and minus points to taking a previously made film and reworking it. Those films that are very close to the original such as the Steve Martin version of *Father of the Bride* (Frances Goodrich and Albert Hackett, Nancy Meyers and Charles Shyer 1991) run a greater risk of having moviegoers say, "What's the point?" Spencer Tracy and Liz Taylor are so good in the original (Frances Goodrich and Albert Hackett 1950), that no matter what Steve Martin does, it looks stilted and pale by comparison.

More successful, especially for the character-centered screenplay, are those projects that make major changes in the original or which work on a foreign film adapted for an American situation. *The Front Page* (1931) began as a Ben Hecht McArthur hit play, became the Lewis Milestone film from their script with Pat O'Brien and Adolphe Menjou, and was remade in 1974 with Jack Lemmon and Walter Matthau (directed by Billy Wilder). But Howard Hawks had Hecht and Charles Lederer transform the whole project by making this newspaperman tale a newspaper WOMAN narrative in *His Girl Friday* (1940). The gender switch, plus the wonderful fireworks between Cary Grant and Rosalind Russell, made for a totally satisfying "new" film.

And filmmakers are always borrowing from other countries (it is a two-way street we might add). Thus *The Magnificent Seven* (William

Roberts 1960) is a remake of Akira Kurosawa's *The Seven Samurai* (1954) which, ironically, was influenced by John Ford westerns! More recently Hollywood has flirted with many French imports including *Down and Out in Beverly Hills*, Paul Mazursky and Leon Capitanos's 1986 retake on Jean Renoir's *Boudou Saved from Drowning* (1932), and Jim McBride and Kit Carson's *Breathless* (1983) even kept the original title of Jean-Luc Godard's French new wave classic picture. As in imaginative adaptation, imaginative remakes do offer plenty of room for creativity. *Note that with remakes you need to know the legal status of using a previously made film.*

6. CHILDREN'S BOOKS

Want to get a good feel for writing screenplays?

We mentioned children's books briefly earlier. Now take a closer look. Check out an armful of children's books from the local library. I'm serious. Comic books do much the same thing—after all, they're written in "frames" with speech bubbles. But children's books have become incredibly inventive and VISUALLY IMAGINATIVE JOURNEYS for kids.

Peter Collington's *The Angel and the Soldier Boy* (New York: Alfred A. Knopf, 1987), for instance, plays with that favorite of all children's narratives: the dream story. In 116 frames with not a single word of dialogue or narration, Collington takes us through close-ups and middle distance shots and long shots of a little girl falling asleep as her mother reads a pirate and treasure story. She clutches two little toy characters: one a soldier and the other a little angel girl, complete with halo. Then the dream narrative takes over and the pirate on the cover of the book her mother was reading comes to life and begins a complicated job of stealing the money from her piggy bank, only to be caught by the toy soldier. But when the pirate's mates capture the soldier, it is up to the angel-girl to come to her friend's rescue, which, imaginatively, she does. By dream's end the two toys are safe with the young waking girl who checks her piggy bank and then drifts off to sleep again clutching the toys and her bank! Simple, compelling, silent! And TOTALLY VISUAL!

NARRATIVE STRUCTURES

So you have selected a tale and your main characters. Fine. Now how to weave your story?

First consider POINT OF VIEW. WHO will tell the story? A film does not just appear before us. There is a NARRATIVE VOICE *which can be defined as the perspective from which we are forced to observe the narrative.* In the classical Hollywood narrative, the narrative voice is traditionally an omniscient distant unidentified narrator: that is, the observing camera that does not call attention to itself.

But narrative voice may matter a lot in many character-centered scripts. *My Life as a Dog* (Lasse Hallstrom 1985) is told in voiceover by the boy himself: we have an immediate bond with the young fellow. In sharp contrast at the other end of the spectrum, we have *Casablanca*, which creates an omniscient point of view beginning with a "documentary newsreel voice of god" showing us maps of the world and images of war as if this film were a documentary.

In terms of narrative structures, consider the following:

1. The Circular Tale

Films that end where they began except for a big difference: we have been through the story itself, thus this similar spot *is not the same*. *Jonas Who Will Be 25 in the Year 2000* opens and closes with one of the main characters buying a pack of cigarettes and both times he complains about the rise in price, yet the rise at the end is because we have been through time together! Circularity gives us a sense of both closure (things are the same) but also of contrast (they are not exactly the same).

2. The Tale Within a Tale: Frame Narratives

One of the oldest forms of storytelling is to create a "FRAME" narrative within which the main tale exists. *Cinema Paradiso* does this as the frame is the present and the tale is the youth of the main protagonist. This also ties into the first type as it tends to be circular. The advantage is to create both distance/perspective and, as in *Cinema Paradiso*, even greater emotion as we feel the added thrust of nostalgia as well.

3. Multiple Point of View Narrative

It's ironic that one of the greatest American films, *Citizen Kane*, breaks all the narrative rules. Instead of one linear plot, we have five major narrative points of view, each about Kane's life, each told in flashback, and all held together by the Reporter whose face we never see. This approach has been used in literature by James Joyce and William Faulkner among others, but it has seldom been handled in American film, though it is the basis of such foreign classics as Andrei Wajda's *Man of Marble* (Poland 1972).

4. Collage Narrative

Dusan Makavejev is, as we have noted, the undisputed master of a cinema of collage narrative. This approach is quite different from multiple point of view: *Citizen Kane* is held together by the fact that all the narratives are about Kane and by people who knew him well; in Makavejev's films, the narratives are a mixture of documentary and fictive elements that appear at first or second or third glance to have no relation to each other. In *W. R.: Mysteries of the Organism* (Yugoslavia, 1972) there are at least five narrative levels that include: captured Nazi films of experiments on prisoners; a story about a beautiful Yugoslav woman who seduces a Russian ice skater in Belgrade and is beheaded with his skate afterward; an old 1950s fictional Soviet film about Stalin; documentary footage about Wilhelm Reich and his theory of orgasm as well as his persecution, imprisonment, and death in prison in the United States; and documentary footage of various noted personalities of the 1960s American "flower child" movement including the editor of *Screw* magazine who has his penis cast in a statue by a famous woman sculptress. The editing between these various narrative elements creates one Collage Narrative in the viewer's mind that can only make sense on an individual level.

This is as far away from Hollywood as anyone can get!

On a less radical note, the French New Wave director Jean-Luc Godard (in fact, many of the directors) experimented with breaking up narrative by various self-conscious techniques including addressing the camera, intrusive title cards from the author, unmotivated camera moves, and so on. And we could point to Monty Python as practicing collage narrative as well—a series of skits loosely joined together.

KERNELS AND SATELLITES

We now turn to the actual construction of any narrative. Traditionally we speak of screenplays as being divided into acts, sequences, and scenes. And these divisions will always have currency for screenwriters. But let us go further and make use of what Steven Cohan and Linda M. Shires speak of as kernel and satellite events in narrative. KERNEL moments "initiate, increase, or conclude an uncertainty" (1988, 54), so they are the major events that advance a narrative. SATELLITE events, "on the other hand, amplify or fill in the outline of a sequence by maintaining, retarding, or prolonging the kernel events they accompany or surround" (54).

Screenwriting books often admonish writers to cut out absolutely everything that is not essential to moving the story forward. But the truth of narrative—even the most plot-driven of plot-driven narratives is always more complex than such a simplistic view of "essential" versus "nonessential" construction would like to think that screenwriting can be. George Lucas's *Star Wars* (1977) gave new meaning to the content of plot-driven narrative. And yet even there it is possible to point to kernel and satellite scenes. Yes, some "business" is covered in the wacky extended bar scene filled with all manner of imaginative creatures. But overall, the scene is there just for the sheer inventive fun of it all! Definitely it is primarily a satellite scene. And the same goes for the well-remembered bicycle scene in *Butch Cassidy and the Sundance Kid* (1969). Of course we can, as we have, talk about the significance of the scene to the film, but overall it is a wonderfully entertaining bridge between their American western experience and their forthcoming travels. It is thus a satellite rather than a kernel moment.

In part 3 we will consider scene and sequence construction in detail. But I feel it is useful here to recognize the division of kernel and satellite scenes and to remark that *in the character-centered screenplay there are likely to be more satellite scenes than would be found in a plot-driven narrative.*

DIGRESSION AS NARRATIVE STRUCTURE

> Digression seems to be my natural way of telling a story.
>
> Luis Buñuel, *My Last Sigh*

Digression is a major error for the classical Hollywood script. Certainly you will find no screenwriting texts that champion the art of digression in screenwriting.

And yet some of the best films made, especially those of Luis Buñuel, proceed by digression rather than by narrative coherence and unity. Of course as a lifetime Surrealist, Buñuel had a passionate mission to destroy logic, narrative, and any other representation of what he saw as bourgeois culture through his often hilarious antipsychological films.

Digression may or may not be important to your script, depending on the characters you have chosen and the general story you have to tell. A single digressing moment in an otherwise "straight" tale is annoying. But if the digressions become a pattern or structure themselves, a statement is being made. Buñuel and Jean-Claude Carriere's *Phantom of Liberty* (1974) leads you to join in the carnival of guessing how small and insignificant a connection Buñuel will weave between the otherwise unconnected scenes as a shot of Napoleon's armies invading Spain gives way to a contemporary playground which gives way in turn to a mass murdering sniper being pardoned in a court and congratulated by the judge and so on. Beth Henley and rock composer David Byrne's nutty *True Stories* (1986) similarly blows apart any appearance of narrative coherence in a film that is more like a randomly shuffled stack of witty postcards than a traditional narrative. We should also add that Robert Altman's best films such as *Nashville* (1975), written by Joan Tewksbury, *A Wedding* (1978), written by Altman, John Considine, Alan Nicholls, and Patricia Resnick, and even *The Player* (1992), written by Michael Tolkin, celebrate digressions to a truly carnivalesque degree. In Altman's hands, however, the effect is one of capturing a sense of the randomness of real life.

And in terms of working on your first draft, you should feel OBLI-GATED to follow any digression that captures your attention. After all, it may turn out to be the main highway to what you really want to say!

CLOSING SHOTS:
THE EMBRACE VERSUS THE LONE INDIVIDUAL

Begin with either your characters or your narrative idea. Either way wherever you end up, that closing will become one of two images: that of several characters embracing each other or of our main character alone to one degree or another. But as you begin, don't worry too much about the "exact" ending of your story. The traditional Hollywood wisdom, of course, is exactly the opposite. Know your ending before you begin. Yet such a rigidly structural approach often works against the richer pleasures that a carnivalesque openness, freedom, and true playfulness can bring.

But do consider the difference between these endings. Either your character is "embraced" and thus left with a sharing of his or her life with others who support, approve, share their lives, too. Or your character must face the world alone like Chaplin walking, his back to the camera, away from us down the highway.

Embrace endings include *Thelma & Louise*, *Boyz N the Hood*, and *sex, lies and videotape*, whereas *Time of the Gypsies* and *The Silence of the Lambs* offer parting shots of loners. "Northern Exposure" as a concept and as a series of episodes celebrates in its clearly carnivalesque form the embrace of a whole community.

Let's take these endings up close: Thelma and Louise "embrace" each other and go to their deaths, joyfully together. Father and son are joined together at the end of *Boyz N the Hood*, thus forming a union that shelters and protects our young determining character from the storms of the "hood." *Time of the Gypsies*, however, gives us a variation on a "loner" ending: Perhan is dead (thus alone!), but his death is celebrated by Grandma and the community (an embrace!), BUT the son (IF he is Perhan's son) steals the coins off his father's eyes and runs off alone hiding in his coveted cardboard box (alone). Plus, the Uncle also leaves the wake and walks, his back to the camera, through the mud and rain into the landscape in an obvious cinematic allusion to the Great Loner, Chaplin (perhaps we should say that alluding to Chaplin in such a shot of an outsider alone is itself a kind of cinematic "embrace" thus adding another layer of texture to the ending). And it is very important that *The Silence of the Lambs* does not end with the "embracing" scene of Clarice's FBI graduation party, but with Lecter alone on the loose.

CHAPTER SIX

PITCHING

BEFORE YOU WRITE

Before you write your script, develop your characters and your narrative into a five-minute oral presentation that draws on all of your talents as a writer and an oral storyteller.

As we shall explore, this progression from the oral to the written makes a lot more sense than writing the script and then trying to construct a short oral presentation based on the feature story. Beginning with the oral storytelling tradition also enables you to perfect many of the techniques mastered in ancient oral traditions that serve any story weaver well. On a very practical level, as Syd Field has written speaking of Hollywood, "You have to win someone over with the energy and theatrics of it" (1989, 138). And on the most cynical of levels, remember that Michael Tolkin's *The Player* (1992) is almost entirely dedicated to pitching as opposed to writing!

•••

We are not suggesting quite as cynical a view as that of Robert Altman and Michael Tolkin in *The Player*. But whatever the degree of truth, the accepted general rule of thumb is that many American producers don't read. That's why they hire Readers. This is an old tradition that goes way back to the early days of Hollywood. Louis B. Mayer, an East European immigrant and founder of MGM, for instance, depended more than most realize on writer Kate Corbaley to report on her readings. And who are the Readers? No special qualifications needed. But it seems Readers, for the most part, aren't Writers. Thus your script more likely than not is read by someone who hasn't written a script and who must write a two- or three-page report on your script—which in most cases will save the producer from having to read your script. One important reader I've met at Columbia Pictures reads ten scripts a week (that's two per working day) and recommends about *two or three a year.*

When you meet a producer, agent, studio executive, therefore, you are trying to *pitch* her or him your script. That means all the work you've done in your head and on paper comes down to five to ten minutes with someone who will *green light* (approve) or *pass* (thumbs down) your project based on what you *say.* And HOW you say it.

THE FIVE-MINUTE PITCH

Needless to say, The Art of the Pitch is fast becoming as important as the craft of writing the screenplay, though as Syd Field wryly remarks, "It is very hard to tell from a pitch if somebody can actually write" (1989, 138). Pitching really is a dramatic performance and you should plan accordingly. Clearly everything you know about screenwriting applies to the Pitch plus the oral skills of the right voice color/tone, pacing, hand gestures, eye contact, and such. Learn from Homer (he had one more advantage: the epics were "sung" to music), the *guslars*—the epic storytellers throughout the former Yugoslavia, your local Tall Tale Tellers, your local bards, and, as we shall explore, your storytelling abilities that any parent must develop in order to survive bedtime rituals. And you will need to practice in front of the mirror, with a tape recorder, with friends, even, yes, in front of a video camera perhaps.

In this spirit, work (and work out!) *a five-minute pitch* that includes a brief *teaser* of an opening—"If you liked *Terminator 2* and *Dances with Wolves,* you'll LOVE this tale of revenge and redemption set against the darkest days of the Revolutionary War when it seemed America would never become free"—a lively plot summary with on-the-nose character descriptions ("like Dustin Hoffman and Woody Allen combined") and a few lines of choice dialogue thrown in along the way ("Everything is perfect except for a few details"—Preston Sturges). And a wrap up. Somewhere within the pitch the GENRE (a romantic thriller with comic moments) and AUDIENCE (like HOME ALONE this film will cross all age groups but will particularly appeal to families) appeal need to be addressed as well.

Hollywood agent Ken Sherman feels the five-minute pitch is an art form one should definitely work on. During a daylong screenwriting workshop in New Orleans (1992), he devoted several hours to having the group listen to pitches and to his critique of each pitch, both for content and delivery. One American Indian participant, for instance, included a wonderful tribal dance in his presentation, but he went on for fifteen minutes. Sherman made it clear that, despite the fine dancing, the writer needed to hold to the five minutes with a tighter focus. "If you have me hooked, I'll ask you to keep going beyond that initial five minutes, but time it so that you say all you NEED to say in that initial period," he remarked.

That's a lot to ask BEFORE writing a script.

But the act of preparing such a pitch, even in rough form, gets you doing what you should be doing a lot of anyway: talking it out with a buddy, friend, pet, and *yourself.* Just thinking, walking, meditating, and drinking endless cups of coffee are not enough. SCREENWRITING IS A SOCIAL ACTIVITY EVEN IF YOU ARE A LONER (there's always the telephone, fax machine, and E-mail!).

Furthermore, if you write out the pitch, you actually have your TREATMENT (see APPENDIX A). And that's a great gift to yourself and your project.

Don't forget a title. Of course many character-centered scripts announce themselves by title: *Harry and Tonto* (1974); *Thelma & Louise; Harold and Maude* (1971); *The Cowboy and the Lady* (1938 with Gary Cooper!); *Babe* (1992); *Bugsy* (1991); and *Victor/Victoria* (1982). Fine. But you may wish to go for a more descriptive, evocative title, and that takes some thinking. Some people come up with titles easily—look at Ernest Hemingway, for instance, with *The Sun Also Rises, For Whom the Bell Tolls,* and *The Old Man and the Sea*—whereas others labor over them. But even a "working title" gives you something to focus on as you write; thus do pay attention to how you title your project. We might add that there's much to be gained from a title with at least a double meaning. In many ways the best American titles are not in the movies, but in that most American of genres: the blues. Louis Armstrong loved to play "Tight Like This" and New Orleans blues queen Charmaine Neville's theme song is "You've Got the Right Key, Baby, but the Wrong Key Hole."

Note: Your pitch may change radically as you begin writing. That's fine. But this exercise is meant only to help you go beyond the act of having characters you are attracted to and project them into a complete tale.

PITCHING II: STORIES FOR CHILDREN

Pitching is a modern branch of the art of oral storytelling. But throughout time, one of the most important forms of storytelling has been creating tales for children. In an imaginative book, *annie stories: a special kind of storytelling,* Doris Brett, a clinical psychologist in Melbourne,

Australia, suggests techniques any parent or would-be teller of tales for children should consider.

Brett understands that, as Bruno Bettleheim has made clear in his study of the uses of "enchantment" for children, stories help the young cope with their fears and help them grow in self-confidence. The "Annie" of the title is Brett's daughter to whom she told stories, all constructed with Annie as the determining character. This technique of inserting your children or children you know into the center of the narrative you unfold either using their real names or ones very close to theirs is at the heart of Dr. Brett's technique.

Brett sees several important outcomes of such a storytelling process. First you learn more about the world of children, for you are forced to "put yourself in their place" (1988, 10). But there is also the bonding comfort that a parent-child storytime offers. Brett notes:

> Quite apart from the content of the story, it means that the child is getting a comforting dose of quiet, loving intimacy with one or the other parent. Thus, at the same time that the story is helping the child deal with her various troubling situations, it is also strengthening the bond between parent and child, which is in itself a tremendous source of security and comfort. (12)

There is yet another lesson the child is learning: the creative use of the imagination and fantasy combined with elements of reality. Yes, it is good to read to children from books. But a regular personalized storytime may do even more for children to not only gain comfort and self-esteem, but also to begin to appreciate the aesthetic pleasures of storytelling itself.

Brett then outlines a variety of sample scenarios for difficult situations that can be woven into stories that help children deal with the first day at school, divorce, a death in the family, a new baby (talk about real trauma!), and good old simple PAIN (an accident, a burn, a broken limb, etc.).

Because too much of our lives these days is centered around *taking in* from television to fax machines, the oral art of creating stories for your children or those of friends is clearly a rewarding experience that can't help but have positive benefits for you as a screenwriter as well. Let me be even more specific. In a recent script course, students found the visit to class by Adella Adella the Story Teller, a well-loved local New Orleans professional storyteller, extremely useful to their writing. Adella performed stories and then discussed her craft with the students. What they learned more vividly than from a book or a film was the importance of presentation, of eye contact, of dramatic movement and sound effects and singing, as well as a certain joyful and, yes, carnivalesque sense of improvisation in re-weaving a basic text.

Their pitches and resulting scripts were all the richer from their contact with a professional teller of oral tales.

NARRATIVE AND STRUCTURE REVIEW

- Think what the Yekuana Indian basket weavers of Venezuela have to teach you as a narrative writer for film: that narratives have the power to do much for people including "conquering death"; narrative itself is much like weaving—the bringing together of different strands in varying combinations.
- The classical Hollywood narrative is a very specific plot-driven, cause-and-effect-organized narrative centering on a central protagonist with a successful ("happy") resolution, a pattern that has not changed since 1917 for most Hollywood films.
- The character-centered script may or often may not adhere to the tight three-act structure often set forth as a model for the classical Hollywood screenplay.
- Begin your script project with either a strong sense of character or with a strong story that appeals to you for whatever reason. Either way is fine.
- Then it is time to begin to shape a narrative. Remember that a story is only a recounting of events in time. A narrative includes the point of view, style, manner, elaboration of the story as *narrated*, presented.
- Determine if your script is to be a narrative of plot, character, or spectacle.
- Beyond the traditional three-act structure, think of any narrative as a continuous play between placement, displacement, and replacement of narrative elements.
- You can also think of narrative as, in Gerard Genette's terms, a process of order, duration, and frequency.
- Duration refers to five ways of building a scene:

  1. Compression
  2. Ellipsis
  3. Screen time equal to narrative time
  4. Stretched/extended time
  5. Frozen or "zero" time

- Search out your narrative from your own life, from an adaptation of a work of literature, from the news, from history, or from particular movie genres or even remakes, and/or from children's literature.

- Once you have a general narrative in mind, think how you wish to structure it. Methods include those of using the circular tale, the tale within a tale frame, multiple points of view, and a narrative of collage.
- Keep in mind that all narratives are made up of kernel events (essential) and satellite moments (nonessential, but important for texture, amplification, development).
- Digression instead of being a narrative weakness may in fact be exactly the carnivalesque structuring mode best suited to your needs!
- Consider endings, but do not feel compelled to know your ending before you begin. Do realize, however, that there are two basic closing shots: that of an embrace of some kind or that of a protagonist alone.
- Work up a five-minute PITCH *before* you write your script. Learn techniques from Homer and other oral bards, singers, storytellers!
- Try your hand at creating stories for children, using them as the main protagonists and centering the narratives on fears/problems they need to address.

WORKS CITED IN PART II

Aristotle. *On the Art of Poetry*. Trans. Lane Cooper. Ithaca: Cornell University Press, 1947. [Originally published 1913]

Bakhtin, Mikhail. *Problems of Dostoevsky's Poetics*. Ed. and trans. Caryl Emerson. Minneapolis: University of Minnesota Press, 1984.

Bordwell, David, Janet Staiger, and Kristin Thompson. *The Classical Hollywood Cinema: Film Style and Mode of Production to 1960*. New York: Columbia University Press, 1985.

Brett, Doris. *Annie Stories: A Special Kind of Storytelling*. New York: Workman Publishing, 1988.

Calvino, Italo. *The Uses of Literature*. Trans. Patrick Creagh. New York: Harvest/HBJ Books, 1986.

Chatman, Seymour. *Story and Discourse: Narrative Structure in Fiction and Film*. Ithaca: Cornell University Press, 1978.

Cohan, Steven, and Linda M. Shires. *Telling Stories: A Theoretical Analysis of Narrative Fiction*. New York: Routledge, 1988.

Collington, Peter. *The Angel and the Soldier Boy*. New York: Alfred A. Knopf, 1987.

Field, Syd. *Screenplay: The Foundations of Screenwriting*. New York: Dell Publishing, 1982.

———. *Selling a Screenplay: The Screenwriter's Guide to Hollywood*. New York: Dell Publishers, 1989.

Frye, Northrop. *Anatomy of Criticism*. New York: Atheneum, 1968.

Genette, Gerard. *Narrative Discourse: An Essay in Method*. Trans. Jane E. Lewin. Ithaca: Cornell University Press, 1980.

Gerzon, Mark. *A Choice of Heroes: The Changing Face of American Manhood*. Boston: Houghton Mifflin, 1982.

Guss, David M. *To Weave and Sing: Art, Symbol, and Narrative in the South American Rain Forest*. Berkeley, Los Angeles, London: University of California Press, 1990.

Homer. *The Odyssey of Homer*. Trans. Richmond Lattimore. New York: Harper & Row, 1967.

Horton, Andrew. *The Films of George Roy Hill*. New York: Columbia University Press, 1985.

Irving, John. Personal interview, New York, 1982.

Keirsey, David, and Marilyn Bates. *Please Understand Me*. Del Mar, Calif.: Prometheus Nemesis, 1984.

Kermode, Frank. *The Genesis of Secrecy*. Cambridge, Mass.: Harvard University Press, 1979.

Lucey, Paul. "Story Sense." Unpublished manuscript.

Martin, Wallace. *Recent Theories of Narrative*. Ithaca: Cornell University Press, 1986.

Muhawi, Ibrahim, and Sharif Kanaana. *Speak, Bird, Speak Again: Palestinian Arab Folktales*. Berkeley, Los Angeles, London: University of California Press, 1989.

Patterson, Francis. *Cinema Craftsmanship*. New York: Harcourt, Brace & Howe, 1920.

Pelton, Robert D. *The Trickster in West Africa*. Berkeley, Los Angeles, London: University of California Press, 1980.

Rosen, Philip, ed. *Narrative, Apparatus, Ideology*. New York: Columbia University Press, 1986.

Sherman, Ken. Screenwriting workshop, New Orleans, April 1992.

Stone, Merlin. *When God Was a Woman*. New York: Dorset Press, 1976.

Sturges, Preston. *Preston Sturges by Preston Sturges*. Adapted and ed. Sandy Sturges. New York: Simon & Schuster, 1990.

Tally, Ted. *The Silence of the Lambs*. Screenplay from the novel by Thomas Harris. First draft: June 6, 1989 (unpublished).

Vonnegut, Kurt. Personal interview, October 1981.

PART III

WRITING

With a good script a good director can produce a masterpiece; with the same script a mediocre director can make a passable film. But with a bad script even a good director can't possibly make a good film. For truly cinematic expression, the camera and the microphone must be able to cross both fire and water. That is what makes a real movie. The script must be something that has the power to do this.

Akira Kurosawa,
Something Like an Autobiography

CHAPTER SEVEN

Prelude to a Screenplay

> So much has been written about the miseries of screenwriting, or, more precisely, about the miseries of the screenwriter's lot, that I, for one, am sick of reading it. I think it is time to redress the balance, to treat Hollywood fairly, and to suggest that screenwriting, far from being hard work, might actually be considered to be a form of creative play.
>
> Larry McMurtry,
> *Film Flam: Essays on Hollywood*

You may already have written scripts. If so, this section becomes a shopping around for ideas that might supplement what you already know and practice.

But in design, this section is aimed at helping new screenwriters find, develop, and flesh out characters in short and, finally, feature screen stories. The two schedules reflect a refinement of years of writing, teaching, and discovering through error often more than trial what "works" best for students of all ages and backgrounds.

THE FOURTEEN-WEEK CHARACTER DEVELOPING SCHEDULE focuses on exercises and short scripts that suggest a carnival of potential approaches to character development, culminating in the writing of an hour-long episode for a network television show that already has its characters set: "Northern Exposure" which has been our sample television example.

THE FOURTEEN-WEEK FEATURE SCRIPT SCHEDULE is exactly that: having explored character development, this schedule gets you through a complete script. Fourteen weeks, of course, represents the average university/college semester. But fourteen weeks is more than an official time period. As three and a half months, it reflects a *comfortable* pace for getting a job done and done well. Some can work much faster. Fine. Yet even fourteen weeks is a push for most people caught up as we all are in a web of other responsibilities. *The hardest part of writing a script is making the commitment to writing the script!* Make the commitment, follow a schedule, and write!

SCRIPT PARTNERS

Find a SCRIPT PARTNER before you write your script and stick with him or her through the whole process. Really. A dozen years of writing and teaching screenwriting convinces me of this need.

WHY? You may write every screenplay alone, but chances are you will work with a partner at some point or another, and you may find that you work best with someone else as a team. But even if you are a loner, screenwriting is, in many ways, a social activity. Writing poetry is as private as writing can be: you write, you submit, you publish. Yes, it becomes social if you also do readings in public. But in terms of writing/publishing, the path is pretty direct between personal expression and finished form. Not true in screenwriting. Let's say you work "alone" on a project. That still leaves you in touch with agents/producers/directors/actors, and more. There are the story meetings, the rewrite conferences, the pitching sessions. In short, being "home alone" is only part of the screenwriting scenario.

Back to the need for a partner. You may or may not work directly with another writer. But you will always need someone or several friends to fulfill the role of the partner: that is, someone you can talk to regularly about your work, bounce questions/ideas off, someone who will give you honest feedback and grief and support when you need it most. The cliché that "Hollywood is the place where you can die of encouragement" is true. Nobody says "no" in Los Angeles or Culver City or Studio City. They just say, "Brilliant, but I really think it is better for television and we don't do TV," or "Hey! You're as good as Bertolucci, so why don't you take it to him since we just do commercial stuff."

So team up with another writer or an honest friend. Talk on the phone, meet for coffee or mineral water or Canadian beer. But talk, discuss, read, and talk some more. Two is more often than not better than one in screenwriting. I once, for instance, had three guys in a script class who got along fine, so they not only fulfilled the assignment of making use of each other as helpful partners working on their own scripts, but they met once a week for an all-nighter and co-wrote a solid action-romance thriller together! That's the best of both worlds, of course: using your partner for feedback on your own project and also teaming up for a "fun" project that can benefit from the yin and yang of both of you saying "what if . . ." and "yes, but we could also have him . . ."

Primary to the relationship is honesty, patience, concern, humor, and an enjoyment of it all. If there's no pleasure in this relationship, it won't work. Of course sometimes partnerships break down. But my experience has been that for the most part they have led to lasting friendships. I've been pleased with how many former student-partnership combinations continue for years after an initial coming together.

TWELVE COMMANDMENTS OF CHARACTER-CENTERED SCREENWRITING

Of course the list could include more than twelve or a quite different line-up if written by others, but here are my twelve commandments to keep in mind in writing your character-centered script and, even more important, in conceiving of your rewrite. Rather than write these as "don'ts" and thus take the usual negative approach we are surrounded by (NO SMOKING! DO NOT ENTER! NO EXIT!), they are written as "do's" and thus as positive steps to consider. Many of the proposed exercises that follow refer to these commandments.

1. KNOW YOUR CHARACTERS BUT NOT COMPLETELY

You do need to know lots about your characters, especially your main ones, before you begin as discussed in part 1. But, as in real life, you can't know everything. Remember if your characters are not surprising you as you go along with twists, gestures, actions, words you did not completely expect (again, as with our real friends and foes), then something is wrong. Once more, this is the "carnivalesque" at work: the spirit of BECOMING as opposed to BEING.

2. PRACTICE THE FREE PLAY THAT THE CARNIVALESQUE SUGGESTS

Character clichés, trite plots, and tired dialogue all come from a failure to keep a polyphony of voices in the air at one time. The complete freedom and fantasy that carnival offers insures that you stay fresh, listen to other "voices," and question yourself constructively. With a carnivalesque attitude, you will see stereotypes and clichés start to fade away. Carnival insures you have a built-in stereotype/cliché monitor at work ready to go off whenever you fall into one or the other. So much extra texture, character, mileage can be had by turning clichés inside out or upside down. This is, for instance, your chance to bring in minorities in certain roles or to expose sexism in speech or whatever. FILM IS A VALUE-CONSTRUCTED MEDIUM and thus anything you can do to destroy clichés/stereotypes counts. Robert De Niro is a "Southern hick" in *Cape Fear* but a very bright hick who has seemingly read all of Western philosophy and literature. That fact destroys any Southern stereotype.

3. THINK CINEMATICALLY

You are not just telling a story; you are SHOWING a story and doing so on film. It is not your job to write lots of camera angles and such, but you are CONCEIVING cinematic moments that will affect us on the screen. The loss of innocence dream sequence in *Time of the Gypsies* makes maximum use of cinema: music, sound, spectacle, action, characterization, camera movement. It's a movie scene! We understand all we need to know through the image and the sound track without a word being said. *Too many new writers focus on dialogue at the expense of "cinema," perhaps because television is such a language-centered medium.* Set yourself the task, for instance, of coming up with a DOMINANT IMAGE that represents your entire film and also one that represents each character. The dominant image is that visual picture that stays with us and conveys a sense of all we need to know about a person, a place, a plot. In a real sense the dominant image of *Boyz N the Hood* is the big red STOP sign that hits us as the first image of the film. Because Singleton is "preaching" to us in his film, his message is clear: stop the killing and, as he expresses in words later, "INCREASE THE PEACE." The dominant image of "Northern Exposure" is very clear: the moose walking down the main street of Cicely, Alaska. That awkward, long-legged, bushy-antlered creature says it all: funny, eccentric, rural, and . . . natural!

The same approach goes for finding a character's dominant VISUAL IMAGE. The image we all remember from *Thelma & Louise*, for instance, is that of both women, hair blowing in the wind, driving down the highway in an open convertible. That image expresses the movement and freedom both women crave.

4. MAKE SURE EACH SCENE HAS AT LEAST TWO REASONS/LEVELS OF EXISTENCE

One level per scene is simply the conveying of information and could best be done by FAX. What interests us is the INTERPLAY OF MULTIPLE LEVELS OF ATTENTION. Usually these multiple levels relate both to deep structure and major plot or subplot, but they may be any combination of levels, depending on the scene or bit. As in character, so in scene and sequence construction: suggest a multitude of voices. At least "two levels" means you need to consider building tension between what is seen and what is said, between foreground and background, between what is said and what is meant, between what WE know and what the

CHARACTERS know. *sex, lies and videotape* begins with the tension between Graham driving down the road and Ann's voice-over discussion of "garbage" with her analyst. That tension is really a puzzle as we wonder, "What is going on here?" It is an excellent intro to these two lives that will come together literally in the same frame by the end of the film.

5. Keep Pace and Rhythm Always in Mind

Like dancing or running or lovemaking among many activities, rhythm, pacing, and the variation of movement count. What we usually think of as mood and tone also come into play here, for part of pacing is knowing when to go from light to heavy and from funny to gut wrenching as well as for how long. *The Silence of the Lambs* is a very talky film, yet the talk WORKS not only because it is fascinating talk (wonderfully delivered by Anthony Hopkins and Jody Foster) but also because of the rhythm of each scene between these two, which is ironically less frantic and more peaceful than the hectic pace of events and relationships outside Lecter's prison.

6. Start a Scene in the Middle and Close It Once Your Point Has Been Made

Narrative in general and film in particular is to a large degree the art of "leaving out." That goes for everything, but especially for writing scenes. Don't tell/show EVERYTHING. Remember those friends who tell you EVERYTHING they do/did. They bore us, even if we must listen to them.

7. Think of the Many Virtues of Humor and Comedy Even in the Most Serious Moments

There are some very funny scenes in Sophocles' *Oedipus*. Comedy is not just slapstick and one-line jokes. It is a deep understanding of the human condition revealed through laughter. Laughter can often coexist well, in fact deeply, with tears, as we all know. That's a complex, satisfying double emotion to aim for. *The Fisher King* (Richard La Gravenese 1991), for instance, is chuck full of such dual pathways to our emotions.

8. Less Is More or Silence May Be Better Than Words and a Static Moment May Be Better Than Noisy Action

How would you tell your whole film as a two-minute silent movie? If you can answer this question, you can begin to see what can be left out. Too much of what we put in is clutter. Hitchcock said it and it is still true: "Film is life with the dull parts cut out." What is dull about many films? Too much is put in, explained, presented. In *The Traveling Players*

(1975), a Greek film written and directed by Theodore Angelopoulos voted by many critics the most important film in the world for the decade of the 1970s, we see a starving Greek population during World War II. How is hunger shown? We see the traveling theater group spot a lone chicken on a snowy mountainside. The group silently forms a wide circle around the chicken. They then quietly converge on the poor creature with a final noisy "attack" by the whole group of twelve or so members as the chicken disappears. No words, one simple shot, and we understand "hunger"!

9. CONSIDER THE VIRTUES OF THE BITTERSWEET ENDING

The cliché is that Hollywood likes happy endings. But most of the films we like best have mixed-emotion endings and fall somewhere in the middle between a "closed" (completed) ending and an "open" (life goes on, and we are not sure how it will work out) closing. In *Casablanca* Rick loses his true love and gains himself, and in *Cinema Paradiso* Toto gains a perspective on his youth, but he realizes his youth has gone as well as his innocence about the joy and mystery of cinema. Both of these examples suggest something lost and something gained.

10. MAKE YOUR SCRIPT A GOOD, FAST READ

I've never read a bad script that was a good read. The two go hand in hand. *Rambling Rose*, which I read as a script before it came out as a film, leaps off the page as story BECAUSE OF THE ATTENTION TO PRESENTATION IN FORMAT AS WELL AS STRUCTURE/CONCEPT. Of course the translation of "good read" really means: setting up the page so that it becomes a movie in the reader's mind.

11. KILL YOUR FAVORITE BABIES

William Faulkner gave this advice, meaning, if something (a scene/a moment/a character) REALLY strikes you as great in your script, it may be "too good" and thus it may be (1) standing out/apart from the rest of the script too much, or (2) too personal to you to actually be as "great" as you think it is. Particularly on the rewrite, you will find some of the material you like best will have to go: it doesn't work, it slows things down, it's out of sync with the whole project. George Roy Hill shot a scene of Butch and Sundance going to the movies in Bolivia and seeing themselves acted out in a silent "cowboy movie." It was a wonderful self-reflective scene in which Sundance objected to the twisting of the facts of their lives and Butch argued in favor of the freedom of fiction to make a good story that the audience would enjoy. Ultimately, however, Hill left the scene on the cutting room floor: he felt that even though it was a splendid scene in and of itself, it nevertheless detracted from the overall effect of the film in that section.

12. Take Risks and Break Any "Rules" Rather Than Write a Weak, Tired, Cliché-ridden Script

Hitchcock kills his main character—Marion Crane—a third of the way through *Psycho*. That's not supposed to happen according to traditional Hollywood wisdom. But obviously Hitch enjoyed playing with his audience and constructing a devilishly clever cinematic mousetrap. We have discussed to what degree each of the scripts we have considered bends, stretches, and breaks the rules.

And there is an unwritten thirteenth rule that should be understood by everyone:

Above All, Enjoy Your Script

That is, once more, in the spirit of carnival, enjoy yourself as you write and think and observe and write again. Find your rhythm, your time and place to write, your way of getting into the mood, of establishing a disciplined schedule so that you can do the writing, and feel free to break your schedule if you need to. And because screenwriting is special, think of things—treats—to do for yourself which will help you continue to realize the magic and pleasure of screenwriting as you go along no matter how small or large that treat may be. A long distance phone call to a long missed friend? A weekend at the beach? A day catching up on four movies in a row? Splurging for tickets to that Neville Brothers concert? A rich gumbo for supper when you are supposed to be on a diet? Whatever it is, be good to yourself, and your characters will be good to you.

CHAPTER EIGHT

The Fourteen-Week Character Developing Schedule

Preparation

1. Locate the videotape of the 1991 Oscar winning short film, *Lunch Date* by Adam Davidson. Contact: The Robert Lantz Agency, 888 7th Ave., New York, NY 10006. Phone: (212) 586-0200. Cost for an individual for noncommercial home use is $25.

Lunch Date is a wry short film in black and white about an upper middle class (or rich?) upper middle-aged woman in a fur coat with a Bloomingdale shopping bag who misses her train in Grand Central Station and winds up having a salad in a station snack bar.

2. Read this text!

3. Useful for short scriptwriting is William H. Phillips, *Writing Short Scripts* (Syracuse University Press, 1991).

4. Find a partner.

5. Make sure you have access to a video camera.

6. Get in the habit of going to at least two movies in a theater each week to keep your finger on the pulse of what's going on in film.

7. As we said in the introduction, live fully and read widely.

8. Locate one of the screenplays to be used in the feature script process, say, *Thelma & Louise* or *The Silence of the Lambs* and read/study for FORMAT just as much as for characterization and structure.

9. Get hold of a "Northern Exposure" episode to study, either through Script City or by contacting: PIPELINE PRODUCTIONS, 3000 Olympic Blvd., Suite 2575, Santa Monica, CA 98404.

Week One: Thinking Visual Stories

Watch *Lunch Date* carefully, noting the absolute simplicity of this two-character short film and yet the cleverness with which it is put together. Note how much depends on gesture rather than dialogue, information withheld rather than presented. Think about the use of 1940s swing music for the soundtrack. What does this add to the character and story? Why black and white? And finally, follow carefully each shot/angle/set up to see how cleverly the story is presented *visually*.

Assignment: Write a two-page (typed/double-spaced: roughly 500 words) story with two characters that depends on *no dialogue*, only visuals and sound. Think about how you can use location, atmosphere, texture, gesture, SOUND, light, and perspective to SHOW character. *Remember: nothing on the page that cannot be seen or heard. Thus no "she thought" or "he remembered": sound, light, movement.*

Meet with your partner and critique each other's stories. Rewrite and polish to your and your partner's satisfaction. *Make sure you have a title for your story.*

Here is a sample written by a young writer, Chris Gibbons:

BEULAH'S

The moon was traveling directly toward the sun, and in a short while there would be a total eclipse.

Mary Jane looked from the sky down at her young hands. She saw their chipped surfaces and rough edges and laid them against her new sunflower yellow suit. Seeing the tags still on the jacket, she quickly ripped them off. The suit fit her slim five foot seven body quite well. She was not particularly striking: her complexion was lightly freckled to match her golden hair, and there were soft pink areas on her nose and cheeks. Her eyes were deep blue and hidden behind her squinting lids.

She walked down the retail store street, past a few proprietors who were standing outside the pawn shop, the shoe store, and the vacuum repair shop. They were already equipped with homemade eclipse glasses. They hung "closed" signs on their doors while Mary Jane walked briskly past.

She finally arrived at Beulah's Beauty and Massage Parlor and noticed Beulah's decorated body. The large Filipino woman wore a brown and gold batik dress with spiral designs. There was a dried chicken leg holding up her bristly black hair and rose quartz crystals swung from her neck as she moved like a hippo to close the blinds of the front window. Her lazy eyelids drooped over her large eyes as she pointed to a chair. Mary Jane slid into the pink and gold speckled chair and studied the scrolls hanging on the water-stained wall she was facing. They had medieval floral decorations and depictions of devilish animals and fiends. They looked old, but the orange and red thumbtacks that held them up seemed to discredit their spiritual nature.

As Beulah did Mary Jane's nails, Mary Jane looked at some other prints, probably made from wood carvings. There were a set of four, black on white. The first was a tribe sacrificing a beautiful bird and the second showed a cow about to be sacrificed. Mary Jane's face tensed with worry but her gaze continued to look at the remaining two prints. Once depicted an infant boy on the sacrificial altar, and the other showed a young woman also about to be sacrificed. Each event occurred under an eclipse of the sun. She looked down at her finished hands and was suddenly brought back to reality by the ugly, rich, golden glow of her nails. She left quickly and quietly, leaving a generous three-dollar tip.

Mary Jane breathed a sigh of relief as she stepped out onto the hard sidewalk, as the beauty parlor door closed behind her. A smart, assertive smile showed that she felt good about herself, and her expression was one of being carefree. She even started swinging her handbag and humming "How Sweet It Is to Be Loved by You."

Then she looked straight at the sun, was blinded, and collapsed not too far from where she first smiled.

WEEK TWO: THE DOCUMENTARY SELF

Rent and watch Michael Moore's documentary feature, *Roger & Me* and/or Barbara Kopple's *Harlan County, USA* (1977), which won the Oscar for Best Documentary. Note carefully how "rounded" each character is simply by being themselves in each film. Study gesture, speech, poise, context, and "narrative" sense within the documentary framework.

Assignment: Take your video camera or borrow/rent one and do the following.

1) Follow somebody you don't know or at least don't know well for at least a few hours. *This person should be someone with quite a different background/job/outlook than yourself.* Of course this means somehow introducing yourself/explaining that you have an "assignment" or whatever you need to say so that person allows you to come along with a camera. *Rather than just an interview of talking heads, try to get that person talking and doing whatever he or she does.* You don't need to keep the camera rolling all the time, but do spend enough time so you capture something of that person's daily life, rhythm, activity, way of talking. A neighbor down the street that you don't really know well? A fellow student you've met in a class? The local mortician? Baker? Policeman? Hairdresser? A crippled Vietnam vet? A Cuban immigrant? An ex-drug dealer? A used car salesman? You choose. Obviously much of

the "quality" of the material you gather will depend both on your choice of subject and of the relationship you establish (the kinds of questions you ask/how you present yourself, etc.) with this subject.

2. Do the same for someone you know very well or pretty well. What you are hoping in this case is to come up with material (talk/actions) that surprises you: things you didn't know! The success of this part of the assignment depends both on how well you manage to capture what you did know and what you didn't.

In both cases try to strike a balance between thinking ahead of things/questions that could be useful, but also allow for improvisation and the chemistry of the moment and build on that as well.

Study your tapes.

Write a 3–5 page (double-spaced) *character sketch* of each of these two subjects. Write these not as a police profile but as a character study that might be submitted somewhere for publication. Include visuals, expressions, snips of stories told, and so on to bring out that character as fully as you can. Be sure to give a sense of the person's public, professional, and personal self (see the character checklist in part 1).

Work as closely as possible with your partner, observing each other's tapes or even working together if you wish as a joint project. Critique each other's character sketches. Polish. (Note: this week's assignment may easily take several weeks depending on the time you have available. Don't, however, cut corners, for this documentary foundation is absolutely necessary as part of the character developing process.)

For your consideration: Two filmmaking brothers in Russia who are even farther away from mainstream cinema than the Coen Brothers or Jim Jarmusch in the United States are Igor and Gleb Alenikov. They combined avant-garde cinema, documentary, and screenwriting in a novel way in 1990. On their tour of America showing avant-garde Soviet films ("parallel cinema"), they brought along a 16mm camera with lots of black and white film. For the several months that they toured the country, they shot everything they wanted to from crawfish boil parties in Louisiana to snowfalls in Ann Arbor and fast burger joints in New York. Whatever they wanted. Then when they returned to Moscow, they developed their film, sat down and watched it, *and wrote a script based on what they saw!* Yes, they even shot extra "studio" shots to make some kind of narrative come together. I have yet to see the film, but imagine trying to sell an American producer on Shoot First, Write Second! Still, for a very personal approach, the Alenikovs may be on to something: a carnivalesque approach to documentary and screenwriting! Anything goes.

When I have used this exercise in class, the results have never been short of mesmerizing. One class, for instance, came up with a young white woman dying of AIDS, a black mother of three flipping burgers in a cafe, a balding middle-aged owner of a French Quarter t-shirt shop, an American Indian 1960s radical finishing his B.A. at age forty-five, a Tarot card reader, and many others. Each was very much him or herself, alive with gestures, phrases, touches that added up to clearly distinct characters.

WEEK THREE: ADAPTING CHILDREN'S BOOKS

I have used this exercise for several years with very good results. Two major goals are accomplished in this rather simple exercise of taking a book written for young children, say for five-year-olds or younger, and turning it into a screenplay. First, you will learn about adaptation: how to begin with someone else's foundation and make it both cinematic and, it is hoped, even better. And second, you will begin to get used to formatting a screenplay. Writing in screenplay format for beginners always means a period of awkwardness until you begin to "think" in format style.

There are variations in what is accepted as FORMAT, especially between television and film, but study various samples, and, in general, keep it simple and, above all, an easy read:

1. Keep description to a minimum.

2. Be very sparing of camera angles/directions and avoid the word "CAMERA" in order that your script reads more like a story. What to use in its place? Use "we see" or simply state, "Thelma started the car and floored it." Directors will direct (producers too!), thus any camera directions often serve more as punctuation, but suggestive punctuation. Several useful directions are: CLOSE ON, ANOTHER ANGLE, WIDER ANGLE, MONTAGE SEQUENCE (followed by END MONTAGE), and POV to emphasize a point of view perspective.

3. Single space everything (television uses various formats which you need to consult for particular shows/genres).

Let's take a sample page of *Thelma & Louise* and note how simple, direct, clean, and lean the page is: the eye glides quickly down the page (I have removed the shot numbers since my version is from the "final shooting script" which is not what you will be writing). Specifics: single-space description and dialogue. Set up headings for shots/scenes in caps as seen below. More traditional than below is to put characters or important objects in caps the first time they are mentioned. Thus HITCHHIKER and the folk in the coffee shop would appear in caps. This excerpt is from page 47 of the shooting script, and it includes picking up J.D. who will become Thelma's lover and Louise's robber.

EXT. CROSSROADS – DAY
Hitchhiker standing on the side of the road. Thelma looks at Louise pleadingly. Louise's car pulls over and he hops in the back seat. An animated Thelma turns around backwards in the front seat to face him.

EXT./INT. COFFEE SHOP – DAY
Hal walks into the coffee shop where Louise works. VARIOUS SHOTS of him talking to other employees. Albert, waitresses, etc. Some cover their mouths as they recognize police sketches of Louise and Thelma. The Day Manager comes over, looks at pictures and talks to Hal.

INT. CAR – MOVING
Thelma passing out beef jerky and Wild Turkey to Hitchhiker and Louise.

EXT. THELMA'S HOUSE – DAY
Hal's unmarked detective car pulls up in front of Thelma's house. A Corvette, completely customized with everything, sits in the driveway.

INT. CAR – MOVING
Hitchhiker leans over resting his chin on the back of the front seat.

THELMA
So, J.D., what are you studying in school?

J.D.
Human nature. I'm majoring in behavioral science.

LOUISE
And whaddya wanna be when ya grow up?

                                    J.D.
    A waiter.

    Louise laughs. He has charmed her too.

                                              (CONTINUED)

That's it! Note that there are no "cut to's" at the end of each shot/scene
these days, though it is still the custom to write "(CONTINUED)" at the
bottom of a page at the far right if the scene is being continued and simply "CONTINUED" at the top left of a page if it is continued from the
previous page.

   Note the general dimensions of margins in inches: left to description:
1½″; left to dialogue: 3″; left to character's name in dialogue: 4″; right
margin to description: 1½″; right to dialogue: 3″; top to script: 1½″; bottom to script: 2″.

   Further note: action belongs in the description outside of the dialogue, not in parentheses under the character's name.

                              • • •

   As for children's books, as we mentioned in part 2, they are an excellent source for material, partially because there is always a need for good
children's programming and also because the books today have become
so wonderfully visual. There is yet another reason to do this exercise:
these books tend to be quite short, thus an adaptation should mean
fewer than twenty pages of screenplay.

   *Study the book you select carefully to see the interplay of picture and
text in the original and thus to figure out how you wish to keep the spirit
of the original but turn it into a film.*

   Then, write!

   Here's a sample opening by an aspiring screenwriter, William Labuda,
adapting a Lousiana children's book, *Cajun Columbus* by Alice Durio
and James Rice.

FADE IN:
MONTAGE SEQUENCE
SCENES FROM THE BAYOU – DAY
1. We hear CAJUN MUSIC rising from somewhere within the wet-
   lands of a Louisiana bayou.
2. CLOSE ON various samples of plant life in the bayou—a moss-
   strewn EUCALYPTUS, a tall BEECH rising from the swamp, a blos-
   soming MAGNOLIA, etc.

3. CLOSE ON various samples of animal life in the bayou—CRAW-FISH, ALLIGATORS, AND PELICANS.

4. We see a PELICAN flap its wings and take flight with a white flower of MAGNOLIA in its beak.

END MONTAGE SEQUENCE
EXT. PARISH CHURCH YARD – TWILIGHT
We slowly move in toward COUPLES twirling and dancing to the up-beat music of a Cajun band we have been hearing. CHILDREN dressed in turn of the century clothing run and play freely over the church grounds.

A YOUNG GIRL, 11, chases a BROWN-HAIRED BOY, 13, who is running off with her bonnet. Another BOY IN OVERALLS, 8, holds a cat by its tail just above the water. Two YOUNG BOYS, about age 5, shout at one another while climbing a large tree.

ANOTHER ANGLE
We see PIERRE LASTRAPPES, a thin and mustached man in his early thirties, stamping his feet while playing on a red windbox. On his head is a ragged felt hat that seems too small to fit his head. As the song ends, we watch him wipe his forehead with his arm, call for his faithful beagle, and stagger outside to the back of the church.

EXT. PARISH CHURCHYARD (BACK) – TWILIGHT
NARRATOR (Cajun accent, male)
Now, once upon a times w'en peoples don't got much educate, an' dey don't got telly vision an' feetsball an bessball to cass an eye on, dere was a poor fella w'at dey call Pierre Lastrapes, him.

And we are definitely off and running. I've never met an aspiring writer who did not learn much and thoroughly enjoy this assignment. And many have remarked that doing this adaptation got them interested in working on children-oriented programming.

Week Four: The Monologue/Voiceover

We are now moving from documentary and other people's work to your own creations.

The focus here is on one character talking. You have two choices: show us the character in action and make use of the voiceover, or, have the character talk on film to us or to him/herself, *but not to others.* We want a single character in isolation who does not have to worry about interactions at this point.

This exercise has another important function. At a time when Hollywood in particular emphasizes snappy dialogue, often of one- or two-word exchanges, there is some real virtue in learning to master the longer character speech in which much is revealed through prolonged talking. Recommended reading includes Sarah Kozloff's *Invisible Storytellers: Voice-Over Narration in American Fiction Film,* which does an excellent job of establishing the roots of voiceover both in literature (first-person narrator) and documentary (all of those old newsreels with voices like those of Walter Cronkite speaking with authority and verve!). And for viewing, try to see at least one of the following: Robert Redford's *A River Runs Through It* (Richard Friedenberg based on the story by Norman Maclean 1992); Emir Kusterica's *When Father Was Away On Business* (Yugoslav, 1985); *Badlands* (written and directed by Terrence Malick 1974); *Blade Runner* (Hampton Fancher and David Peoples 1982); *My Life as a Dog* (Lasse Hallström, Reidor Sönsson, Brasse Brännstrom, and Pelle Bergland 1985); *Annie Hall* (written and directed by Woody Allen 1977); *All About Eve* (written and directed by Joseph Mankiewicz 1950); *Jules and Jim* (François Truffaut and Jean Gruault 1962); *The Road Warrior* (Brian Hannant, Terry Hayes, and George Miller 1982); *Rashomon* (Shinobu Hashimoto 1951); *The Power and the Glory* (Preston Sturges 1933); *The Naked City* (Albert Maltz and Malvin Wald 1948); *Stand by Me* (1986); *Taxi Driver* (Paul Shrader 1976); *The Lady from Shanghai* (Orson Welles 1948); or *Double Indemnity* (Billy Wilder and Raymond Chandler, from the James M. Cain novel, 1944).

What you should appreciate is the truly carnivalesque potential that the voiceover as well as the direct camera address have for character development. Either way, what the monologue does is to establish a personal, direct link with us, the viewer. It is an opportunity for a personal cinema. Of the two, the on camera address is more limiting in the sense that character and voice must be the same.

But think of the potential for the voiceover to create contrast, distance, as well as personality, warmth, involvement. François Truffaut felt a strong affinity for the personal quality of this technique; in his early short about young boys, *Les Mistons* (1957, 17 minutes), who are beginning to become interested in women, he uses a voiceover of a man obviously in his late twenties or early thirties who is thinking back on his youth. A wistful sense of nostalgia hangs around the energetic images we see (in black and white) of young boys following a beautiful young woman who is in love with a young man. The kids are, as the title suggests, real brats. Without the voiceover, this short would be closer to slapstick. But the voiceover *told from the present looking back* does what cinema can do so well: makes us simultaneously aware of two times, two feelings, two voices.

Each of the films listed above takes a different perspective on voiceover ranging from a disembodied narrator who is never identified (*Jules and Jim*) to a mixture of on camera direct address combined with voice over (*Annie Hall*) and on to the convention of the voiceover for hardboiled genre detective/crime films which grew out of the hard-boiled novel genre such as *Double Indemnity*—a fine example of this is Orson Welles's wonderfully modulated Irish voice in *The Lady from Shanghai*.

Assignment: Either take one of your two previously written character sketches or, if you wish, start from scratch with a new character and create a monologue in either voiceover or direct address in screenplay format. Work carefully on voice color, on pacing, on dialect, vocabulary, and texture. Do make your monologue a complete piece and do *pay attention to visuals*. Length: no more than five pages.

An extra assignment that may be enjoyable to try as a preview for the "Northern Exposure" workout would be to script a monologue for Chris, the eclectic D.J. Here's a sample in which Chris takes on the universe and democracy from the "Democracy in America" episode written by Jeff Melvoin:

INT. HOLLING'S BAR – DAY
As Joel and Maggie join the others.

CHRIS (O.S.)
"Though passion may have strained, it must not break, our bonds of affection."

As Chris CONTINUES, we get a final look around the bar, everyone eating, drinking as usual.

CHRIS (O.S.)
Lincoln's words to a divided nation. My counsel to a divided Cicely. Holling Vincoeur, you're still first in the hearts of your fellow Cicelians. Today, the people simply said they want Edna to run things for a while. And that's cool. If it doesn't work out, we'll have another election. It's not perfect, but it's the best system anyone's come up with. As Justice Holmes said, the Constitution is an experiment, as all life is an experiment. Apropos of that, final words tonight belong to Thomas Jefferson, third President of these United States, who gave us this to chew on: "Sometimes it is said that man cannot be trusted with the government of himself. Can he, then, be trusted

with the government of others? Or have we found angels in the forms of kings to govern him?"

EXT. CICELY – NIGHT
The light from the radio station shines like a beacon.

CHRIS (O.S.)
"Let history answer this question". . . You're listening to K-Bear, 570 a.m., the voice of the Borough of Arrowhead County . . .

FADE OUT

Clearly anyone writing a Chris monologue has to map out a list of literary/authority quotations/allusions and a theme to hold them together. That's the trick.

WEEK FIVE: SELF STUDY

I have waited this long to get at the center of all carnivals: you. By week five you should be comfortable with format, with adaptation, with visuals, and the beginning of spoken language.

This week, put yourself through the hoops your characters must pass through.

1. Write up a brainstorming kind of informal list that answers many of the questions/items on the character checklist about yourself.

2. Find at least a dozen photos that you feel best represent your life, from your earliest baby picture on. Try to include at least a few shots that have your parents or parent and brothers and sisters, if any, and/or closest friends. Arrange these photos in an order that most pleases you and add a few lines or a paragraph or even a page or two if you wish about the memories/feelings each photo calls forth from you.

3. Use both of the above as part of what Gregory Ulmer has called a *"mystory."* A *mystory* is meant to be a free-form work produced by you which can contain just about anything in the way of language and images that you feel represents you. Ulmer's feeling is that we are living in a time of such informational overstimulation that we have not yet found appropriate ways to digest and make sense of the world around us today. In this spirit, he feels the *mystory* is a step toward assembling the fragments that could later become part of a basis for self-analysis as well as for further self-expression. As he states in *Teletheory: Grammatology in the Age of Video*, "Write a mystory bringing into relation your experience with three levels of discourse—personal (autobiography), popular (community stories, oral history, or popular culture), expert (disciplines of knowledge). In each case use the sting of memory to locate items sig-

nificant to you" (1989, 209). Try for at least twenty pages incorporating your photos, notes, passages you write about yourself, memories you have, quotes from songs or stories that mean something, or lines from poets or writers, as well as "expert" pieces that appeal to you. *This should have the appearance of a kind of carnival montage on paper. Do not try to create a systematic order or a disciplined structure. The quality of the fragments and their juxtapositions to each other and your overriding attraction to them are what counts.* Many voices may speak here, often overlapping, perhaps reappearing. You decide. And, as always, share with your partner.

4. Finally, get your partner to write his/her character sketch of you. It need be about a page or two. No more than three or four. If he or she is also working as a writer, have that person try to add characteristic habits, phrases, gestures, attitudes. Meet for coffee or whatever and go over this analysis of your partner. What do you think? How does it match up with yours? (For best results, don't pass on your *mystory* until your partner has completed his/her analysis profile of you.)

What is being accomplished here? Not an exercise in self-therapy exactly, nor is this purely an attempt at autobiography. What I hope comes through is an effort to begin to see how much you do and don't know about yourself and the many voices within you. You just might uncover some rusty or dusty voices you either forgot about or were not sure were ever there that could be very useful and pleasing to you later.

More? Read a good filmmaker's autobiography such as Luis Buñuel's *My Last Sigh*.

WEEK SIX: DIALOGUE

Two characters talking. Suddenly a character must react and interact as well as express himself/herself.

Go back over the videotapes you've made and study again how people talk, respond, choose their words, make their delivery. Focus not only on the speaking but on *the listening* as well. Often the camera can tell us more about a character through how she or he listens than how they speak or what they say.

Try also taping conversations with an aural tape recorder to further study speech patterns, manner, delivery. Study pacing and the use of silences as well. Of course you can do the same with films, but I do recommend beginning once more at the documentary level. One of my favorite documentaries is a half-hour piece called *Yeah You Rite* (1986) by Louis Alvarez and Andrew Kolker, which focuses on the way people talk in New Orleans (purchase through The Center for New American Media,

524 Broadway, Second Fl., New York, NY 10012-4408). The rich gumbo of dialects, special vocabularies, and accents in the city is truly amazing as well as vastly amusing.

But the point is that anyone who is not from New Orleans who sees the tape will instantly understand that none of the films that comes out of Hollywood ever gets New Orleans speech right, including especially Oliver Stone's *J.F.K.* (1991) and Jim McBride's *The Big Easy* (1986). My point is clear: if you begin with a false sense of speech, how can you be expected to build a true sense of character?

The week's assignment is to write a 4–7 page dialogue scene in script format between two characters, one of whom is a homeless person and the other who clearly has a much more stable economic life. The two must also be different in two of the following three: race, gender, general attitude/abilities/interests.

As you write this exercise, you really are learning the basics of scene construction and the interplay between speech and action, foreground and background, and the need to construct texture within a scene. How much action and how much dialogue? You decide, but no talking heads simply sitting around a table with nothing else going on. Remember commandment number 4 that there should be at least two levels to every scene, that is, either cross purposes, or a tension between foreground/background, or between other elements in the scene.

Here is an exchange between Garp and his feminist nurse mother, Jenny, in Steve Tesich's adaptation of John Irving's novel, *The World According to Garp* (directed by George Roy Hill, 1982). Garp is a serious writer, the father of two boys, a home-based husband and something of a womanizer. Jenny is, to say the least, an unconventional mother who conceived Garp from the sperm of a dying amputee soldier in an army hospital during World War II. Part of what we sense in any exchange between them, therefore, is the cross purposes of two very different characters who happen to be related by blood. In this scene they are commenting on each other's writing: Garp has been writing fiction and Jenny has finished writing about her life in a simple and straightforward prose style.

> JENNY and GARP are sitting at the table next to their respective manuscripts, GARP next to thin, JENNY next to thick, drinking coffee. JENNY looks at Garp's manuscript.

JENNY

It's kind of thin.

GARP

It's not the quantity that counts.

JENNY

Thank God for that . . . I better take my typewriter back.

GARP

Aren't you going to write anymore?

JENNY

Whatever for? I've written all I wanted to write.

GARP

But you might want to rewrite.

JENNY

Rewrite what?

GARP

What you've written.

JENNY

Whatever for?

GARP

To make it better.

JENNY

Better for who?

GARP

WHOM.

JENNY

WHOM. Better for whom?

GARP

For you. I mean for yourself, that's for whom.

JENNY

It's good enough for me.

GARP

That's not very artistic.

JENNY

I'm a nurse not an artist.

GARP

Well, I want to be an artist, and I want to know what you thought of it.

JENNY

I'm not sure I understand it.

(pp. 53–54)

Oscar-winning screenwriter Steve Tesich manages to capture the essence of the difference between this loving mother and son duo who are quite literally going in opposite directions. Each embraces a multitude of voices within his/her character, and what we sense is how different these separate carnivals are. They are in this brief scene simultaneously mother and son, man and woman, serious writer and utilitarian author, artist and nurse, as they themselves finally declare.

Simplicity of construction. But look at how important the set-up is: the mere fact that they are side by side, sharing a single typewriter and both engaged in the same activity—writing—suggests the strength of their relationship despite their differences.

Note also the simplicity of the exchanges. Of course there are times in a dialogue when one or the other character needs to speak in more detail as Garp does in the very next exchange after Jenny's line, "I'm not sure I understand it":

GARP

It's simple. He can do wonders when he's wearing his magic gloves. His wife is sad. He touches her with his gloves and she's happy. His kids are crying? He touches them and they smile. But he can't feel them. And he yearns to feel. He can keep death away with his magic gloves but he can't feel life. So he takes them off . . . and he dies . . . but he feels life as he flies into the arms of death.

Thus after an almost matter-of-fact series of exchanges, we suddenly glimpse exactly what kind of writer Garp is. But the rhythm of the scene depends more on the brief exchanges set up above.

Meet with your partner once you've done your dialogues and read each other's piece out loud. Listen for rhythm, flow, development, and make any changes that actually HEARING your lines read need to be made. Furthermore, experiment with changes in some of the lines before considering your scene complete. Is one character more verbal than another? Garp and Jenny are pretty evenly matched, but many characters are not. That's for you to discover and decide.

WEEK SEVEN: THREE CHARACTERS

It may surprise you how much of most films breaks down to a series of dialogue scenes between two characters. Think how much of *The Silence of the Lambs* depends on the one-on-one scenes between Lecter and Clarice, while clearly *Thelma & Louise* is very intensely a two-character film punctuated by their contact from time to time with others. Of our sample films, only in Kusturica's *Time of the Gypsies*, with its focus on a constantly crowded frame as a reflection of gypsy culture, do we see a very different set-up. Part of Kusturica's message is very definitely that in such a culture, finding a place and time to be alone as one or as two is very difficult.

Clearly the dynamics change when three or more characters interact. Review the scene in *Thelma & Louise* that begins with the attempted rape of Thelma and ends with Louise shooting and killing the rapist.

We can break down the scene into the following movements: (1) Harlan coming on strong with Thelma who begins to reject his advances; (2) Louise, now outside, looking around as Harlan's advances become uglier ("There is no trace of friendliness in his face now") after Thelma hits him. His reaction is to depersonalize her and control her as he turns her around "pushing her face down onto the back of the car." The next (3) movement begins as Louise, off camera, says "Let her go." In parts 1 and 2, Louise has been present but not interacting. Now, with this third part of the scene, all three are directly involved. This segment ends as Louise's use of Thelma's gun leads to Thelma's escape. Now, in (4), the tension is between Harlan and Louise with Thelma in the background. The power structure has been reversed and Harlan is now trying to get out: "We were just havin' a little fun." Louise's motherly character comes on strong here as she feels obligated to lecture him: "Just for the future, when a woman's crying like that, she's not having any fun." Part 4 is over as she walks off. That could have been the end of it. But it's not Harlan's character to let Louise lecture him after having already humiliated him (in his eyes). Thus his two exchanges (movement 5) which lead to Louise's unexpected shot at his face. The final part of the scene is the reaction, as both women begin to realize what has happened and what they must do. What we see is that Louise has taken command ("Get in the car"), though Thelma drives and that Louise is still letting go of what she has done: "You watch your mouth, buddy," she whispers to herself, a line that tells us much about what she is feeling. As the scene ends, they are ready to hit the road and to begin their life on the run. Three characters and three pages and six movements within one scene.

Note that since this is basically a two-character film, each additional character added must help focus and bring out the two main characters.

Harlan's actions show us that Thelma attempts to resist, but is ineffectual. Louise proves herself to be a strong woman capable of pulling a trigger *not because of the physical act of the attempted rape but because of his filthy language afterward.* It is Harlan's tongue, not his penis, that kills him. The killing comes as a surprise, for we are suddenly face-to-face with Louise and a deep structural level of her character which is never revealed or explained away in the film. Yes, shoot the man in the foot or arm for his behavior, but the clear, deliberate shoot-to-kill action ("Louise takes two long strides back towards him, raises the gun and FIRES into his face") clues us in that we do not know all there is to know about Louise.

Assignment: Write a three-character scene that has at least five movements to it in which the nature of the relationship between the three characters shifts clearly from section to section. (3–6 pages)

Go over it with your partner and polish.

Week Eight:
The Extended Character-Centered Scene

So many plot-driven films seem to zip along at an MTV speed with almost no letdown from beginning to end. All our sample films discussed, however, make use of extended character scenes which often go on for minutes at a time. Many other examples abound. Part of the significant success of *Howard's End* (Ruth Prawer Jhabvala's screenplay from E. M. Forester's novel, 1992) has to do with an ensemble cast of characters allowed to play out extended, complex scenes.

Of course it's much easier to do short action scenes. But for those interested in character-centered films, the ability to handle the extended scene well is essential. What is an extended scene? For our purposes we can say it is any scene longer than three pages. In our close-up on *The Silence of the Lambs,* we saw that the Clarice-Lecter exchanges all run more than six pages.

Assignment: Take one of our four sample films and study it carefully for the use of extended scenes. Then weave one yourself. There should be at least two characters involved. You choose the circumstance, the characters, the actions. Build on previously done work if you wish. Share with your partner, and polish.

Week Nine: A "Northern Exposure" Treatment

Now that you have worked on many of the basics of script writing, try your hand at being a true professional. If you feel you are ready to start your own script, then fine. Go on to the fourteen-week feature script section immediately.

But my logic in concluding the character development sequence with a known national television program is both to introduce you to the freedoms and restrictions of such work and to help you begin to realize that television today is where the bulk of writing is required.

Beginnings: Watch "Northern Exposure" as often as possible, taping it and seeing some episodes a second or third time to get used to the characters and format. Review our comments in part 1. Think of the truly carnivalesque structure and characterization of the main figures. Write a brief character sketch of each of the main characters. And study the script you obtain from CBS.

Note that the page-a-minute formula tends to hold true, with most scripts for an hour show weighing in at 45–58 pages. What is extremely significant to understand is that for an hour-long show, you are to come up with a four-act narrative.

William Coveny, the former Director of Current Programming at CBS, puts the concept/structure of a "Northern Exposure" episode this way: "You tend to see a central idea or theme for each episode around which three or sometimes four plots are built" (1992). "Spring Break," which we quoted earlier, concerns how spring can bring out those wild (carnivalesque!) spirits within us; "Democracy in America" was exactly that; and the last episode of the 1991–1992 season focused on the founding of Cicely, complete with a discussion of its lesbian cofounders, Cicely and Rosalyn.

Let's be even more specific. In the "Spring Break" episode, we learn the ice is beginning to crack and everyone is acting "out of character." This particular episode has four narrative lines: Joel and Maggie actually KISS after having exotic/erotic fantasies of each other; Holling wants to pick a fight; someone (Chris!) is stealing electronic equipment all over town; and Maurice as a suddenly uncharacteristic, domesticated, "sensitive" male attempts romance with a very masculine female police officer.

If you know the characters on the show and have a feel for the wildly diverse topics and actions the show embraces, then you should have a field day listening to many carnivalesque voices that speak within you. In fact, I can think of no better further preparation for "Northern Exposure" work than that of reading several comedies by the ancient Greek master, Aristophanes. In *Peace*, for instance, a disgruntled farmer, tired of the war going on between Athens and Sparta, decides to conclude his own separate peace. To do so he flies to the heavens on a dung beetle, which is propelled by the power of farting. Zeus does conclude peace with the farmer and also throws in his daughter in the bargain. The rest of the play has to do with the celebration of peace and the first example of group sex in Western literature, as one after the other of the farmers makes love to Zeus's daughter, Peace. The spectrum of comedy embraced by Aristophanes ranges from the scatological to the sublime. His choruses always manage to come up with some of the most beautiful lines in Greek poetry, much as Chris's voiceovers wrap up and introduce themes/ideas/feelings for Cicely. Remember that Athens was still at war when the chorus sang these lines:

> CHORUS OF FARMERS
> What a pleasure, what a treasure,
> What a great delight to me,
> From the cheese and from the onions
> and the helmet to be free.
> For I can't enjoy a battle,
> but I love to pass my days
> With my wine and boon companions
> Round the merry, merry blaze,
> When the logs are dry and seasoned,
> And the fire is burning bright,
> And I roast the peas and chestnuts
> In the embers all alight,
> Flirting too with Thratta
> When my wife is out of sight.
> (*Aristophanes* 1971, 220)

Let the spirit of Cicely speak to you, and see what concepts you come up with!

Your assignment is to write a 5–7 page treatment for a proposed "Northern Exposure" episode making sure you identify where the acts divide. Also add an opening summary/conceptual paragraph that gives an overview of your whole treatment. Your partner and perhaps other friends who watch the show should be asked to pay especially close attention to your treatment. Listen to all suggestions: in this case because you have a show that others know, you may very well get some excellent feedback.

WEEK TEN: "NORTHERN EXPOSURE": ACT 1

With your treatment refined and in mind, begin writing! Note that you need a 2- or 3-page "prologue," which is standard in such a format to introduce and hook your audience before, of course, going to the first commercial. What is it you can do in two pages that introduces your theme/characters/circumstance? In a sense your treatment tells you, but in the specifics of writing, you need to be even more concrete. For "Spring Break," the prologue is a surprise fantasy (we don't know this at first) in which Fleischman and Maggie meet in a tropical garden and Maggie comes on strong. We learn, of course, in the following scene that Maggie has been dreaming and her boyfriend Rick is going off on a trip. "Spring Break" is David Assael's script and the prologue is as follows:

FADE IN
EXT. TROPICAL GARDEN – DAY
Lush, misty, exotic. Birds CAW and monkeys SCREAM. Maggie and Joel stroll through the foliage.

> JOEL
>
> Why'd I listen to you? Why'd I let you drag me out here?

> MAGGIE
>
> It's beautiful.

> JOEL
>
> It's a jungle. There're tarantulas here—tropical diseases—you ever hear of elephantiasis? Your leg swells up like a telephone pole. We didn't have any shots.

> MAGGIE
>
> This is paradise. We don't need shots.

> JOEL
>
> These banana trees are probably full of primates.

> MAGGIE
>
> Fleischman, will you relax.

> JOEL
>
> A-ha!

> MAGGIE
>
> A-ha, what?

> JOEL
> (pointing)
>
> That's a snake, O'Connell. A snake.

Maggie gently strokes the chin of a small garden snake.

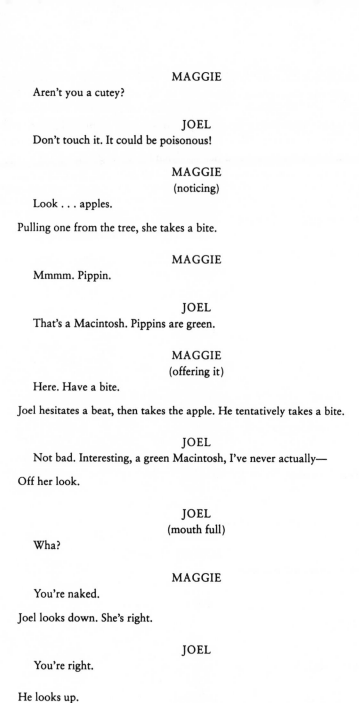

MAGGIE

Aren't you a cutey?

JOEL

Don't touch it. It could be poisonous!

MAGGIE
(noticing)

Look . . . apples.

Pulling one from the tree, she takes a bite.

MAGGIE

Mmmm. Pippin.

JOEL

That's a Macintosh. Pippins are green.

MAGGIE
(offering it)

Here. Have a bite.

Joel hesitates a beat, then takes the apple. He tentatively takes a bite.

JOEL

Not bad. Interesting, a green Macintosh, I've never actually—

Off her look.

JOEL
(mouth full)

Wha?

MAGGIE

You're naked.

Joel looks down. She's right.

JOEL

You're right.

He looks up.

MAGGIE

What?

Off Joel's look, Maggie looks down. She's now naked too.

> MAGGIE

Oh . . .

> JOEL

You know, normally, I don't like being naked in public. I get self-critical—embarrassed. But I don't feel that way now . . . Do you?

> MAGGIE
> (turned on)

No. Actually I feel very . . . very . . .

She moves to embrace him. As their lips touch—

The cut is to Maggie waking up and discovering this opening has been a dream. The prologue clearly serves to hook us on the episode and to introduce a major narrative concern: what will Joel and Maggie do about their budding passion for each other? Within the overall context of "Spring Break" each character will be forced to deal with his or her passion. But this two-pager compactly and economically sets up the rest of the hour: fantasies will be dreamed, lived out, acted upon, and, finally, embraced.

Act 1 of "Spring Break" is sixteen pages and divided into twenty-two shots or scenes. Note that although "Northern Exposure" does allow space for more development than most programs, scenes rarely run longer than four pages for a key kernel scene, and that many of your satellite scenes are actually only transitional shots.

Assignment: Write act 1!

Once written, do run off copies and try to get enough friends together to do a reading. With the feedback from your partner and from the reading, you will have an excellent sense of what is and is not working for you.

WEEK ELEVEN: "NORTHERN EXPOSURE": ACT 2

Assignment: Write act 2.

Act 2 tends to be short: roughly 7–10 pages.

Ask yourself the following question: Am I being carnivalesque enough? The danger in writing for a set show is that you too will become too predictable, too close to shows you have previously seen. What "Northern Exposure" allows you is the chance to open up any particular character of idea and bring out a "voice" we haven't fully explored before. With such a bevy of characters, the possibilities of variations are tremendous. The "Fling" episode, for instance, in which Chris decides to fling a cow across town but ends up flinging a piano as an example of performance art, gives Chris the spotlight, whereas "Animals R Us" brings Marilyn, the Native American assistant, more to the front as she confronts Maurice's wild scheme to raise ostriches.

Note: When I visited the set of "Northern Exposure" (December, 1992) in Redmond, Washington, I was struck by how much the actors have "become" the characters they play so that the give-and-take between writers-directors-actors is extremely important in the continued growth and health of a show that hopes to go on season after season. Director (and a writer/co-executive producer) Rob Thompson made it clear that it is a great advantage for the writers to see what kinds of "carnival" each actor is able to bring to his or her role. Thus note the increased role Marilyn (Elaine Miles) has been playing as the writers have become comfortable and intrigued with her "complex simplicity."

WEEK TWELVE: "NORTHERN EXPOSURE": ACT 3

Assignment: Write act 3, roughly 10–12 pages.

Question: Have you included at least one substantial voice-over monologue for Chris to express many of the major themes you wish to highlight?

WEEK THIRTEEN: "NORTHERN EXPOSURE": ACT 4

Assignment: Write the final act, roughly 15–18 pages.

Question: How far can you go in exploring set characters? Answer: Pretty far. Take the episode in 1992 in which Maggie and Joel wind up sharing a room in a hotel at a convention in Juno. They actually decide they WILL MAKE LOVE. That's going far given their characters as previously established. And yet, there is an out: Maggie falls asleep! As we know, the 1993 season opened up new avenues for the relationship as Maggie and Joel do come together in the "Ill Wind" episode (February 15, 1993).

Since you are writing "on spec" you need perhaps to play it in the middle. You wish to show that you have some feisty and original ideas, and yet you can't have Ed suddenly become a serial killer or Chris go for a sex-change operation. Stretch, bend, rework character, but don't completely go outside the established territory.

Finished? Congratulations! Time for celebration.

After the celebration do try for a complete reading and session with your partner.

Then give it a rewrite fixing what needs fixing (see part 4 on rewrites). You then have a writing sample you can feel proud of.

Once more, it is becoming very common for agents, producers, talent scouts, to want to see not only original work, but samples of what you can do with a given show. I've had students write episodes of "Northern Exposure," "Cheers," and "Rosanne" and quite frequently they have gotten jobs, graduate school appointments, and so forth, based in part on their TV episode scripts.

WEEK FOURTEEN:
SELF-CRITIQUE AND THE ART OF THE REWRITE

When you reach this point, you've done a lot of work and, hopefully, begun to learn much about yourself as a writer of screenplays. More important, you will have put a theory of character to practice: you will have begun to explore the carnivalesque world of character.

Time to take stock and review your own accomplishments and frustrations. Look over the Self-Critiques in the Appendix and discuss your whole situation with your partner.

Final assignment: Go back over your work and select one early exercise. Rewrite it making one major change: if the monologue is a woman, change her to a man; if she is black, why not try for Native American. Whatever. Just make sure you've made one major character change that forces you to see that character from a different perspective.

Where do we end this fourteen-week commitment?

Why not listen to the words of director François Truffaut who said, "Cinematic success is not necessarily the result of good brain work, but of a harmony of existing elements in ourselves that we may not have even been conscious of: a fortunate fusion of subject and our deeper feelings, an accidental coincidence of our own preoccupations at a certain moment of life and the publics" (1985, 15).

CHAPTER NINE

THE FOURTEEN-WEEK
FEATURE SCREENPLAY

She's got something in her throat.
>   Clarice, on finding the cocoon in a
>   victim's throat, *The Silence of the Lambs*

The frame through which I viewed the world changed too, with time.
Greater than scene, I came to see, is situation. Greater than situation
is implication. Greater than all of these is a single, entire human
being, who will never be confined in any frame.
>   Eudora Welty, *One Writer's Beginnings*

Word has it that Paul Schrader wrote *Taxi Driver* in three days. And one
book, Viki King's *How to Write a Movie in 21 Days* suggests a three-
week model. But in my experience either scenario is the exception rather
than the rule. Especially for those taking on the task for the first time.

My suggestion is for a fourteen-week frame. I have worked within
this structure because it fits the typical university semester. But years of
experience in teaching the feature script have shown me that this time
line allows for growth, maturity, a bit of revision, and still that necessary
sense of the clock ticking which SHOULD HELP rather than hinder creativity. I am, of course, speaking of a first draft only. Though since almost everyone these days composes on the computer (and would be fool-
ish in so many ways not to), a "first draft" incorporates any changes
made along the way.

Add, subtract, speed up, slow down from the pace set here. It's up to
you to decide how best to write. But this schedule will get you through
and allow for some breathing space and time to think it all through. In
over a dozen years of teaching the feature screenplay, I've never had a
student who didn't finish a script. The pace is roughly ten pages a week
once you begin the actual script, but some write more, others less.

Should you rewrite as you go along? I don't encourage a fixation on perfection. Keep the pages coming with your initial drive and vision. And rewrite later. Having said this, however, I have found that many enjoy "tinkering" as they go along. In fact, they tell me it's hard to resist. If you can write new material and tinker too, fine. But don't let the need to make it better get in the way of simply getting it done.

Obviously if you have worked through the previous schedule, you will be in a particularly strong position, psychologically and in terms of training, for the "marathon" itself. Because so much has already been covered, I will be much more brief in this section, viewing this truly as much more of an outline than a "how to" that deserves another text.

PREPARATION

1. Order copies of the following scripts:

sex, lies and videotape. New York: Harper & Row, 1990.
The Silence of the Lambs (Script City)
Thelma & Louise (Script City)
Boyz N the Hood (Script City)

SCRIPT CITY carries most of the xeroxed copies of scripts for popular films that have not been published. To get on their mailing list write to SCRIPT CITY, 1765 N. Highland Ave., #760, Hollywood, California 90028. Their "hot line" phone is (213) 871-0707.

2. Watch the video of *Time of the Gypsies* (available in most video shops as a Columbia Pictures release) and *Cinema Paradiso*, as well as the films listed in (1).

3. Complete as much of the previous schedule as you can.

4. Brainstorm on the film you want to write and the characters you wish to center upon. Let the characters and their narrative situations simmer within you for *several months* if possible. Keep a notebook, and jot down bits of dialogue, rough ideas that might become scenes, images that strike you. Anything. *What is very hard to do—in fact almost impossible—is to simply "come up" with an entire story and characters on the spot during the first week.*

5. Choose a partner, or, if your previous partner has worked out especially well, gear up for the full experience.

6. Continue to live fully, read widely, watch carefully, listen attentively, and take chances.

WEEK ONE: DEVELOPING THE PITCH

I like to go against the grain.

Screenwriter Steve Tesich
(Academy Award: *Breaking Away*)

In part 2 we discussed where stories come from, and the possibility that you might begin with a character or with a narrative idea. Let's simply add, building on Eudora Welty's splendid insight at the beginning of this chapter, that you might begin with a situation or an implication, or even one specific image. *Something grabs your attention for some reason: follow it through to discover why.*

This first week is devoted to generating characters, exploring them and their narratives, and weaving these into the five-minute pitch. *This first week is the most important: do your exploring and weaving well, and your next thirteen weeks will be much more pleasure than pain.*

Maybe you will come up with three or four ideas. Fine. Let your partner be your sounding board and see which idea begins to move to the front. Explore, don't force. Discover, don't impose. POKEY GOT AIDS reads a spray-painted bit of graffiti in my racially mixed New Orleans neighborhood. Who is Pokey? How did he get such a suggestive name? Did he (and I'm already making an assumption in terms of gender!) get AIDS? And who felt it necessary to spray the abandoned house opposite St. Cecilia's church with this message? Is it a warning to those in the 'hood? My imagination begins to work because my curiosity won't let go of this image and those words.

Let your pitch evolve as it will. Fashion your narrative from a carnival of voices that begin to take focus into clearer patterns. Make use of all the previous material in this book, including the review lists. Who, for instance, is your main character and what is his or her core characteristic/experience? *Without a core experience, you do not have a pitch or a movie.*

Thus by the end of a week, you should have a five-minute pitch that you and those you try it on are pleased by, enticed by, and pulled into.

In addition: Read and study *Thelma & Louise* and *The Silence of the Lambs* and compare/contrast the scripts with the films/videos in light of the discussion of these works in this text. Write a two-page character sketch of either Thelma or Louise including her childhood and youth not covered in the script (backstory), including all points in the character checklist from part 1.

WEEK TWO: THE WRITTEN TREATMENT

Without realizing it, the individual composes his life according to the laws of beauty even in times of greatest distress.

Milan Kundera,
The Unbearable Lightness of Being

Assignment: Write a 5- to 10-page treatment of your oral pitch, elaborating, exploring further. Where does the extra material come from? Clearly the written treatment allows you to flesh in not only more about the main characters and their actions, but to add much more about the minor characters and subplots. Note: don't ever feel tied down to this treatment: it is only a blueprint to get you started, to give you something to refer to as you work. In the spirit of carnival, you may very well find after a few weeks that you need an entirely new subplot or embracing figure or dividing character. No problem. At least the treatment pointed a way.

Based on feedback from your partner, refine your treatment.

In addition: Review part 2 and the script for *sex, lies and videotape* and watch the video for the film and for *Time of the Gypsies*. Outline the structure of the film in terms of scenes and sequences to get a feeling for how it is constructed/structured.

WEEK THREE: BEGINNINGS

This is the story of two men who met in a banana republic. One of them was honest all his life except one crazy minute. The other was dishonest all his life except one crazy minute. They both had to get out of the country.

The opening epigraph in Preston Sturges's
The Great McGinty

Come up with a *dominant image* for your script that best captures your main character and his/her core characteristic/experience *visually*. There is no question in *A River Runs Through It*: the opening shot is a close-up of running water: CLEAR running water! The image sticks with us throughout this film about fishing and family, identity and growth. In contrast, it's ironic that the dominant image for *The Silence of the Lambs* is not that of, say, the lambs being slaughtered, but of a young woman's face (Clarice's) with a death's head moth on her lips: thus death, the cocoon clue left by Buffalo Bill in each murder, and the "silence" (covering the lips) are all suggested in one image. Note that the image itself does not appear in the film, just the poster. Likewise, you may find that your dominant image does not work its way into the script, and yet there should be some visual motif we strongly associate with the main character. *Howard's End* opens with the lush image of Ruth (Vanessa Redgrave) walking through the thick uncut grass of her country estate, Howard's End, as night falls. Although most of the film then takes place in the bustle of London during the early part of the century, that image of the rich vegetation and peace of a country location is what Ruth's friend Margaret (Emma Thompson) is finally drawn to. That image represents both women and helps to center our feeling for the whole narrative. And for "Northern Exposure" there is no question: the image of the moose ambling down main street is the clear logo/trademark/dominant image that opens and bridges many of the scenes of the show.

Assignment: Write the first 10 pages of your script. Go over the "Fade In" section, which follows. In theory your pitch and treatment should already have determined your opening. But think again, and make sure that what you have chosen is the most effective way to launch your script.

In addition: Study the script and film (video) of *Boyz N the Hood.* We have said it is a "preachy" film. Is there any way to present Singleton's characters in a different, less didactic manner with the same effect? Discuss with your partner. Study the use of the *soundtrack* including the importance of sirens, helicopters, street sounds. Discuss with your partner also which characters you would develop further if it were your project.

For your opening, consider these options:

Fade In: Opening Shots and Scenes

You have your narrative, you have your structure and even a treatment. Now to get started. You've heard you need to hook the audience in the first few minutes. It's true, but how you hook is the rub. You don't have to BLAST the audience out of its seats. If you do, chances are you'll never be able to keep up the pace. But to a large degree your opening is determined by your overall structure as we shall see. Preston Sturges, for instance, was always fond of overturning conventions and expectations, so *The Palm Beach Story* (1942) is a romantic comedy that BEGINS in the credit sequence with the couple getting married. That's supposed to be the ending of romantic comedies! Obviously Sturges has our attention.

Let us turn to ten possible openings for consideration. As one overall comment, however, remember it is important to try and establish some dominant *image* or *mood* as soon as possible. Remember too that openings might combine several of the following in imaginative ways. For *Driving Miss Daisy* (1989) it is the automobile that we see in the first scene.

Your main goal is to establish the conflict, characters, atmosphere, sense of your narrative world. *Remember that you wish to draw the viewer into your world, but you don't want to drown him or her in the first ten minutes.*

1. PROTAGONIST UP FRONT

Here, as in *The Silence of the Lambs*, we start immediately with our hero or heroine from the first fade in. Advantages are that we know who's who right away.

2. FROM MACRO TO MICRO STORY

As in *Casablanca*, this approach means framing the inner story the script will focus on with the macro view. Here we get the context first and then the protagonist and his/her plight. But the macro view suggests the overall struggle of the characters. Advantage is that we get "the picture" before we meet our main characters. Foreshadowing, in other words. The hot Russian *glasnost* hit, *Little Vera* (Marina Khimelik 1987), does the same. We begin with shots of the ugly industrial wasteland in which Vera lives before we meet Vera. Then we close in on her house, her balcony, her life.

3. VOICEOVER FIRST-PERSON INTRO

Films like *My Life as a Dog* which begin with the main character speaking to us in voice over establish an immediate sense of closeness with us: what follows is extremely personal and we are in on it. If that's the level you wish, this "literary" technique may work well for you. Note that voiceover is used sparingly and doesn't have to dominate the rest of the film. In fact, the tradition is to open and close and use only a few other times. *sex, lies and videotape* is an interesting variation, for it begins with a voiceover, but it quickly becomes apparent that it is not a traditional direct voiceover *for us*, but rather that it is a session with a psychotherapist that we happen to hear.

4. DIRECT CAMERA ADDRESS

Annie Hall and *Time of the Gypsies* both effectively employ the device of shattering our invisible status as an audience by having a character open by staring at us (the camera) and speaking. Like the voiceover, this establishes an immediate bond with the audience, but even more so because of the eye contact and the "violation" of the unspoken rule that, particularly in Hollywood films, characters don't look at "us," this technique "grabs" us. Note that the technique is almost never used in the rest of the film. It is primarily a way of getting started.

5. MONTAGE OPENING

The use of a number of brief shots/scenes to open a film works if the primary goal is to create an atmosphere/a mood/a brief feeling of time passing to create, like the macro to micro intro, a sense of context and, especially, an emotional context. This is true of *Raging Bull* in which the montage of ring images centering on the "raging bull" alone, prancing in slo mo in the ring, becomes a haunting background for the rest of the film.

6. THE CROSSCUT OPENING

Butch Cassidy and the Sundance Kid and *Thelma & Louise* both begin with a crosscutting between the two main characters to establish each before the main action gets started. In a sense, of course, you could consider this a variation of number 1 since you actually have two protagonists, even though the narrative in each case is weighted toward one more than the other.

7. IMMEDIATE PROBLEM TO BE SOLVED

Vittorio De Sica's *Bicycle Thief* (Italy, 1948) introduces the hundreds of unemployed workers waiting for an assignment in the opening shot. Very quickly Antonio appears, but this is different than number 1 or 2 since we get the situation/problem/conflict first and then the character.

8. THE FRAME OPENING

More often than not, but not always, the frame device of opening and closing with a narrative structure outside the main narrative of the film means you are beginning in the present, flashing back to the past, and ending the film in the present, as in *Citizen Kane, Gandhi,* and *Cinema Paradiso.* The sense of closure of such a circular structure can be, as noted earlier, very satisfying.

9. THE EXPLODING ACTION OPENING

A lot of Hollywood films like to start very fast and then slow down to a long exposition sequence. *Beverly Hills Cop* works this way as does *Raiders of the Lost Arc* and *Rocky.*

10. THE SLOW, DIALOGUE-CENTERED OPENING

People tend to forget how slow and how dialogue-weighted the opening sequence of *The Godfather* is. Yes, it could be said to use number 2, as we move from the Corleone wedding to the Corleone office, but the major section of the opening centers on the group of men in the Don's office, talking. This is not an easy feat to pull off. The Coen brothers wrote a brilliant long opening of this type for *Miller's Crossing*, but it was clearly too much for audiences, which did not show up to watch the film. *Casablanca* is slow in getting to Rick, but the set-up happens in short, fast scenes.

That's it. As for credit sequences, you don't label them as such in your script. The producer and director will do so. But you can certainly keep this in mind.

Week Four: Shading Character

The people I show, don't dramatize crises, they deal with them quietly as is normal with these kinds of men.

Howard Hawks, in Joseph McBride,
Hawks on Hawks

We have talked much about character in part 1. But how do you actually represent the process and discourse of character on screen? Think what is available to you:

1. A character's speech
2. A character's actions
3. A character's silence and nonaction/reaction
4. A character's environment: place and time
5. Other characters as they embrace or divide him/her
6. What is said and done when the character is not present
7. The use of representative objects or creatures (pets, favorite items we come to associate as "being" a part of the character)
8. Music (theme motifs) and sound/noise.

How well you shade in your character depends to a large degree on your imaginative weaving of many or all of these elements. Rick in *Casablanca* is best shaded by the haunting tune "As Time Goes By" for it evokes his core experience, love and hurt, which he must learn to transcend. However, gestures such as the final "thumbs up" from the Terminator as he sacrifices his own existence (I almost said "life"!) to save his adopted son and wife-figure in *Terminator 2* can say much more than long monologues. *Even if you have worked out a pitch, treatment, and character study, you still need to find those means to best portray your character on screen.* What individualizing traits become motifs?

What seemingly minor details gradually add up for the audience over the course of your narrative? All these issues have to do with shading in, filling in, your character.

Assignment: Write 10 more pages (pages 10–20).

I need not repeat that continual contact with your partner over your work is essential. Establish a regular meeting time/method. Coffee in a café? Late-night phone calls? The regularity of your meetings will be soothing to you as you work on your script.

In addition: Watch *Time of the Gypsies* again. Now watch *The Godfather.* Discuss with your partner the similarities and differences to character and narrative and texture as well as to *culture* taken by Francis Ford Coppola, Mario Puzo, and Emir Kusturica respectively.

WEEK FIVE: SCENES AND SHOTS

> I want to exist somewhere in between the American mainstream and the individualized European style.
>
> Jim Jarmusch, in Leonard Klady, "Jim Jarmusch"

Read over this section on building the scene which follows.

Ask yourself this: do I really need a scene at all, or is what I have to say really simply a shot between scenes or other shots (montage)?

Assignment: Write 10 more pages (pages 20–30).

In addition: Review *Cinema Paradiso.* Jarmusch speaks of wanting to exist as a filmmaker somewhere between Hollywood and a European cinema of character. To what degree is *Cinema Paradiso* actually like a classical Hollywood narrative and in what ways does it differ? What features of the film do you admire most? Of characterizations? Is there a pattern to the film clips shown in the movie theater? We have touched on the core experience need for a father figure. Explore this point further. To what degree are the characters also emblems of an Italy that no longer exists? What are some of most stunning visual moments? Is there a dominant image?

Building the Scene

It's normal to construct a scene with your main characters on screen talking and/or carrying out some action. But the character-centered script often experiments with even this "given" practice. In *Adam's Rib* (Ruth Gordon and Garson Kanin 1949), Katharine Hepburn and Spencer Tracy are high-powered lawyers on opposite sides of a case and they happen to be man and wife. In one scene as they get ready to go out, the camera holds on their empty bedroom while we hear them carry on a conversation from both sides of the screen as each makes use of his/her own bathroom adjoining the bedroom. As we have stated before, every scene needs at least two levels or reasons to exist. The trick is to make sure those levels are sufficient enough to reveal character strongly, clearly. In the above scene we learn both that each is a strong-willed professional and that what holds them together is their mutual attraction, represented by the marriage bed!

In the spirit of the carnivalesque, think of what might be the typical way of setting up a scene and then think again about how to "open it up" to new possibilities.

We've already said much about scene construction during the Character Development schedule. But let us emphasize how effective *simplicity* can be in a character-driven scene. Take almost any moment in Yasouri Ozu and Kogo Noda's *Tokyo Story* (1953) and you can see how effective simplicity can be. At the end of the film the old father figure has suffered rebuffs from his children in the city and the death of his wife. He sits alone in his now empty house looking out over a river that is highly industrialized. The camera holds on him alone in his house with no music on the soundtrack. What we feel in that silence are all the voices he has come in contact with throughout the narrative. Part of Ozu's genius is that of realizing less is more, very much in the tradition of Japanese painting and haiku poetry.

WEEK SIX: SEQUENCES

I don't think I need quite as much narrative. It's allowable to let fewer things happen, to give a fuller sense of character and small truths rather than the Big Truth.

> Writer/director Paul Schrader, in
> John Brady, *Craft of the Screenwriter*

What happens when we think of our own life in terms of sequences? Do we see both similarity (continuity) and difference (displacement) in the rhythm of our own lives?

Study the section on sequences.

Do a simple diagram based on what you have written and your own script. Can you determine roughly eight to twelve sequences within your script? How does each relate to the other? Do you see a definite development of character from one sequence to the next?

Assignment: Write 10 more pages (pages 30–40).

In addition: Identify the sequences and their patterning in *Thelma & Louise*.

Sequences

Sequences are to scripts what chapters are to novels. They unite minor scenes (bits) and major scenes as a complete unit within the total structure of your narrative. The average feature film contains between eight and twelve sequences. *The Silence of the Lambs* can be divided into ten sequences.

The structure of a sequence is similar to that of the entire script and may be divided into exposition, complication, and reversal/resolution usually capped with a "bridge" bit or scene that moves us into the next sequence (think how the "Raindrops Keep Falling on My Head" scene in *Butch Cassidy and the Sundance Kid* bridges Butch and Sundance's dead-end present and their decision to leave the country: Paul Newman riding backwards on a bike and crashing is a funny visualization of where he's been, where he is, and what will happen).

Not enough attention is paid by most script writers and screenwriting manuals to how important it is to have at least a rough idea of what your sequences will be.

Sequences, once more, suggest flow/variation/development/unity. The advantage, of course, of keeping your sequences in mind is that you have a "half way" means of keeping your whole script in your head as you write. It's easier to tell yourself that you are deep into your fifth sequence than to face the wall of only being "half way" through your script!

...

A sequence checklist:

1. Is there a beginning, middle, and end to each sequence?
2. Does the sequence contain at least one key scene and a variety of shorter scenes/bits?
3. Do I know what the tempo/rhythm/pace of my sequence should be?
4. Have I created a bridge into the sequence and out?
5. Is there an overall theme/unity/mood/atmosphere and/or texture to the sequence?

The opening sequence of *Time of the Gypsies* is geared to plunge us into the midst (and mud!) of gypsy life. Since we are not gypsies and thus are entering another world, each scene or bit reveals an important perspective on how we shall experience and come to terms with the narrative that will unfold, including the fat bride talking to "us" and the gypsy telling us that God took one look at the world of gypsies and left!

This is followed by the gambling scene, long tracking shots of the muddy village, the home life of Perhan, his sister, grandmother, uncle, and, yes, turkey, and quibbling neighbor, and Perhan's boyhood sweetheart who will later become his wife and mother of (his?) child. The unity of the sequence is "gypsy life." When the opening sequence finishes, we are, in effect, ready for anything.

Note also the importance of how you join scenes/bits together. Think of the wide variety of CUTS available to you in moving from one scene to another:

1. Music bridge: Using music to connect two (or more) scenes.
2. Sound/voice bridge: Same as above, sometimes used as a brief intro as the sound/voice/music is actually from the scene about to appear and thus glides us into what will happen next. Observe how well this technique is used in *Slaughterhouse Five* (1972) in which the protagonist, Billy Pilgrim, is "unstuck in time" and thus the voice/sound becomes critical in fading between the past/present/future.
3. Match cuts: Cutting between two similar actions/objects/colors/characters/moods/locations.
4. Contrast cuts: The opposite. Cutting to emphasize difference: From babies playing to an old man dying or from a romantic couple at night by a lake to hard hats pouring concrete in the glare of a summer's day.
5. Smash cut: The same but in aces. A cut that rubs our nose/eye in the total difference (sound/image) between shots/scenes.
6. Dissolves or overlaps or wipes. Each has a reason, an effect as opposed to a simple cut. Do you want to emphasize a certain point? One of these transitions might do it.

WEEK SEVEN: MINOR CHARACTERS AND SUBPLOTS

This is a big town now, Eddie. Some very tough people have checked in here lately. The penalty of growth.
Marlowe to Eddie Mars, in Raymond Chandler's
The Big Sleep

And Raymond Chandler knew how to populate that big town with some of the most darkly appealing minor characters of any American writer past or present.

Assignment: Yes, 10 more pages (pages 40–50).

Review minor characters (part 1) and study the subplots remarks that follow.

Rent Fellini's *Amarcord* (1973) and enjoy the Italian master of the carnivalesque as he presents a highly personal view of his own childhood seen almost literally through the eyes of a small town carnival (the film begins with a feast dedicated to burning Old Man Winter). Note that the whole film is constructed around a gallery of minor characters who make up one large character: a semiautobiographical Fellini. Thus here is a film in which subplots become major points and digressions lead directly to personal truth. See how well Fellini chooses real characters from his locations to populate his films. Each minor character is a distinct type, figure in Fellini's landscape. Taken all together, they add up to the circus (his favorite image) of his life.

Contrast Fellini with *sex, lies and videotape*. Minor characters? Their roles? Subplots? Soderbergh, of course, is the extreme opposite. This is a minimalist landscape that he has portrayed. But, as we have mentioned earlier, part of what is fascinating is how what seems like the main narrative thread is actually the subplot in many ways: the attraction of Graham and Ann for each other.

Let your partner help you decide if you have too many or too few minor characters and subplots. Are they perhaps too strong and dominant? Use this week to help balance these elements with your main protagonists and narrative.

Subplots

Minor characters exist in both the main plot and the subplots. Subplots are clearly that, however: they either intersect with or run parallel or in contrast to the main narrative. Much of what we have said for minor characters applies also to subplotting. How many you need and how you develop them depends on the nature of your main narrative. The major subplot in many films that are not romances on the first level is romance. That is true in *Raging Bull, Thelma & Louise, Cinema Paradiso, My Left Foot,* and *Time of the Gypsies.*

But there are many shades of subplots that also, like the minor characters, mediate, muddle, or carry messages for the main narrative. *It is important to remember that the main character may or may not figure in the subplot(s).*

Similarly, it is necessary to know the difference between your story narrative and your character narrative so that you then can identify everything else as a subplot. Remember we have said that *The Silence of the Lambs* has a story narrative about Clarice wanting to become an FBI agent. Her character narrative has to do with her need to come to terms with her childhood, which involves the death of her mother/father and the lambs.

What else does that leave? There are numerous subplots in *The Silence of the Lambs*, but let us mention five, beginning with Buffalo Bill himself and his murders. He is *not* connected directly with either the story narrative or the character narrative! Yes, it is the most important subplot, but it is only that. A second subplot is a romantic one: will Clarice form an attachment with her boss? Third, there is the friendship that develops between Clarice and Hannibal Lecter. Her avoidance of Dr. Prentiss becomes another subplot, and the female Tennessee senator's efforts to save her daughter from being murdered by Buffalo Bill comprise yet another. All of these taken together reflect, as through a prism, Clarice herself, her conflicts, her desires, her hopes, her fears.

"Subplot" is, of course, ultimately an unsatisfactory term. These plots are not "sub" so much as they are, as noted above, "parallel," "counter," or "interwoven."

WEEK EIGHT: MIDWAY BLUES

You should look straight at a film: that's the only way to see one.
Film is not the art of scholars but of illiterates.
                    Werner Herzog, in Carter J. Wiseman,
                    "The German Film Renaissance"

This whole book has been aimed at helping you become more illiterate in Herzog's sense of acquiring "direct vision."

Assignment: Finish the first half of your script (roughly through page 60).

Half way. Perhaps all has gone smoothly till now. But for many, half way means you feel you will never finish: there's a feeling you've worked hard, said what you had to say, and another sixty pages seem impossible.

Obviously you've been very close to your project for a relatively long time. Take time out and close down the computer. Do something else for a few days. Maybe take the week off if you need to. *Assignment: Do something "uncharacteristic" for you to help clear your head, get a fresh perspective on your project.*

Afterward, and only then, go over this checklist, which should help you get over any midway blues, realizing that with such a fresh glance, you may be able to follow Herzog's advice and look at your own work (with your partner's help) like an "illiterate":

1. Review your treatment. To what degree do you wish to change it or to what degree has it changed on its own?
2. Have you engaged us in a narrative about a determining character with a compelling deep structural need?
3. Is there enough at risk in the first half to hold us for the second half?
4. Have you brought out all the "voices" within the main characters as you wished to do?
5. Have you made use of drama, too, if you are writing a comedy, and vice versa?
6. Have you created the texture and sense of resonance you wish your film to have?
7. Do your characters and narrative continue to surprise you or have you plotted all too carefully?

WEEK NINE: EXPLORING THE SOUNDTRACK

When I was young, I wanted to make complicated films about simple people. Now I wish to make simple films about complicated people.

Yugoslav filmmaker Lazar Stojanovic,
who went to prison for three years (1971–1974)
for his film *Plastic Jesus*

As one young writer told me after listening to this Yugoslav director speak and show his film, "I would love to make a film so dangerous that the authorities would consider throwing me in prison for three years." Unfortunately, such chances appear limited at the moment. But there is much that one can do that is subversive in film, including the often ignored soundtrack.

Assignment: Write pages 60–70.

Consider all the ways in which the soundtrack can strengthen your script. Much attention has already been paid to the use of voiceover and off camera dialogue/speech.

Music has always been important to film, especially to help create and direct appropriate emotional responses. Think of the strong effect *The Crying Game* evokes by beginning in Ireland with Percy Sledge's "When a Man Loves a Woman" and ending in London with "Stand by Your Man." The whole film is summed up in these two songs and their implications for Neil Jordan's narrative. And what would the ending of *Rocky* (1976) be without the strong blaring of the theme song and the super close-up of Rocky's badly battered face?

Thus part of what makes the classical Hollywood film classical is such a heavy-handed use of music to manipulate the audience. But what happens when music becomes counterpoint? Jean-Luc Godard created unusual effects by starting and stopping music at random. Thus there was no way for the audience to simply be pulled through a scene, a sequence, or a film without being forced to think, "Wait a minute. Why is the filmmaker doing this to me?" Obviously Alan Parker got an unusual effect out of American black pop music in *The Commitments* (1991) by having the songs played by young Irish bands. That kind of counterpoint on the soundtrack adds much to our viewer participation in a film.

Similarly, the use of sound (and silence) can be extremely imaginative. What if a typical love scene is playing itself out as two young lovers talk, but a jet flies overhead and we miss what they say to each other? The point is, we KNOW what young lovers say, so why do we need to hear it? Thus the jet could be both a contemporary sign of the times and yet another way we have blown up another movie stereotype.

In addition: Study the sound carefully in one of our five films. Note that *Time of the Gypsies* makes the richest use of music because it is appropriate to the gypsy culture. And hear how silent and insulated a world the characters in *sex, lies and videotape* live in.

Week Ten: Refining Dialogue

No one can articulate a syllable which is not filled with tenderness and fear.

> Jorge Luis Borges, *Labyrinths*

Assignment: Write pages 70–80.

Dialogue has been discussed earlier. Refining it, developing a better ear for it, knowing when to speak and when to have the characters be quiet takes time. Write out all the dialogue you think you need in a scene. Then go back and see how much you can cut out. I still find about a third of the dialogue gets cut as I look back over a script. Don't rewrite your whole script, but do run the experiment of looking at a scene and seeing what you could cut without losing the effect of the scene.

Also keep the "dialogue" between action and speech in mind. A page of only talk suggests only one level of tension. Work to imagine what your characters are DOING while talking. Instead of just talking over coffee in a café, are the two college students tossing pizzas at a part-time job? The action can compliment or work as counterpoint to the dialogue.

The Coen brothers balance action and speech well in their script for

Raising Arizona. The following page is from a scene in which H. I. and Ed who have just stolen a baby to be their own are visited by two of H. I.'s prison buddies, Gale and Evelle, who have just escaped from the penitentiary. At this moment all are eating breakfast in Ed and H. I.'s trailer home. The format in this excerpt is that of the published version:

GALE

... Whyncha breast feed him? You 'pear to be capable.

ED

Mind your own bidnis.

(Through a mouthful of cornflakes):

EVELLE

Ya don't breast feed him, he'll hate you for it later. That's why we wound up in prison.

(Gale blows out smoke and picks up his spoon to start back in on his cornflakes)

GALE

Anyway, that's what Doc Schwartz tells us.

(He is walking in, yawning) (1988, 57)

Dialect, humor, action, all come together with a tension between what is said and what is meant: the two escaped prisoners are suspicious of how H. I. and Ed came to have a baby in so short a time.

Look at your own dialogue work. Is there, as Borges claims, both tenderness and fear? Are there, in other words, various voices being heard through each character's speech?

WEEK ELEVEN: HUMOR AND DRAMA

How can I lose? Twelve ball. How can I lose? Because you were right. It's not enough that you just have talent. You gotta have character, too. Four ball. Yeah, I sure got character now. I picked it up in a hotel room in Louisville.

Paul Newman, in The Hustler

Rain Man (Ronald Bass and Barry Morrow 1987) was one of the more serious films to come from Hollywood in recent years. And yet at the most tense moments of this drama about a greedy brother who must learn to connect and be more selfless (Tom Cruise) and an older one who is an autistic savant (Dustin Hoffman) and who must face the reality that he will never be "normal," humor is brought in to express the deepest feelings. The ending in which the two brothers are parting is actually an embracing ending. For despite the forthcoming separation, the newly formed concern for each other which we have witnessed has assured them and us that distance cannot erode the effects of shared love they have experienced. We are waiting for some very serious words to be expressed on both sides, but instead we have Dustin Hoffman saying "Screw K-Mart." Everyone laughs, but most of us have tears in our eyes as well. For the truth is that humor can make a dramatic moment even sharper. "Screw K-Mart" tells us that Dustin has learned from his bullheaded brother, admires him, and will carry his spirit with him to the home he must go to.

Think of deepening the dramatic effect in your serious scenes with humor.

The opposite is true as well: deepen a comedy with drama. Joe Dante's *Matinee* (1992) stars John Goodman as a sleazey William Castle–styled cheap horror flick maker touring his own films from town to town. But the film is given resonance by darkening this carnival as the context for the times—1962—is the Cuban Missile Crisis that was such a very real fear at the time. Thus the true fear of nuclear war is played off against the "movie fear" of cheap horror films in a way that takes the script beyond the level of simple *Ferris Bueller's Day Off* (John Hughes 1986) slapstick.

Assignment: Complete pages 80–90.

Week Twelve: Final Reversals

Nature, Mr. Allnut, is what we are put into this world to rise above.
Katharine Hepburn to Humphrey Bogart,
in *The African Queen*

Two important reversals happen at this 90–100 minute mark in *Time of the Gypsies* to set up the final "replacement" that will occur: Perhan is reunited with his sister after years of separation and, in one more embracing movement, he is joined with the young boy she claims is his son. These two events set into motion the conclusion of the film which is Perhan's desire for revenge against the Godfather who had cheated and lied to him and who had thus denied him even the substitute blessing of a substitute father.

In writing this week, you must be sure to have your final reversals in place. What event(s) will lead your main character to his or her final embrace or separation? Finally, is that reversal strong enough to sustain all that you have built before it?

Assignment: You should arrive at page 100 or close to it this week.

WEEK THIRTEEN: PARTING SHOTS

> Made it, Ma. Top of the world!
>> James Cagney, before dying in *White Heat*

Do not draw out your ending. Cagney's dying words are brief and terribly ironic. We hate and admire him at the same time as the kid who had nothing, gained the world dishonestly, and died for it. This does not mean that the last scene has to be very short, but it is to say you should return to your closing image (has it changed or are you still satisfied?) and *simplify it* so that it has the final impact you want it to have. *Annie Hall* ends with a shot of a busy New York street with Woody Allen no longer facing us on camera, but speaking to us, alone, from off camera. *He still has a relationship with us the viewer even if the relationship with Annie is over*, and the last image of the street connects him with an ongoing life that he must return to. Simple, strong, effective, and, in this case, open-ended.

Many critics have pointed out that cinema is a medium of excess: they mean that there is so much to take in within the frame and in the flow of a film that no filmmaker can control all responses, effects created. And Wallace Martin has remarked about narrative in general that "narratives, no matter how peppered with generalizations, always provide more information or food for thought than they have digested" (1986, 187). *Thus, as you reach page 110, make sure you have sharpened your closing images.*

WEEK FOURTEEN: A TIME OF RELEASE

> Go, and never darken my towels again!
>> Groucho, in *Duck Soup*

Relief and release are the order of the week. You are completing your journey and should celebrate with your own carnival. In the next section we discuss what to do once the time of release comes to an end and you are ready to look at your rough draft again.

But before writing "the end," take a long moment to ask yourself: has the core characteristic need of my character been met, resolved, or at least framed clearly, strongly enough to leave my audience with the overall feeling I want them to leave the theater with?

If so, congratulations!

If not, do what you need to do so that you can write "the end" with a feeling that you have truly ended your script and not just stopped writing.

Do, however, consider the following:

Endings

In part 2 you were asked to choose your final shot: either one that leans toward an "embrace" or one that "divides" by leaving the individual alone.

Generally, Hollywood pushes for the upbeat ending with an embrace. It seems to be part of the fabric of our culture: no matter how bad things get, there is always some hope. But upbeat does not necessarily mean simplistic, unrealistic, sugar-coated. In fact, note how the MIXED ending, what we could perhaps call the BITTERSWEET ending, predominates: E. T. goes home (that's what "it" wanted) leaving all the Earthlings tearful as well as pleased; Clarice becomes an FBI agent, but Hannibal Lecter is loose and ready to strike again; Thelma and Louise establish an honest, joyful friendship but die; Rick in *Casablanca* acts with honesty and courage in helping the cause of freedom, but it costs him his one true love; Perhan kills the gypsy godfather, but he in turn is killed, and his son perpetuates the gypsy ethos by stealing the coins from his father's eyes; Rocky wins the love of Talia Shire and his own self-esteem but loses the boxing match with the Champ; the main protagonist in *Cinema Paradiso* relives the pleasures and pain of his childhood in a small Italian town, but he has lost his mentor, his youth, a more simple Italy that is gone forever. "Upbeat" in this sense suggests not a fantasy triumph over simple evils, but an often painful acceptance and transcendence of the protagonist's situation.

Finally consider the difference between the open and closed ending. The closed ending suggests the narrative is, for all purposes, completely over. We are not really invited to think of what happens the next day or in a possible sequel. The open ending suggests that the narrative has been a slice of life, a part of an ongoing reality and thus *the story is not over*. Consider these possible endings in relationship to your script:

1. THE CIRCULAR ENDING

We end as we began, but with an important difference: your story has taken place. Martin Scorsese's *Cape Fear* ends with the daughter, the narrator, once again facing the camera (us) and concluding the tale. *Cin-*

ema Paradiso ends with the main protagonist in the present again, facing his life as an adult after reliving his childhood. Both of these examples could also be called FRAME ENDINGS since the opening-closing scenes frame the rest of the narrative occurring at a separate (flashback) time. A nonframe circular ending would be like the one in Alain Tanner's *Jonah Who Will Be 25 in the Year 2000* (1976) in which one of the main characters buys cigarettes in the opening, complaining about how expensive they are and then, in the final shot, returns to the same shop only to find the price has gone up yet again. Time has passed, but his behavior is the same.

2. The Fantasy Triumph Ending

The Coen brothers' *Raising Arizona* (1987) ends with H. I. once again narrating to us (thus circularity as noted above), but this time he fantasizes the future in which they are grandparents surrounded by family and kids at a Thanksgiving dinner. It is clear, however, that this is taking place only in H. I.'s mind; thus we feel the poignancy of the moment.

3. The Embrace/Blessing

Films that are character- and relationship-centered as opposed to issue/location/justice oriented must show us a coming together, an acceptance, a passing of the blessing of love/friendship/bonding by the end. Whether this is the last shot/sequence or simply the highlight of act 3 is another matter. But ending on the embrace, the kiss, the hug signals healing, community, family, or joined lives. *Rocky* ends not with the fight but with his embrace of true love, played by Talia Shire. In *Down and Out in Beverly Hills*, Nick Nolte, the street bum who has shaken up a rich and spoiled California family, is accepted back into the family as all embrace him. They need him!

4. Goin' Down the Road . . . Alone

Chaplin made a career out of the Tramp, his back to the camera, going down the road . . . of life . . . alone. Being alone may be the message and thus should be the image. This is true also for "justice"-oriented films (genres of determinate space) such as the western and the gangster/crime film: Henry Fonda riding off into the landscape in *My Darling Clementine* or Bogart as detective going off down the street in any number of detective/crime films.

5. The Freeze Frame Ending

The emphasis here is on technique for either of the above purposes. François Truffaut's *400 Blows* captured world attention in 1959 as his troubled young protagonist escapes from a reform school and runs to the sea only to discover he really has no place to go and nobody to turn to: freeze frame on his troubled face. Used well, the freeze frame simply states: we are not ending, we are just STOPPING. *Butch Cassidy and the Sundance Kid* uses the freeze frame for a slightly different effect. Butch and Sundance run into the open and die in a storm of Bolivian bullets. The freeze frame spares us their violent death, allowing us to savor them as they were while the soundtrack continues complete with the volleys of bullets reminding us of the reality of what is happening. Beware, however. The freeze frame has for many films become an awkward cliché that says "we don't know how to end so we will just STOP!"

6. The Layered Ending

Some films delight in giving us a series of endings, as if to say, (1) it is never really over, (2) choose your own ending. *Time of the Gypsies finally* ends in a freeze frame of the Uncle a là Chaplin, alone and with his back to the camera. But there are at least four other endings: (1) Perhan being shot (again) by the angry new bride of the godfather and his body falling onto a passing train (defeat); (2) the FANTASY TRIUMPH vision he has as he lies dying on the train (personal victory); (3) the ritual celebration of Perhan's death as everyone gathers, including his son (community continues); (4) his son's stealing of the coins from his father's eyes and his escape outside, alone (focus on being alone). Careful, if you use this approach, that you don't appear to be simply inconclusive!

7. The Extreme Long Shot

Use this shot for character(s) in a landscape, the long view of . . . life, everything. *Alice in the Cities* (Wim Wenders 1977): We leave the intense interior close-up in a train on Alice and the "guardian" and move to what becomes a reverse zoom bird's-eye view of the train moving along through the countryside along a river with the sea in the distance. A chance for the audience to breathe and put all in "perspective" after the "close-up" of the narrative.

Works Cited in Part III

Allen, Woody. *Four Films of Woody Allen.* New York: Random House, 1980.

Aristophanes. *The Complete Plays of Aristophanes.* Ed. Moses Hadas. New York: Bantam, 1971.

Borges, Jorge Luis. *Labyrinths.* New York: New Directions, 1964.

Brady, John. *The Craft of the Screenwriter.* New York: Touchstone Books, 1981.

Chandler, Raymond. *The Big Sleep*. New York: Ballantine Books, 1939.

Coen, Joel, and Ethan Coen. *Raising Arizona*. New York: St. Martin's Press, 1988.

Coveny, William. Personal interview, New Orleans, March 1992.

Kalmer, Bert, and Harry Rubin. *Duck Soup*. 1939.

Kellog, Virginia. *White Heat*. 1949.

King, Viki. *How to Write a Movie in 21 Days*. New York: Harper & Row, 1988.

Klady, Leonard. "Jim Jarmusch." *American Film* (October 1986): 46.

Kozloff, Sarah. *Invisible Storytellers: Voice-Over Narration in American Fiction Film*. Berkeley, Los Angeles, London: University of California Press, 1988.

Martin, Wallace. *Recent Theories of Narrative*. Ithaca: Cornell University Press, 1986.

McBride, Joseph. *Hawks on Hawks*. Berkeley, Los Angeles, London: University of California Press, 1982.

McMurtry, Larry. *Film Flam: Essays on Hollywood*. New York: Touchstone Books, 1988.

Stojanovic, Lazar. Personal interview. Ann Arbor, November 1991.

Tevis, Walter. *The Hustler*. Screenplay by Robert Rossen and Sidney Carroll.

Truffaut, François. *The Films in My Life*. Trans. Leonard Mayhew. New York: Touchstone Books, 1985.

Ulmer, Gregory. *Teletheory: Grammatology in the Age of Video*. New York: Routledge, 1989.

Welty, Eudora. *One Writer's Beginnings*. New York: Warner Books, 1984.

Wiseman, Carter J. "The German Film Renaissance." *Newsweek*, 2 February 1976, p. 44.

PART IV

LAUNCHING YOUR SCRIPT

I read recently that Americans are buying used cars for an average of $6,000 and I thought, Why don't they take the bus to work and make a feature film instead?

Rick Schmidt,
Feature Filmmaking at Used-Car Prices

CHAPTER TEN

From Rewrite to Screen: An Overview of Options

Screenwriting Computer Software

I find that there is no universal or even majority consensus on the value and/or use of screenwriting software. Some swear by these programs, other writers I talk to are still writing scripts by long hand, and Anna Hamilton Phelan who wrote *Gorillas in the Mist* reportedly writes her scripts on one continuous piece of butcher paper! I have not yet made the move to the following software programs, but I offer information for those who wish to try:

COLLABORATOR
Collaborator Systems, Inc., P.O. Box 57557, Sherman Oaks, CA 91403. Phone: (818) 980-2943.

FINAL DRAFT
MacToolkit, 1234 Sixth St., Suite 204, Santa Monica, CA 90401. Phone: (310) 395-4242.

MOVIE MASTER
Comprehensive Cinema Software, 148 Veterans Drive, Northvale, N.J. 07647. Phone: (201) 767-7990.

SCRIPT PERFECTION
ScriptPerfection Enterprises, 3425 Lebon Drive, Suite 725, San Diego, CA 92122-5243. Phone: (619) 455-6635.

SCRIPTOR
Screenplay Systems, 150 East Olive Ave., Suite 203, Burbank, CA 91502. Phone: (818) 843-6557.

Truby's Writers Studio, 1739 Midvale Ave., Los Angeles, CA 90024.
Phone: (800) 33-TRUBY.

THE WARREN SCRIPT APPLICATIONS FOR WORD FOR WINDOWS
The Writers Computer Store, 11317 Santa Monica Blvd.,
Los Angeles, CA. 90025. Phone: (310) 479-7774.

REGISTERING YOUR SCRIPT

So you've finished your script. *Register it immediately*. This should come automatically: you write "the end" and then drop a copy in the mail to the Writers Guild of America either east or west; it doesn't matter, though most writers tend to use "west" simply because it is in Hollywood. The address is:

WRITERS GUILD OF AMERICA WEST, INC.
8955 Beverly Boulevard
Los Angeles, CA 90048
Phone: (310) 550-1000

Registration is $20. Remember that registration is excellent *insurance* but it is not total protection. As the Guild states: "Registration does not confer any statutory protection. It merely provides evidence of the writer's claim to authorship of the literary material involved and of the date of its completion" (application form).

Publicity Director Cheryl Rhoden of the Guild does make it clear that the legal department settles hundreds of arbitration cases a year and thus is a well-respected force in the filmmaking process. She also suggests that those who are eligible to join the 7,000-plus membership gain many advantages since the Guild is extremely active on many fronts including workshops, screenings, social action (a team of screenwriters went to Bosnia to assess the situation firsthand in 1992), and research.

Even for those who are not members of the Guild (and the Guild is speaking of changing the membership requirements to include authors of books as well as of scripts), it is possible to subscribe to their worthwhile journal, *The Journal of the Writers Guild of America west*. Contact through the above address and send $40 for nonmembers, $20 for members.

The Rewrite

Finishing your script is cause for celebration. So celebrate! A party, a week at the beach, a trip abroad, a month of sleeping late. Whatever you wish! You deserve it.

But after the celebration, my advice is to take a break and forget about the script for as long as it takes to feel refreshed, relieved, recharged.

Then read it again with a calm, clear eye, make notes, and then make changes. Big ones if you have to. Only then, when you are pleased with your first rewrite, make five copies and pass them out to those you trust to tell you the truth. Better yet, try to give one to a close friend, one to a medium-close friend, and one to a colleague or acquaintance you don't know too well. That leaves two more: try for someone older than you and someone younger than you and/or male if you are female and vice versa. That should guarantee some good feedback.

Listen closely to what these readers say. Maybe you think they are picky, maybe too one-sided, but never mind. Hear them out and then sort out what you've heard and think through these comments before going for another rewrite.

Then rewrite.

Are you more pleased? Good. Now seek out any professional help you can in your community. Is there a professional screenwriter in town and will he/she agree to read your work for a reasonable fee? If so, it's money well spent. Is there a screenwriters' network or "workshop group" that meets once a month or every other week? If so, join. If not, maybe you can start one. The support members of such groups give each other is extremely valuable. Remember, two people and you have partners; three and you have a support group. *The worst thing a screenwriter has to fear is not so much fear itself but ISOLATION.* Find kindred souls!

When your script sparkles and shines as brightly as you can make it sparkle and shine, then see about what follows in this section: that is, what to do with your work to gain recognition and reward.

SCREENWRITING CONTESTS

Screenwriting contests are good news for new writers. With each year that passes, more industry officials recognize that one of the best ways for them to find out what new voices are Out There is to look over the winners of national or even local screenwriting competitions. India-born writer Radha Bharadwaj, for instance, lives in the Los Angeles area but had not been able to get studio folk interested in her scripts. But once she entered and won the Nicholls Competition for her two-character script, *Closetland*, she found Ron Howard Productions contacting her and becoming the producer of this $2 million project. Hers is not an isolated story. So the gospel is, Thou Shalt Enter!

Note: contests come and go and change form constantly. Thus the need to check on each of these and keep your eyes open for new contests as they appear.

THE AFI MINORITY SCREENWRITER CONTEST
$500 plus a scene showcase. Limited to ethnic minorities including blacks, Latinos, Asians, and Native Americans. Send SASE to MINORITY SCREENWRITER'S CONTEST, AFI Alumni Writers Workshop, P.O. Box 69799, Los Angeles, CA 90069.

AMERICAN INDEPENDENT PRODUCTIONS SCREENPLAY CONTEST
A new contest on the block, which began in 1992. It is truly a national contest and cash prizes are offered. Contact: Screenplay Contest, P.O. Box 16526, Hattiesburg, MS 39402.

AMERICA'S BEST
$25,000 in prizes. Contact: The Writer's Foundation, Inc., 1801 Burnet Ave., Syracuse, NY 13206. January deadlines.

AUNT JACK PRODUCTIONS SCREENWRITING COMPETITION
A new contest focusing on "stories based on Southern themes." A $1,000 winning prize and one-year option by Aunt Jack productions. Aunt Jack Productions, 354 S. Orange Dr., Los Angeles, CA 90036. $15 fee.

CHRISTOPHER COLUMBUS SCREENPLAY DISCOVERY AWARDS
1. Up to twelve scripts selected for development based on "execution, salability and originality."
2. Discovery of the Month: a script introduced to top agents, etc.
3. Options up to $10,000 per screenplay.
4. Screenplay Discovery of the Year.

Contact: The CCS Entertainment Group Christopher Columbus Screenplay Discovery Awards, 433 N. Camden Dr., Suite 600, Beverly Hills, CA 90210. $45 fee.

THE FLORIDA STATE SCREENWRITERS' COMPETITION
$500 for the winner who happens to be a Florida resident with a script 75 percent set in Florida! Contact: Florida Screenwriters'

Contest, Division of Humanities, Box GD, Jacksonville University, Jacksonville, Florida 32211.

THE HOUSTON INTERNATIONAL FILM AND VIDEO FESTIVAL

Five categories and four winners in each. Application = $80. (Comedy, Dramatic/adaptation; Dramatic original; Historical Period film; Fantasy/Science Fiction). Contact: Worldfest/Houston, P.O. Box 56566, Houston, TX 77256.

MALCOLM-VINCENT SCREENWRITING COMPETITION

Application fee: $45. $5,000 first prize, $2,500 second, $1,500 third, and $1,000 fourth. Deadline tends to be late January. Address: 279 S. Beverly Drive, Suite 17, Beverly Hills, CA 90212.

NATE MONASTER MEMORIAL WRITING COMPETITION

Sponsor: UBU Productions and the University Film & Video Association. Scripts accepted in the following genres: half-hour television comedy, one-hour television drama or television movie. TELEVISION SCRIPTS ONLY. No application fee. For information, contact: THE NATE MONASTER MEMORIAL WRITING COMPETITION Communications Dept., Loyola Marymount University, Loyola Blvd. and W. 80th St., Los Angeles, CA 90045. Phone: (310) 338-1855 or call Marlene Saritzky at UBU Productions, (213) 204-0404.

THE NEW PROFESSIONAL THEATRE SCREENWRITING/
PLAYWRITING FESTIVAL

$1,500 grant. "NPT is a company with an emphasis on providing minority employment, however all writers are encouraged to submit scripts." Send scripts with SASE to: New Professional Theatre, Sheila Davis, 443 W. 50th St., New York, NY 10019.

SCRIPT

(Screenwriting Coalition for Industry Professionals and Teachers), a constituency group of the University Film & Video Association (UFVA) often sponsors television and film script contests. Contact: William Miller, School of Telecommunications, Ohio University, Athens, OH 45701-2979.

THE TELEFILM CANADA PROJECT

$15,000 to write up story ideas that win. Requirement: you must be a citizen of Canada who has had at least two scripts made previ-

ously (now *that's* restrictive!). Contact: Telefilm Canada, Tour de la
Banque Nationale, 600 de la Gauchertierre St. West, 14th Fl.,
Montreal, Quebec H3B 4L2.

THE VIRGINIA STATE GOVERNOR'S SCREENWRITING COMPETITION
$500 first prize. Must have lived in Virigina during the past year.
And—get this—at least 75 percent of the script must take place in
Virginia! Three winners in 1991. Contact: Virginia Film Office,
1021 East Cary St., Richmond, Virginia 23219.

THE WARNER BROS/LORIMAR TELEVISION SERIES WRITING COMPETITION
Prizes for half hour and hour series entries. Deadlines tend to be
June 1. $20 entry fee or $10 for students. Contact: William Miller,
Coordinator School of Telecommunications, Ohio University,
Athens, OH 45701-2979.

FELLOWSHIPS

It's an encouraging sign that there appear to be more organizations, studios, and groups interested in setting up fellowships for filmmakers including screenwriters. The idea is simple: those new writers who show
some talent should be encouraged. This list is not complete, for the field
is changing constantly. But take this as a beginning and stay alert to
other script internship/fellowship possibilities.

I have not listed the endless number of sources—local, regional, and
national—to which you can apply for grants of various sorts. Let it suffice to say that grants for screenwriters are most likely offered by everyone from your state's arts council and state's humanities council up to
and including the National Endowment for the Arts and the National
Endowment for the Humanities, and a newcomer, ITS (Independent
Television Service), which was set up in 1990 as an alternative to what
they see as a status quo–oriented PBS television. Their mission statement
is encouraging: "To bring to public television audiences innovative programming that involves creative risks and which addresses the needs of
unserved or underserved audiences, particularly minorities and children." For more about ITS, contact: ITS, P.O. Box 65797, Saint Paul,
MN, 55165. Phone: (612) 225-9035.

THE AMERICAN FILM INSTITUTE
GARY HENDLER MINORITY FILMMAKERS PROGRAM
Period: 10 months. Stipend: $1,200 a month. Screenwriting is one of

six "tracks" offered. Contact: 2021 North Western Ave.,
Los Angeles, CA 90027. May deadlines.

THE NICHOLL FELLOWSHIPS
These offer up to five awards of $20,000 each to new screenwriters.
Deadlines are usually May 1. For information write: The Nicholl
Fellowships, Academy of Motion Picture Arts and Sciences, Dept. F,
8949 Wilshire Blvd., Beverly Hills, CA 90211-1972.

THE PARAMOUNT/EDDIE MURPHY FELLOWSHIPS
The Paramount Fellowship is open only to graduate students at
NYU, Columbia, USC, UCLA, or AFI. For the Eddie Murphy–
Paramount Fellowship, you must be enrolled at Howard or Hanson
Universities in Washington, DC. Fellowships provide $20,000–
30,000 and a year at the Paramount Studios program.

THE SUNDANCE INSTITUTE
Founded by Robert Redford, Sundance now sponsors the well-
respected January Festival for American independent cinema. And
though its guidelines have changed from year to year, the Institute
has nourished many regional and aspiring filmmakers over more
than a decade with an intensive program that selects and brings a
handful of fellows to Utah or California to be teamed up with some
of the best professionals in the field to look over their shoulders and
help out. Glen Pitre, a Harvard-educated Cajun from Cut Off,
Louisiana, for instance, was selected back in 1985 and wound up
completing his nineteenth-century Cajun story about a male
"healer" and his love for a married woman, *Belizaire the Cajun*
(1986), thanks in large part to the support that Sundance provided.
It's mission statement says, in part, "The Institute provides a context
in which writers, directors, producers, and others with film projects
of appropriate nature can advance their skills." Contact: Sundance
Institute, 10202 W. Washington Blvd., Columbia Pictures Entertainment, Culver City, CA 90232.

THE WALT DISNEY STUDIOS FELLOWSHIP PROGRAM
In 1992, the Walt Disney Pictures and Television Studios offered up
to twenty-five year-long fellowships for writers at $30,000 each.
Deadlines are February 1 and submissions include either a com-
pleted original screenplay or a three-act play. For television you
may submit a half-hour script for a current program. Contact:
Brenda Vangsness, Program Administrator, The Walt Disney
Studios, 500 South Buena Vista St., Burbank, CA 91521-0880.
Phone: (818) 560-6894.

THINK GLOBALLY:
THE JOYS OF FOREIGN PROJECTS/CONTACTS

My own personal experience as a screenwriter living in New Orleans and working in Hollywood, New York, Belgrade, Athens, Moscow, St. Petersburg, Budapest, and elsewhere convinces me that *screenwriters today must think globally in terms of working with foreign filmmakers who need American screenwriters, in terms of foreign investment for American productions, and in terms of coproductions set abroad.* No writer today should ignore the fact that we are a global television village despite ethnic hatreds and rising nationalism. Add to this the Hollywood statistic that over 50 percent of its income is from abroad, and you begin to see how seriously you should take foreign involvement at whatever level of script development, packaging, producing, distribution/consumption.

"It's now cheaper for Russians to buy a bad American film than to make a good Russian one," commented one Russian friend in 1992. The Russian box office is now dominated by many American films I have never heard of and I'm sure you haven't either (they do not have the hard currency to buy recent hit releases). And turning on television anywhere in the world these days (yes, even in Albania now!), American product comes back to you. Yes, the smallest Russian village watches CBS's "Santa Barbara," and "Dallas" has been memorized by audiences everywhere.

Think globally and write locally, to modify the popular bumper sticker.

All this points to the need for you to learn as much as you can about the foreign markets and to make connections. How do you do this without leaving the country? Film festivals and film markets such as the very important Los Angeles Film Market held in February each year.

You can, of course, travel and meet filmmakers abroad. But that is expensive and based on a large element of chance. Better to strike up an acquaintance at a festival and then follow through. I am speaking about the need to familiarize yourself with the foreign films shown at a festival, and then the need to try and meet the filmmakers at whatever spot seems the most likely depending on the festival: press conferences, parties, hotel lobbies, whatever.

You can't imagine what an opportunity this may be for someone wishing to start out, for at least five good reasons:

1. Foreign filmmakers now realize they need American writers to produce stories/characters with the "American touch" that they know sells. It's not enough for a film to be in English, as an endless list of losing foreign-produced films have shown. *They need you!* This means they

may need you to flesh out one of their ideas or to take on your script and ideas. Either way, you win. One Hungarian director friend, for instance, asked me to send him a screenwriter. "What about the young Hungarian writers who should be lining up to work with you?" I replied. "There are no young Hungarian screenwriters!" was his answer. Thus, upon return I found that several talented young writers were indeed ready to pack and fly. As well they should be!

2. Many foreign producers have money and are eager to invest in English language films that may be shot in their countries. I met an Indian producer living in London once who realized he had learned enough from watching the biggest filmmaking industry in the world—the Indian film business—to move on to the international scene. When I met him, he had productions going, all in English, in Russia, England, France, and elsewhere.

3. My experience is that foreign filmmakers often are much, much faster in getting a film made than Hollywood. Because production units are smaller and, in many countries, made up of people who really do know each other well, time, money, energy are saved. Thus you do have a solid chance of seeing your script on the screen in a relatively brief period of time.

4. Foreign or coproduction films tend to pay a lot more attention to the screenwriter. It's fun and satisfying to be included on a project from beginning to final answer print. Often, for instance, as an American writer, you may be asked to sit in on the editing so that the film has an "American pace" or "American flavor" in editing.

5. Who would turn down the chance to travel anyway? There is something exciting about filming abroad as opposed to Gary, Indiana or in a small town in Texas. As I write this, I have been asked to be a consultant on a Russian kind of *E.T.* film being shot in St. Petersburg. Fine. I enjoy the chance to visit Russia, see friends, see new sights. Also I am currently involved in projects with filmmakers in Greece, Hungary, and what remains of Yugoslavia. More than the money—which of course is much less than offered by Hollywood when Hollywood finally does get around to writing checks—I've savored the friendships, the travel, the experiences, and even the frustrations of work abroad.

We should add to the list the perk that if you work with someone you probably met at a festival, the chances are your film with him or her will also wind up on the festival circuit. Nothing wrong with that either!

But I've saved till last the most important reason a new American screenwriter should think about working with a foreign filmmaker: you will learn a lot. Remember that, in general, much of foreign cinema is much more character-centered than American cinema has tended to be. The experience of trying to find a happy middle ground between your

"American" perspective and the foreign filmmaker's view of narrative, culture, character, life, cannot help but be an engaging, growing adventure. Such a cross-cultural carnival often ends in both parties being enriched.

STALKING NORTH AMERICAN FILM FESTIVALS

One of the best guides to all film fests as well as to what is happening around the world each year in film is Peter Cowie's *International Film Guide* published by *Variety* in London and Hollywood each year. It's not always easy to find in the bookstores, so you may wish to order it. Address: Cahners Publishing, Ltd., 34-35 Newman St., London, WIP 3PD, England.

August-September

THE MONTREAL WORLD FILM FESTIVAL
Especially strong in foreign filmmakers and films. The Montreal Festival takes place at the end of August for 10 days through the Labor Day weekend. Over 300 films from over 50 nations are screened in 7 theaters with lots of chances to meet filmmakers. For information, contact: THE MONTREAL WORLD FILM FESTIVAL, 1455 Boulevard de Maisonneuve Ouest, Montreal, Quebec, Canada H3G 1M8. Phone: (514) 933-9699. FAX: (514) 848-3886.

TORONTO INTERNATIONAL FILM FESTIVAL
This fest, which takes place for roughly 10 days overlapping with the Montreal festival, has become the largest in North America. Especially important for the many American as well as foreign filmmakers/producers/executives who attend. Hundreds of films in a variety of theaters. Contact: The Toronto International Film Festival, 70 Carlton St., Toronto, Canada M5B 1L7. Phone: (416) 967-7371.

TELLURIDE FILM FESTIVAL
A well-established festival high in the Rockies that is small, expensive, and fun if you can get there and stay there, held at the end of August and into early September, overlapping with Montreal and Toronto. Contact either National Film Preserve, P.O. Box 81156, Hanover, NH 03756, or 119 Colorado Ave., Telluride, CO 81435. Phone: (303) 728-4401.

THE NEW YORK FILM FESTIVAL

It's surprising how much attention this festival gets, given its small size—roughly 20 films most of which have already played Cannes, Montreal, or Toronto. Nevertheless, it is a window of opportunity for those on the East Coast to catch some of the best new films, foreign and American. Opportunities to meet filmmakers are not as many as at Montreal, Toronto, or some of the other festivals, but where there's a will there's a way. Contact: The Film Society of Lincoln Center, Lincoln Center, 140 West 65th St., New York, NY 10023. Phone: (212) 875-5610.

VANCOUVER INTERNATIONAL FILM FESTIVAL

A "quiet" festival that deserves more attention than it gets. It spans the end of September into the first two weeks of October. Smaller than Montreal and Toronto but larger than New York. Those who attend like the more laid-back atmosphere and eclectic program of past and present, East and West, mainline and experimental films. Contact: #303-788 Beatty St., Vancouver, BC, Canada V6B 2M1. Phone: (604) 685-0260. FAX: (604) 688-8221.

October

CHICAGO FILM FESTIVAL

Since 1964, this modest fest with a strong track record has been a showcase in the Midwest. Contact: Chicago Film Festival, 415 North Dearborn Ave., Chicago, IL 60610. Phone: (312) 644-3400.

January

PARK CITY: SUNDANCE U.S. FILM FESTIVAL

Now considered the number one festival for new American cinema, especially minority and independent productions. This is the fest that discovered *sex, lies and videotape* and other films that began as independent productions and managed to find wide distribution. Contact: Sundance U.S. Film Festival, 19 Exchange Place, Salt Lake City, UT 84111. Phone: (801) 329-3456.

February

AMERICAN FILM MARKET (LOS ANGELES)

Beginning in 1981, this market has become more important than Cannes for the business of film for American film companies and foreign companies wishing to crack the American market. Held in late February in Los Angeles. Contact: The American Film Market Association, 12424 Wilshire Blvd., Suite 600, Los Angeles, CA 90025. Phone: (213) 447-1555.

April

SAN FRANCISCO INTERNATIONAL FILM FESTIVAL
For over thirty years, this festival has been one of the very top American showcases for important foreign films as well as new independent voices in cinema. Contact: San Francisco International Film Festival, 1560 Fillmore St., San Francisco, CA 94115. Phone: (415) 567-4641.

AFI (AMERICAN FILM INSTITUTE) LOS ANGELES FILM FESTIVAL
A relative newcomer, this festival has grown to be a real eye-opener in the past few years. End of April and early May, with about 200 films around the city. For information, call (213) 520-2000.

WRITING, DIRECTING, AND
PRODUCING YOUR OWN SCRIPT

The irony of filmmaking in our time is great: although Hollywood has come up with ever-increasing bloated budgets, the means of production—especially in the field of video technology—have steadily fallen into the hands of the average consumer. The means of distribution have also increased with the rise of cable television, made-for-video markets, and the growth of foreign sales.

Yes, it's good to keep one eye on the Industry and learn all you can as you write scripts you hope you can find an agent for—so that an agent can represent you and help you get a foot in the door. *But you should also think small and try your hand at a script that could be shot in your area for next to nothing.*

Start by reading Rick Schmidt's *Feature Filmmaking at Used-Car Prices: How to Write, Produce, Direct, Film, Edit, and Promote a Feature-Length Film for Less Than $10,000.* Read it forwards and backwards. Even more important than the step-by-step details is Schmidt's spirit and vision: DO IT! One former student wrote and starred in a feature film shot for $2,000. It's not a masterpiece, *but it is a completed film!* And as I write this, it is already playing at its third film festival and being invited to its next.

Consider these points:

1. There is absolutely no reason why you can't write and film scenes on a simple video camera and use this approach to refine your craft.

2. More than likely, there are local film/video organizations in your area that can help you with cheap-to-rent equipment for filming and editing. More films, especially documentaries, than I care to count have been made with such support in the New Orleans area through the New Orleans Video Access Center. Also in this category would be local Cable Access channels. Sign up and show up and make use of what they have to offer. And then:

3. Get your project on local cable or local television. It should not be that hard.

4. Then begin to be more ambitious: think about a feature script that is either a "chamber piece"—made for just a few characters with very few locations (*sex, lies and videotape* is such an easily controlled project), or one that can take advantage of events, locations, talent you know of. I've lived in Greece for six years. How can you rival the scenery? You've already saved millions! Now to find the slimmest of stories and you see how you could make either your own tragedy like Cacoyannis' *Iphigenia* (1977), comedy like Jules Dassin's *Never On Sunday* (1960), or Hollywood erotic teen pic like *The Blue Lagoon* (Douglas Day Stewart 1980).

Screenwriter Manny Kotto whose script *The Ticking Man* was part of the 1990 rush for selling scripts for over a million dollars (the film is as yet to be produced) says he got his foot in the door another way. First he had the good fortune to go through the AFI fellowship program. But then he met actress Tippi Hedren while working a minor job and asked if she would consider starring in a short he wished to put together. She agreed, he shot it, and he had a fine classy sample to show around Los Angeles. We could go on for pages with such creative examples. The point, however, is clear: be creative not only on paper but in planning what and how to shoot!

5. Think about the growing made-for-video market, especially for genre pictures. Horror and porno top the list, of course, in this area. Former students have shot and sold cheapie horror films to national video chains where millions of viewers apparently will forgo all technical accomplishments to find new chills. Or maybe the rough edges of such productions provide part of their charm. Either way, this market will continue to grow.

6. If you are going for a truly character-centered script that you have shot yourself, think of aiming the final film at festivals. As the founding father of the New Orleans Film and Video Festival, I have encouraged local filmmakers to premiere their works and enter other festivals else-

where with many promising results. One New Orleans local hour-long piece, *Maggie May* (Markia Menutis and Robert Surgi 1990), went the festival circuit from New Orleans to Chicago to Berlin and to AFI in Los Angeles. That's a lot of attention and the beginning of many important industry connections.

Finally, I have no section on how to get an agent and break into Hollywood. I bow to the industry-driven books in this area, including Syd Field's *Selling a Screenplay: The Screenwriter's Guide to Hollywood* (see the Appendix listing of books). Everyone offers his or her advice in this area, thus I would rather concentrate on the do-it-yourself area—for my experience is that too few in the Industry really think people can go out and make their own works that are every bit as good or, in many cases, much better than the studios crank out. Yet I think it's possible. I do have an agent, but I have gone years without one and sold and optioned my scripts by myself living in New Orleans. Phones, faxes, and airplanes help a lot. Once again, however, what is most exciting for the beginner is the chance these days to go the distance with a little help from your friends and experience both the frustrations but certainly also the joys of seeing a film to completion.

Remember there is nothing more depressing than knowing you have the desire to write and the ability to do good work and yet feeling that, for whatever reason, you are not getting off the ground with your scripts. *If you have talent and energy and modest means, you can make a film and then SOMEBODY will notice you!* Lawrence Kasdan once said that those who succeed are those who do not give up.

Appendix A: Coverage

Part of being able to write well is the art of reading well. Screenwriters should not only see films as a steady part of their diet but also read scripts regularly—professionally produced scripts and those of your friends, acquaintances—to get a feel for everything from format and set-up to actual character development—on paper—and structure.

An exercise that goes beyond reading is learning to write a brief "coverage" of a script. Coverage is what script readers write in Hollywood, for agents and producers alike. The points to be covered are: an idea of the story, of the characters, of the potential for audiences/filming, the problems, and finally, a recommendation: yes or no. It is an excellent exercise to try your own hand at writing one.

Here is an actual sample of coverage that was written for Columbia Pictures on *Presumed Innocent*:

> A compelling and intelligent murder mystery/courtroom drama, this necessarily talky screenplay adaptation of the novel conveys (usually clearly) its complex plot developed from a strong dramatic and commercial premise. The ending revealing the murderer's identity is a strong and effective surprise. However, besides some required clarifications of plot detail, a bigger concern is the general emotional detachment of the characters, which slightly dampens one's involvement in the story.
>
> The characters are efficiently and believably drawn through jargon, naturalistic dialogue, and manner. This is especially so of Rusty and those who populate the professional world of the law. But even in that arena, his relationships are somewhat detached, even with mentor Raymond. Rusty is a cool character, sympathetic for his situation, but hardly engaging. Although this may be suited to his character as an analytical legal mind, it works against our emotional identification.

This situation is exacerbated by his home life. While that's just the point—he's neglected his home life for work and comes to suffer the consequences—there needs to be more clarification in the relationship between Rusty and his wife Barbara. She needs to be better defined and more of some kind of presence. Similarly, another scene would be useful to better define what's missing in Rusty's relationship with his son Nat, rather than simply make the boy a virtual nonpresence.

Thanks to its inherently compelling premise, the heavily detailed narrative maintains interest despite some rough spots, especially concerning finer points of certain evidence and its significance. The setup is quite long, and the story doesn't really take off until halfway through the script when Rusty becomes the primary suspect in the murder he's investigating. This set-up includes a sequence of selected intermittent flashbacks which describe chronologically the backstory of Rusty's meeting, seduction by, then rejection by ambitious Carolyn, the murder victim. As flashbacks go, they are effective and fit with surprising smoothness into the structure. The ending is intellectually satisfying but, again, its effect is diluted by the emotional vacuum.

Minor clarification of story details and modifications to certain characters and relationships will help this piece to achieve its already great potential as a highly successful star vehicle. RECOMMEND.*

* David Bruskin, 8/04/90.

Appendix B: Self-Critiques

Giving coverage on someone else's script is one skill. Harder and ultimately more necessary is giving coverage on yourself. You don't have to
write out a self-report as the three sample student critiques here provide.
But whether you critique yourself to yourself, or through a friend being
present, or in a letter to yourself, the self-critique is definitely part of the
process.

All three were written in a feature script class at the University of
Michigan, Fall 1991. They were asked to review their experience in writing a feature script and to look toward their future plans, all in less than
500 words.

Critique #1 (Male)

I guess you could say that I feel a lot like Hannibal Lecter right now for I
must point that high-powered perception at myself. I assume that the
itch here is simply being honest, and believe me, I knew when I was
making it happen and when I wasn't. Writing a feature script under the
constraints of three other classes is no cake-walk, but to tell the truth, it
was often a welcome escape from the monotony of Thomas Hardy and
Henry James.

I'm happy with my script, *Swimming West to Spawn*, however, I am
not very confident about the finished product. I feel as though I've created some very warm, strange, and original characters, yet I think some
of them lack the depth of character that they deserve. Bush, the main figure, seems very superficial and I think that that's a large problem, for no
one wants to sympathize with a character like his when his world seems
to crumble all around him. In addition, he is stagnant—we do not see
him undergo a real change (at least one worth waiting for). When he
does finally come to some sort of realization, it's not until page 100.
Further, this script lacks a clear narrative. Granted, it's ok—it doesn't
have to be your typical Hollywood narrative, but I think that it could

use some closure, something that pulls it together. I mean, the story literally drops off. I NEED AN ACT III!

I introduce a love interest (I think with a lot of potential to be interesting and funny) on page 94 and ten pages later the mother dies and the story ends. This could use a major overhaul. Looking back at my outline, I see that the flow of action gives new meaning to the word "haphazard." I do, however, like the fact that this script is weird. I think that structurally it's very open. Perhaps this is why my characters seem to merely "play" in each of their scenes with little happening. I know what needs to be done; I think it is mostly a matter of a rewrite.

This script is very different from my earlier script, *The Victors*. *The Victors* is much more a linear story in which we follow the protagonist from goal to its completion. My method of writing *The Victors* was much less hampered as well. *Swimming West to Spawn* emerges out of a pressure cooker of other pressures. I am happy, though, to have another story down on paper.

This term has been nothing short of enlightening, only confirming my desire to make this my life's work. I think that film, be it writing, directing, or what have you, is something that requires a certain passion, a passion that I would one day like to harbor into movie theaters everywhere.

CRITIQUE #2 (FEMALE)

I originally took this class simply to learn about one area of filmmaking that I knew nothing about: screenwriting. I think it is important to know the difficulties and tasks of all of the individuals that work on creating a film. I also wanted to be in the position to better judge and appreciate film writing. I was not, however, prepared to write an entire full-length feature script on my own.

I began with nothing: no story I'd always wanted to tell, no scraps of paper with ideas from my childhood, no folder full of newspaper articles. When I was forced to come up with an idea, and quickly, I was pleasantly surprised that I had several and, after some effort, was able to combine those that would work together, and discard the rest—because my script really was a combination of several entirely different story ideas. Being a percussionist, I began by setting out to use the advertising power I had as a screenwriter to do, for something, what Hitchcock did for percussionists in *The Man Who Knew Too Much*. I quickly decided to use tennis as the tool through which to tell my story (the rise of a young tennis player was one of my early, less appealing ideas). I then chose a genre and an atmosphere, a kind of mystique I would feel and try to convey, whenever I wrote my script. Once I got the plot worked out and had established the main characters, the story almost wrote itself.

I did, however, have problems choosing situations for scenes that would move the plot and tell something about the characters. I'm still not entirely happy with some of the characters, and hope to develop them much more in the rewrite.

Twenty pages or so into my script, I was surprised to discover that I really liked doing it. I find it terribly frustrating, but even more satisfying. I had never considered writing as a career, though, so I was hesitant about pursuing it, especially when I was beginning to feel discouraged about the whole field of filmmaking. Some of the guest speakers this term really helped me in this respect. I wish I could credit all of them, but a few stand out in my mind [*editor's note:* she lists guest speakers and their influence].

I also enjoyed the foreign filmmakers. Film as art is much more appealing to me than film as Arnold Schwarzenegger. I saw in each of the foreign filmmakers a preciousness that in my opinion is missing in the majority of commercial American films.

My future is uncertain. I'm thinking about composing for commercials or television or sound editing in film. I'm definitely not abandoning the idea of screenwriting, though. I'm not sure I like the way the majority of screenwriters (and scripts) are treated in the USA, so if I were to pursue writing, I'd prefer to work in Europe. Europe also seems more suited to my tastes. As things stand now, I would like to plant my feet in New York or Orlando with one eye on Europe and the other on Hollywood.

CRITIQUE #3 (AFRICAN-AMERICAN FEMALE)

Screenwriting is definitely a process. It is a long and arduous process. Never in my life have I done anything that has been so many things to me at once. Screenwriting has given me a tremendous amount of pleasure. On the other hand during moments of intense frustration, I have had to fight off the overwhelming desire to take a baseball bat and smash my computer to bits. I can honestly say that writing the feature-length screenplay is the one thing that I have both loved and hated.

I call it process because most of the term it was an uphill battle for me. In September I had absolutely no idea what I was going to write. As bad as my first draft is, I am really amazed that I was able to create something that I care about. I have seen my script metamorphose before my eyes. At some points it felt as if I wasn't writing the script, but that my screenplay was writing itself. This was especially true during my first revision. Most of the time I felt as if I was knocking my head against a brick wall.

Now that I have written my first draft of my first script I know that I can write a screenplay. But the next ongoing goal is to write screenplays well. My future as an auteur demands this. I hope I have the ability to tell good stories well. I know I can write the typical Hollywood screenplay but I want to write above those limitations.

Appendix C: Your Personal Screenwriting and Video Library

There are lots of books that will help you, but the following are some personally recommended items to purchase and put on your shelf. In terms of screenplays, remember that just about every script is available through SCRIPT CITY, Phone: (800) 676-2522.

Videos

Of course videos are for sale and rental everywhere. But many of the classics, foreign, and off-Hollywood films are often difficult to locate. Two excellent sources are the following: FACETS VIDEO, 1517 West Fullerton Ave., Chicago, IL 60614, Phone: (800) 331-6197. And FOOTHILL VIDEO, P.O. Box 547, Dept. MCW, Tujunga, CA 91043, Phone: (818) 353-8591, is fine on many foreign classics and older American films, almost all offered for $14.95 plus a free one for every three purchased.

Finally, a wonderful thirteen-and-a-half-minute video produced by the Writers Guild of America and directed by Chuck Workman is *Words*. Workman won an Oscar for *Precious Images*, a similar montage of hundreds of famous shots from Hollywood films all presented in about ten minutes and he has done the same with a focus on famous lines from Hollywood. I've watched this tape many times and I come away each time with a sense of awe and pleasure at how many memorable films there are. It's a video that makes you feel good and gives you courage to keep on writing. Contact the Writers Guild of America west, 8955 Beverly Blvd., West Hollywood, CA 90048. Phone: (310) 550-1000.

BOOKS

GENERAL

Bakhtin, Mikhail. *Rabelais and His World*. Trans. Helene Iswolsky. Boston: M.I.T. Press, 1968. No, this is not about movies or screenwriting. But Bakhtin's analysis of the "carnivalesque" is an important influence on my concept of creating screen characters and I thus highly recommend this important study.

Bergan, Ronald, and Robyn Karney. *The Farber Companion to Foreign Films*. Boston: Farber and Farber, 1992. An excellent listing with critiques of many of the best foreign films around which are, for the most part, character centered.

Bresson, Robert. *Notes on Cinematography*. New York: Urizen Books, 1977. Bresson's book is leaner than a honed-down haiku. There are maybe six sentences per page and each is worth considering in depth as every aspect of filmmaking is distilled to its essence.

Buñuel, Luis. *My Last Sigh: The Autobiography of Luis Buñuel*. Trans. Abigail Israel. New York: Alfred A. Knopf, 1983. A year does not go by that I do not reread, refer to, think about, and quote Buñuel on Buñuel, cinema, life. His wickedly healthy laughter is a welcome relief from all that is stereotyped, formulaic, and deadening. How can you not enjoy an autobiography full of lines such as, "The idea of burning down a museum has always seemed more enticing than the opening of a cultural center or the inauguration of a new hospital" (107)?

Egri, Lajos. *The Art of Dramatic Writing*. New York: Simon & Schuster, 1949. Reprinted 1960. Still the best overall book about writing plays/films/television.

Filmmaker: The Magazine of Independent Film. This is a new magazine that has excellent coverage of off-Hollywood films, filmmakers, screenwriters, news. Contact for info and subscriptions: The Independent Feature Project, 5550 Wilshire Blvd., Suite 204, Los Angeles, CA 90036-3888. Phone: (213) 937-4379.

Naremore, James. *Acting in the Cinema*. Berkeley, Los Angeles, London: University of California Press, 1988. The more a writer knows about cinema and the making of films, the better a chance you have of writing scripts that you *know* will work on the screen. I can think of no better book on film acting than this. Naremore is theoretical and specific as he considers Chaplin, Cary Grant, Marlon Brando, Katharine Hepburn, and others in detail.

McMurtry, Larry. *Film Flam: Essays on Hollywood*. New York: Touchstone Books, 1987. McMurtry, novelist by trade and screenwriter "for the fun of it all," has given us everything from *The Last Pic-*

ture Show to *Lonesome Dove* and also this fresh set of essays that puts Hollywood in perspective.

Schatz, Thomas. *The Genius of the System.* New York: Pantheon Books, 1988. Schatz provides you with an excellent understanding of the historical development of the major studios in Hollywood and the transitions they have gone through as television became a major or, in many cases, the major player in entertainment in recent years.

Squire, Jason E. *The Movie Business Book,* 2d ed. New York: Simon & Schuster, 1992 [originally published 1988]. Full of very useful essays written by filmmakers themselves, including producer David Puttman, writer-director Joan Micklin Silver, story editor Eleanor Breese, and screenwriter William Goldman.

Skorman, Richard. *Off Hollywood Movies: A Film Lover's Guide.* New York: Harmony Books, 1989. Four hundred and forty-five reviews of mostly character-driven movies from *Harold and Maude* and *Harlan County, USA* to *Pixote,* Tati's *Playtime,* and Nicolas Roeg's *Walkabout.*

ON SCREENWRITING

Bernays, Anne, and Pamela Painter. *What If? Writing Exercises for Fiction Writers.* New York: HarperCollins, 1990. Not a screenwriting book, but one very useful nevertheless for the scope and variety of exercises it suggests, including keeping a journal in the third person for a few days and creating a story built around a minor character in a major work of fiction (and we could add, film!). Imaginative work.

Corliss, Richard. *Talking Pictures: Screenwriters in the American Cinema.* New York: Penguin, 1974. Still a solid survey of "classical" American screenwriters.

Field, Syd. *Selling a Screenplay: The Screenwriter's Guide to Hollywood.* New York: Dell Publishing, 1989. In this intro to the complicated world of pitching, selling, and marketing your work in Hollywood, Syd Field lays out the landscape clearly and with solid common sense–oriented advice.

Froug, William, ed. *The New Screenwriter Looks at the New Screenwriter.* Los Angeles: Silman-James Press, 1992. A follow-up to Froug's 1971 collection of interviews, this timely collection includes lively exchanges with everyone from Anna Hamilton Phelan (*Gorillas in the Mist*) and Daniel Pyne (*Doc Hollywood*) to Joe Eszterhas (*Basic Instinct*) and Diane Frolov who writes for "Northern Exposure."

Goldman, William. *Adventures in the Screen Trade.* New York: Warners, 1983. Still the best single insiders' guide to the Industry told with wry and often cynical insight by one of the best screenwriters of the past thirty years.

Josefsberg, Milt. *Comedy Writing*. New York: Harper & Row, 1987. An excellent, no nonsense, often funny book on comedy written by a writer who made millions laugh for years.

Lucey, Paul. "Story Sense." No publisher yet announced. Paul Lucey has been teaching screenwriting for years at USC and is currently the Director of the Undergraduate Screenwriting Program. His book is the culmination of the very useful insight he has gained into narrative over the years of observing the Industry and working with his students.

Schmidt, Rick. *Feature Filmmaking at Used-Car Prices: How to Write, Produce, Direct, Film, Edit, and Promote a Feature-Length Film for Less Than $10,000*. New York: Penguin, 1988. A funny, practical, and true account of how to do it all yourself. Even if you don't plan to go this route, you do need to read how Schmidt did it and how overinflated Hollywood has become in comparison.

Seger, Linda. *Making a Good Script Great*. Hollywood: Samuel French, 1987. A level-headed guide not only to the art of the rewrite but of screenwriting in general.

———. *The Art of Adaptation: Turning Fact and Fiction into Film*. New York: Henry Holt & Co., 1992. Seger does a convincing job of demonstrating how much of film and television depends on adapting previous material, eitherfrom literature, drama, or also the news and "true life."

Wolff, Jurgen, and Kerry Cox. *Successful Script Writing*. Cincinnati: Writer's Digest Books, 1991. This overview goes into almost no detail in any one area, but it covers a little of everything from writing for Animation to writing Movies-of-the-Week.

SCREENPLAYS

Do get your hands on the screenplays of the four films mentioned in this book through SCRIPT CITY, or any other source you may have. (Note: the script for *Time of the Gypsies* is not available anywhere as far as I can tell and certainly not in English.) Beyond those, here are a few to purchase and study:

Allen, Woody. *Four Films of Woody Allen: Annie Hall, Interiors, Manhattan, Stardust Memories*. New York: Random House, 1980.

Coen, Joel, and Ethan Coen. *Raising Arizona*. New York: St. Martin's Press, 1988.

De Sica, Vittorio. *The Bicycle Thief*. Trans. Simon Hartog. London: Lorrimer, 1968. Of course you will want to read American scripts. But it's also important to read as many of the best European scripts as you can to get a feel for how they do what they do well. There are six writers named on this classic of Italian neo-realism, including Vittorio De Sica, the director. Read, noting the extreme simplicity of character, narrative, resolution.

Klotman, Phyllis Rauch, ed. *Screenplays of the African-American Experience*. Bloomington: Indiana University Press, 1991. A pioneering effort to bring African-American screenplays written by independent filmmakers to a wider audience. Includes scripts by Bill Gunn, Charles Burnett, Charles Lane, Alile Sharon Larkin, and Julie Dash.

Rohmer, Eric. *Six Moral Tales*. Trans. Sabine d'Estree. New York: The Viking Press, 1980. Rohmer's case as writer-turned-filmmaker offers an interesting "crossover" case for any writer to think about. Many of his best films, including *Claire's Knee, Love in the Afternoon*, and *My Night at Maud's*, all began as decidedly literary short novellas that he wrote "at a point when I did not yet know whether I was going to be a filmmaker" (p. v).

Thomas, Sam, ed. *Best American Screenplays*. New York: Crown Publishers, 1986. This first volume of American scripts provides you with the complete scripts for such classics as *Casablanca, Meet John Doe, Rebel without a Cause, Bonnie and Clyde, Butch Cassidy and the Sundance Kid,* and *The Graduate*.

Truffaut, François. *The Story of Adele H*. New York: Grove Press, 1976. A sample script by one of Europe's best filmmakers shows the collaborative effort of Truffaut together with, on this script, Jean Gruault and Suszanne Schiffman with the help of Frances V. Guille who wrote *The Journal of Adele Hugo* on which the script is based.

APPENDIX D: AT LONG LAST THE RECIPE FOR A SCREENWRITERS' GUMBO WITH CHARACTER!

We began this odyssey stating that much of Hollywood's standard fare in recent years resembles microwave cooking. The contrast offered was that of New Orleans cooking, which, in a gumbo, for instance, means you need to carefully prepare a *roux*, the deep structure without which the rich stew-like mixture would simply taste like canned soup.

Now at last a recipe for a screenwriters' gumbo with character!

This is a variation on that offered by my friends Rima and Richard Collin in their book, *The New Orleans Cookbook* (1989). Prepare, cook, and serve to the small group of friends you've had over to read the first draft or fifth draft of your latest script, out loud.

SCREENWRITERS' CHICKEN AND SAUSAGE GUMBO

A true Cajun gumbo that is hearty and full of character in the most car-nivalesque of ways: many voices adding up to a single joyful taste!

THE GUMBO BASE
A 3–4 lb. fryer, cut up
1½ lbs. Creole (or Polish will do) smoked sausage sliced into
     ½-inch pieces
½ lb. lean baked ham cut into ½-inch cubes
2½ cups chopped onions
1 cup thinly sliced shallots
¾ cup chopped green pepper
2 ribs chopped celery
3 Tbs. finely minced garlic
3 Tbs. finely minced parsley

Place all prepared ingredients, EXCEPT fryer, in a large bowl and set aside.

THE ROUX
⅔ cup olive oil (Greek, if possible)
½ cup flour

THE LIQUIDS
¼ cup cold water
2 qts. chicken stock

THE SEASONINGS
1 tsp. salt
1 tsp. freshly ground black pepper
½ tsp. white pepper
¼–½ tsp. cayenne pepper
1¼ tsp. dried thyme
1 tsp. oregano
3 whole bay leaves
2 Tbs. file powder

Measure all seasonings, EXCEPT file, into small bowl and set aside.

MIXING THE INGREDIENTS
Measure olive oil into a heavy 7- to 8-quart pot or kettle. Heat the oil over high heat. Brown the chicken parts in the hot oil, turning them over to ensure even browning. Remove to a platter and set aside.

Deep Structure: Make the roux by gradually adding flour to the heated oil remaining in the pot while STIRRING CONSTANTLY. Reduce heat to low and keep stirring until a medium-brown roux the color of hazelnuts or rich peanut butter is formed.

When the roux reaches this critical color, immediately toss in the ingredients for the gumbo base (contained in large bowl). Cook over low heat, stirring constantly, for ten minutes. The vegetables will have a glazed appearance.

Add the water, browned chicken pieces, and the seasonings contained in the small bowl (i.e., all except the file).

Mix thoroughly.

Gradually stir in the chicken stock.

Raise the heat until the gumbo comes to a boil, then lower the heat and simmer for an hour. Stir frequently.

Remove from heat and let the simmer die down.
Then and only then add the file and stir.
Let the gumbo stand another five minutes.
Serve over boiled rice.

There you have it! Core character, the carnivalesque, and deep structure. What more can you ask for? Seconds, anyone?

· · ·

As a screenwriter, script consultant, teacher, and, after all these years, still an avid moviegoer, I invite readers to share their experiences with their work as it relates to this book and its proposals. Comments, complaints, suggestions are welcome. I can be reached at:

Andrew Horton
English Dept., Box 50
Loyola University
6363 St. Charles Ave.
New Orleans, LA 70118
Phone: (504) 865-2260
FAX: (504) 948-2948

INDEX

Designer:	Robert Ross
Compositor:	Prestige Typography
Text:	9.5/12 Sabon
Display:	Sabon
Printer:	BookCrafters, Inc.
Binder:	BookCrafters, Inc.